By the Power of God

Other Titles by Dick B.

Dr. Bob and His Library: Books for Twelve Step Growth

Anne Smith's Journal, 1933-1939: A.A.'s Principles of Success

The Oxford Group & Alcoholics Anonymous:
A Design for Living That Works

The Akron Genesis of Alcoholics Anonymous

New Light on Alcoholism: God, Sam Shoemaker, and A.A.

Courage to Change (with Bill Pittman)

The Good Book and The Big Book: A.A.'s Roots in the Bible

That Amazing Grace:
The Role of Clarence and Grace S. in Alcoholics Anonymous

Good Morning!:
Quiet Time, Morning Watch, Meditation, and Early A.A.

Turning Point:
A History of Early A.A.'s Spiritual Roots and Successes

HOPE!: The Story of Geraldine D., Alina Lodge & Recovery

Utilizing Early A.A.'s Spiritual Roots for Recovery Today

The Golden Text of A.A.: God, the Pioneers, and Real Spirituality

By the Power of God

A Guide to Early A.A. Groups & Forming Similar Groups Today

Dick B.

Paradise Research Publications, Inc.
Kihei, Maui, Hawaii

Paradise Research Publications, Inc., P.O. Box 837, Kihei, HI 96753-0837

This Paradise Research Publications Edition is published by arrangement with Good Book Publishing Company, P.O. Box 837, Kihei, Maui, HI 96753-0837

Cover Design: Lili Crawford, Maui Cyber Design

The publication of this volume does not imply affiliation with nor approval or endorsement from Alcoholics Anonymous World Services, Inc. The views expressed herein are solely those of the author. A.A. is a program of recovery from alcoholism—use of the Twelve Steps in connection with programs and activities which are patterned after A.A., but which address other problems, does not imply otherwise.

Publisher's Cataloging-in-Publication
(*Provided by Quality Books, Inc.*)

B., Dick.
   By the power of God : a guide to early A.A.
groups & forming similar groups today / Dick B.
   p. cm. -- (Why it worked : A.A. history series ;
no. 3)
   Includes bibliographical references
   LCCN: 99-76227
   ISBN: 1-885803-30-3

   1. Alcoholics Anonymous. 2. Alcoholics
Anonymous--History. 3. Alcoholism--Treatment.
4. Twelve-step programs. 5. Alcoholism--Religious
aspects--Christianity.   I. Title.

HV5278.B34 2000   362.29'286
               QBI99-1653

To: Frederick Robert Johnston, Maui, Hawaii
Bishop Frank Costantino, Orlando, Florida
Larry Webb, Buffalo Bill Tobicoe & Tony Stark, California

Let the heavens be glad, and let the earth rejoice: and let *men* say among the nations, the LORD reigneth.

1 Chronicles 16:31

Many, many a time Frank [Buchman, founder of The Oxford Group] has taken the passage . . . [i.e., Ephesians 3:20, 21–cited below] and shown its wonderful meaning in this way:

God through Christ is able to do for you

all that you ask or think—

above all that you ask or think—

abundantly above all that you ask or think—

exceeding abundantly above all that you ask or think!

—in you, by you, for you, through you.

Miles G. W. Phillimore

Just for Today

Now unto him that is able to do exceeding abundantly above all that we ask or think, according to the power that worketh in us, Unto him *be* glory in the church by Christ Jesus throughout all ages, world without end. Amen.

Ephesians 3:20, 21

Contents

Foreword

In reading *By the Power of God*, my heart soared as once again I realized how many biblical principles were deeply imbedded in the A.A. program as it was originally practiced.

From the Oxford Group to the early groups in Akron, Cleveland, and New York City, the roots of A.A. cannot be denied. From Dr. Bob's "Christian Fellowship" to Bill's note that, "A.A. is but a spiritual kindergarten," the God of the Bible has been the power that has made all things possible.

Dick B.'s thoughtful and extensive search for the truth has made the lives of the founders and early AAs come alive for all of us. He has renewed our hope that there can be Pioneer Groups in A.A. today and that the guidelines are already in place.

I applaud Dick B.'s encouragement to work *within* the A.A. program by keeping history alive, studying the biblical principles that worked for our founders and countless others, and by contributing fully to the primary purpose of helping the suffering alcoholic in a way that would meet the approval of our Lord, Jesus Christ.

I pray that there will always be places where our Christian heritage can be remembered, where the love of Christ can be spoken, and where we will never forget where we came from.

OZZIE LEPPER

President/Managing Director
The Wilson House
East Dorset, Vermont
[Birthplace and also the final resting place of A.A. co-founder Bill Wilson]

Preface

As the readership of my titles on early A.A.'s real spiritual roots has grown, so has the volume of communications as to how to apply the roots in today's A.A. and other Twelve Step fellowships.

Reflected in the letters, phone calls, faxes, and emails I have been receiving in ever-increasing numbers is a hunger for "How to Do it Today!" Of course, the A.A. of yesteryear is truly gone forever. There is no Dr. Bob—physician, Bible student, "Prince of Twelfth-Steppers," ambassador for Christ. There is no loving Anne Smith—"Mother of A.A.," "Founder," nurse, evangelist, employment agent, and dispenser of "spiritual pablum" each morning in the Smith Home at 855 Ardmore in Akron. There is no Quiet Time (in or out of meetings)—where the Bible is studied, devotionals are read and discussed, prayer is made to God, God's voice is listened for, and journaling occurs within the A.A. framework. And yet there are so many who not only want to do those things, but want documentation that they were done. There also are many who want a guide to doing them today.

There is now a Good Book/Big Book group in Southern California which is listed in an A.A. meeting schedule. There also is a "Safe to Talk about Jesus" meeting. There is a Big Book/Bible study meeting in Florida. There are spiritual retreats for AAs and their families in at least seven locations in the United States, and one in England. There are other A.A. groups where these practices occur; but AAs have been so cautious or so intimidated that little has been said about them. Where such groups become known, there have also been outcries that these are "heretical" groups. Yet they *do* continue.

There is almost certain to be no return to Christianity in A.A. There is almost certain to be no abandonment of the god of lightbulbs, chairs, Gertrude, trees, and lizards. There is almost certain to be no attempt at A.A.'s world headquarters to cease publication of more and more "any god" materials or to return to the First Edition of *Alcoholics Anonymous* and its personal stories of how the early AAs studied the Bible, read *The Upper Room*, and relied upon the Creator after coming to Him through His Son, Jesus Christ.

So this present title is no guide for A.A. as a whole. It is not even a report concerning early A.A. that will appeal to the fellowship as a whole, or its present trustees, or to most of its delegates, or to most of its groups. But *it is* a solid effort to put together a review of early A.A.'s spiritual roots, to publish a study of those roots and pioneer practices in light of A.A.'s present Traditions; and to provide a guide as to how early A.A. really operated and recovered by the Power of God. And can today where its members choose to do so.

God could and would if sought, today's Big Book still says. God can and will, some earlier editions said. God can do exceeding abundantly above all that we ask or think according to the power that worketh in us [those who have become children of God by a new birth. See Ephesians 3:20-21]. And God *has relieved of alcoholism, healed, and delivered out of countless problems*. He has for me and for many others. He certainly did for the A.A. pioneers. He can do it for you if you seek Him by following His Word.

You begin by starting! If you want to.

Here's a guide for those who want a starting point.

Part One

The Starkness and Darkness of the Problem and the Simplicity of the Early Solution

"As we became subjects of King Alcohol, shivering denizens of his mad realm, the chilling vapor that is loneliness settled down. It thickened, ever becoming blacker. Some of us sought out sordid places, hoping to find understanding companionship and approval. Momentarily we did—then would come oblivion and the awful awakening to face the hideous Four Horsemen—Terror, Bewilderment, Frustration, Despair. Unhappy drinkers who read this page will understand!" (*Alcoholics Anonymous*, 1st ed., 1939, p. 165).

"Remember, Bill, let's not louse this thing up. Let's *keep* it simple!" (*DR. BOB and the Good Oldtimers*, 1980, p. 343, emphasis added). These were A.A. co-founder Dr. Bob's very last words to co-founder Bill Wilson on Dr. Bob's deathbed.

1

1

My Personal Debt to, and Opportunities from, A.A.

I'm one of those drunks who ought to have been in A.A.

And fortunately, I wound up there at almost sixty years of age. Like some, I had success as a part of my background—Eagle Scout, top student, Army service, fine university, Phi Beta Kappa key, fine law school, case editor of the law review, excellent law associates, long—though ultimately dissolved—marriage, two great sons, community service and recognition, successful solo law practice, and a creditable stewardship of assets. *Accompanied* by a long-standing addiction to sleeping pills, and a shorter span of ever-increasing alcoholism.

At the suggestion of my former wife, with a stamp of approval from my psychiatrist, and the support of my own Bible fellowship friends, I entered A.A. after nine months of depression, disgrace, fear, secrets, guilt, troubles, and un-wanted focus in the public eye by the news media. Somehow, the open door of A.A. beckoned; and I loved it.

There are those today who read my many books on the spiritual history of early A.A. and conclude I am trying to return A.A. to Christianity. Or that I am buttressing the arguments of A.A.'s many critics. Or that my historical focus on early A.A., its biblical roots, and its astonishing successes is too narrow. None of these suppositions is correct.

3

I *am* an AA; and I am *in* A.A. I chose it. I dived into it. I seemed to need it. I received completely new information from it. I found a home when I seemed to have none. I found new friends when I seemed to have lost mine. I helped hundreds of others when my focus in previous life seemed, at the end of it, to be primarily on helping myself. I stopped drinking at once and almost immediately ended my use of sleeping pills. And then began a new life which continues to this day. I therefore owe a deep personal debt to Alcoholics Anonymous which I have tried to repay by attending, and serving in, its meetings; sponsoring its newcomers; studying its basic text (*Alcoholics Anonymous*); learning, practicing, and teaching its Twelve Steps of recovery to others; and thoroughly enjoying and touting its fellowship. All continuing to this very writing.

There is a good deal more, of course. There have been the many miracles resulting from my return to reliance upon God: recovery from alcoholism and addiction; survival of grand-mal seizures; an end to five years of delayed withdrawal "shaking;" deliverance from endless insomnia; and the receipt of appropriate solutions for many legal, financial, and personal problems.

Out of it all came an opportunity. I had resigned from the State Bar in despair. I was frustrated at being too sick to work. I was bewildered by my memory loss, my faltering mental capacity, my horrendous life problems, and my "how-did-this-happen-to-me" questions. And I was terrified. There were enough legal problems, publicity problems, financial problems, housing problems, family problems, friendship problems, loneliness problems, and vocational problems to make my status *unique* (terminally unique, some like to say), unsolvable, endless, and bottomless in its downward descent. At least that is what I *thought*.

I don't need to tell my drinking story, my A.A. experience, or my deliverance specifics, in detail, or even in a general way. There are countless stories at any meeting, in A.A. literature, in popular books, and in not-so-popular books. Some are not particularly accurate or inspiring. Some are not even truthful. But there *are* those which underline what can happen to an AA who relies upon God, stays sober, endeavors to change his life, and works at helping others not yet delivered.

I do want to point to some major things that happened to me personally. And comment briefly on the opportunity that came to me almost exclusively from being an active, recovered AA. One who did not and does not hold himself out as an expert, a counselor, a detractor, or one who knows all the facts about the A.A. picture and its beginnings. And the following are some of the major things that have occurred:

- Immediate welcome at the door, specific suggestions as to what I should do, many meetings which I was told to attend, lots of phone numbers I could call, and some guides in the form of meeting schedules, the basic text, the script of the Twelve Steps on the wall of many rooms, and a much-needed opportunity to fill my hours with sober people who were doing sober things at sober places.

- A strong suggestion that I obtain a sponsor immediately; clear instructions from my sponsor as to meetings, phone calls, Steps, Big Book study, and fellowship involvement. For a time, he set an excellent example by doing himself what he suggested I should do. He kept in touch daily, figuratively saved my life when I had seizures at an A.A. meeting, and worked with my son to get me into immediate hospitalization and then a treatment program.

- Total lack of condemnation from other AAs despite bad personal habits, withdrawal symptoms, crazy thinking, unceasing jabber, confusion, fear, and legal or other problems which are the common lot of the alcoholic-addict today.

- Zealous involvement in helping and sponsoring and guiding newcomers through the mine-field, the Big Book, the Steps, and—where they wanted it—through their life problems when I was equipped to help. This involvement was in fact the high point of my A.A. membership. It has been the highest A.A. reward. And it was the focal point for the opportunity that opened.

- A growing awareness that some things were amiss. People left A.A. in large numbers. People returned to drinking and drugs in large numbers. There was far less mention of God than there was of some nebulous "higher power" and absurd names for it. There was ceaseless talk about "spirituality" with no apparent explanation or understanding of what that meant. There was resentment and point-blank open criticism from many in meetings when God, the Bible, Jesus Christ, or some religious belief was mentioned. There was no clear guide as to prayer, healing, forgiveness, deliverance, and the other things I was beginning to assimilate from my ever-growing study of the Bible and participation in a Christian Bible fellowship. There was objection from my sponsor and his sponsor when I introduced my own sponsees to my own understanding of God, the Bible, Jesus Christ, and so on. Finally, as I grew in my convictions, and as the men I sponsored fanned out, I began to hear in and out of meetings that I and they were "Jesus freaks;" that people who read the Bible returned to drinking; that A.A. had left the Bible behind in the 1930's; and that people went to church for religion and to A.A. for alcoholism—whatever that meant.

- An exposure to A.A.'s real past when a young man, now dead of alcoholism, told me that A.A. was based on the Bible and suggested I read *DR. BOB and the Good Oldtimers*. Absolute amazement when I did just that, and began to read the other two A.A. histories (*Pass It On* and *Alcoholics Anonymous Comes of Age*). An awakening when I realized that the A.A. of yesteryear was nothing like the

A.A. of today. For the early days involved explicit mention of the Bible. Specific mention of God Almighty. Unhesitating references to Christianity. There was individual prayer. There was Bible study. There was group prayer. There was an unending quest for the guidance of God among the individuals and within the group. There was Christian fellowship. And that was enough to spark my interest. Yet there were simply *no specifics about* the early beliefs and no clear indication of what the Reverend Sam Shoemaker, the Oxford Group, Dr. Bob's wife Anne, the early Christian literature, Quiet Time, or even the Bible itself had contributed to the A.A. program of recovery and fellowship.

● So there was presented to me an opportunity to start a new life *in, within, and about A.A. as it used to be.* And why not! I was welcomed in talks with survivors of the founders, with survivors of the Oxford Group, and with cohorts of Sam Shoemaker. I met people, in and before A.A., who observed quiet time. I studied archives which contained tapes and transcripts of the very few oldtimers who really knew the score about the earliest practices, principles, and successes. I was not a scholar, a doctor, a psychologist, a clergyman, an historian, a professional writer, or a reporter looking *into* A.A. I was not someone who ignored A.A. Traditions—often using his or her full name and frequently attempting to concealed actual or possible A.A. connections and alcoholism. This was an opportunity for some one *in, and still within* A.A., who had been there, who was still there, who actively studied and practiced and taught the program within A.A. And who was able to search for, and interpret as a recovered member, find the facts, study the evidence, and report it all.

- And did I have a bias? I sure did. I believed and still believe that I, and the many men I have sponsored, have fully recovered from our malady and are adequately dealing with life's problems by the very same reliance upon God, the accomplishments of His son Jesus Christ, and the truths of the Bible that early AAs used with astonishing and continuing success. Therefore, the more I could unearth about where the pioneers got their ideas, what they studied, what they believed, and what they did, the more I was able to confirm the successes of those, including myself and my sponsees, who followed their path. A path that began with intense and enthusiastic participation in the fellowship and recovery program of Alcoholics Anonymous itself. Bias? Yes. Opinions and conclusions? Yes. And the objective? Information and service to others with like problems or convictions or needs.

I said I didn't need to share my drunkalog, and I won't. But there are a couple of things you need to know. I learned these as I groped my way through early sobriety. Within a very few days, I was terrified, ashamed, shaking, guilt-ridden, and in despair. I got no solace from my sponsor or from others in the fellowship. And it happened that my deliverance really began at about six months of sobriety in the V.A. psych ward in San Francisco. A gentleman in my Bible fellowship whose name was Chuck kept calling me long-distance every day. This was something he could barely afford. Yet I kept him on the line for a long time each day, whining, groaning, and complaining about my fears.

Finally, that wonderful gentleman asked me why I didn't quit trying to program my life. He said quite simply, *Why don't you let God guide you!* Now there was a novel idea! And then he said I needed to read about Peter walking on the water. I told him he was in error—that it was Jesus who walked on the water. He replied that there were two in the walking-on-water club—Jesus *and* Peter. He told me to look it up in the Bible.

Out came my King James. Probably just to correct Chuck's idea that Peter walked on the water. My memory was terrible. My mind was foggy. I had no Bible Concordance. So on and on I searched. Finally, I found it—in Matthew 6:25-27. It said:

> And in the fourth watch of the night, Jesus went unto them, walking on the sea. And when the disciples saw him walking on the sea, they were troubled, saying, It is a spirit; and they cried out for fear. But straightaway Jesus spake unto them, saying, Be of good cheer; it is I; *be not afraid* (emphasis added).

There it was. *Jesus walked* on the sea! But something caught my eye. The next verse mentioned *Peter*. On I read:

> And Peter answered him and said, Lord, if it be thou, bid me come unto thee on the water. And he said, Come. And when Peter was come down out of the ship, he walked on the water to go to Jesus (Matthew 14:28-29).

Sure enough, Peter walked too. But there was more to the story for me than that. And that is why Chuck told me to read it in God's Word for myself. The account continued:

> But when he [Peter] saw the wind boisterous, he was **afraid**; and beginning to sink, he cried, saying, Lord, save me. And immediately Jesus stretched forth *his* hand, and caught him, and said unto him, **O thou of little faith, wherefore didst thou doubt** (Matthew 14:30-31, bold face added).

So that was what Chuck was driving at. I was filled with fear. I was trying to think it out and walk it out *alone*. Yet God's own Word was filled with assurances that fear was my enemy, and that I needed only to trust God and obey His commands to come out OK.

> The fear of man bringeth a snare; but whoso putteth his trust in the Lord shall be safe (Proverbs 29:25).

The Lord *is* my light and my salvation; whom shall I fear? the Lord *is* the strength of my life; of whom shall I be afraid (Psalm 27:1).

Yea, though I walk through the valley of the shadow of death, I will fear no evil: for thou *art* with me; thy rod and thy staff they comfort me (Psalm 23:4).

Fear not, little flock; for it is your Father's good pleasure to give you the kingdom (Luke 12:32).

Jesus said unto him, If thou canst believe, all things are possible to him that believeth (Mark 9:23).

For God hath not given us the spirit of fear; but of power, and of love, and of a sound mind (2 Timothy 1:7).

Ye are of God, little children, and have overcome them: because greater is he that is in you, than he that is in the world (1 John 4:4).

Trust in the Lord with all thine heart; and lean not unto thine own understanding. In all thy ways acknowledge him, and he shall direct thy paths (Proverbs 3:5-6).

These verses flooded my mind. I tried to commit them to memory. More important, I *believed them*. I believed them in the nut house. I believed them in Vacaville State Prison. I believed them when I went before the Judge and pleaded guilty. I believed them when I realized that because I had come to God through His son Jesus Christ, I had the power of God within me. And the fear was gone! The obsession to drink had left the moment I arrived in A.A. and asked God for help. Now I was able to face all my problems, trust in God, and be delivered from the power of darkness, the encasing chains of fear, and the problems that had seemed insurmountable.

And I passed this on to my sponsees. Then, when I discovered A.A.'s roots, I realized the same faith and results were available in early A.A. when the success rate was so high. Words that are often meaningless to new AAs became meaningful because of my increasing understanding of their biblical roots. And let's notice a few of them in A.A.'s basic text (Third Edition):

Seemingly he could not drink even if he would. God had restored his sanity (Big Book, p. 57; See 2 Timothy 1:7).

He humbly offered himself to his Maker—then he knew (Big Book, p. 57. See James 4:10).

When we drew near to Him He disclosed Himself to us (Big Book, p. 57; See James 4:8).

For we are now on a different basis; the basis of trusting and relying upon God. We trust infinite God rather than our finite selves (Big Book, p. 68; See Proverbs 29:25).

In meditation, we ask God what we should do about each specific matter (Big Book, p. 69; See Proverbs 3:5-6).

. . . [A]sking each morning in meditation that our Creator show us the way of patience, tolerance, kindliness and love (Big Book, p. 83; See 1 Corinthians 13, James 5:8-9; Matthew 7:1-5).

Love thy neighbor as thyself (Big Book, p. 153; See James 2:8).

Faith without works is dead (Big Book, p. 88; See James 2:20).

Thy will be done (Big Book, p. 88; See Matthew 6:10).

As you can see from my writings, there are many many more. Yet how long it took me to make the connection. How bereft of explanatory material were the meetings and the A.A. literature. How many hours are continually wasted by people speculating about God's will concerning honesty, purity, unselfishness, love, day-to-day alternatives, ill-health, disasters, and fears. How negative are the comments when only *believing* what God says is the requirement. My profit and opportunity, then, were to take my own experience with alcoholism, withdrawal, seizures, ill-health, fears, angers, guilt, shame, dishonesty, and just plain problems and shine the light of God's solutions on all these. God heals. God forgives. God delivers. God tells us in His Word about His love, His peace, His protection, His healing, His moral standards, His grace, and *His mercy*. Thank goodness for the mercy of God and what His son accomplished for us in wiping out the transgressions of those who choose to accept him as the way, the truth, and the life.

That's the real profit—the real opportunity. The one that captured the hearts and actions of early AAs who were powered by the love of God. The message was one you could find spelled out in the literature A.A. pioneers read and the actions they took:

> And as ye go, preach, saying, The kingdom of heaven is at hand. Heal the sick, cleanse the lepers, raise the dead, cast out devils: freely ye have received, freely give (Matthew 10:7-8).

> Jesus answered and said unto them. Go and shew John again those things which ye do hear and see: The blind receive their sight, and the lame walk, the lepers are cleansed; and the deaf hear, the dead are raised up, and the poor have the gospel preached to them (Matthew 11:4-5).

That's the message that caught me. I haven't restored sight, healed deaf, cleansed lepers, or raised the dead. But I have sure dealt successfully with some moral lepers, some AAs who could barely walk, some AAs who could barely hear God's promises, and some AAs who—for a long time—had been unable to see the obvious through a mind clouded by alcohol, drugs, and insane thinking. And how did they and I recover? By the power of God.

2

What Believers Involved in Today's Twelve Step Programs May Be Seeking

"God knows we've been simple enough and gluttonous enough to get this way, but once we got this way [i.e., became real alcoholics], it was a form of lunacy which only God Almighty could cure." (Transcript of remarks by A.A. co-founder Bill Wilson to T. Henry Williams in a December 12, 1954, interview. Transcript located in A.A.'s GSO archives in New York).

You walk into your first meeting of Alcoholics Anonymous. You may be there because the court or probation officer or parole officer told you to go. You may be there because your treatment center brought you there in a van with a group of its patients. You may be there because your therapist said you would not be treated unless you also went to A.A.

You are a male and believe you would be most comfortable in a "men's group"—even a "men's stag group." Can you find one? Or you are female and prefer to be in a "women's group." Can you find one? You are gay or lesbian, and you want to be with AAs of that persuasion. Can you find a gay or lesbian group? You are an airline pilot, a lawyer, a policeman, or a doctor. Is there a meeting for people of your "kind?" You are an atheist and don't want to be with people who believe in God. Is there an A.A. group for atheists? Finally, let's assume you don't believe or want to believe in anything at all? Has A.A. made a place for you?

The clearcut answer in today's A.A. is that each and every one of the foregoing people can find a group specifically established for "their kind!" There are men's groups; women's groups; gay and lesbian groups; groups for pilots, lawyers, policemen, priests, artists, and doctors; groups for atheists; and plenty of A.A. Conference Approved literature telling you that you can believe in something or nothing or anything or a radiator or Gertrude or a lightbulb or a doorknob. So you will not feel alone, alienated, intimidated, or ostracized if you are one of these people. In fact, you can speak up loudly in any meeting about your "relationship" with another AA, your sexual orientation, your occupation, your atheism, your "child within," or your belief that your "higher power" is Santa Claus, the Big Dipper, the group, or a chair. There is a hundred to one bet that not one person will challenge or criticize you or try to quash such statements about who you are and what you believe or don't believe.

Moreover, you've got A.A.'s literature and the Twelve Traditions of A.A. to back you up. In fact, one of the older and more well-known histories of A.A. is titled *Not-God* which tells its readers that A.A. is all about "not-God-ness." A much more recent handbook tells AAs they can get well in four simple lessons and need not worry about God or the 400 times He is specifically mentioned or referred to in A.A.'s basic text. Bringing further comfort to the unbeliever's soul, this handbook adds:

> Alcoholics Anonymous is not a religious program. We're free to call this Power anything we wish, as long as it is a Power greater than ourselves. The "Big Book" authors use many different names for this Power including Creative Intelligence, Universal Mind, Spirit of Nature, Czar of the Heavens, Creator, Father of Light and the Great Reality, among others. Quite a few times they call this Power, God, but they *use the word God merely for expedience* rather than for any religious purpose. Please refer to this Power by any name you believe in or feel comfortable with (*Back to Basics*, pp. 38-39, emphasis added).

And, consistent with such opinions, a large number of AAs do today refer to this "expedient any god" by such titles as Good Orderly Direction, the group, a chair, Ralph, a bulldozer, a tree, a radiator, the goddess, "Her," "It," a lightbulb, a rock, Gertrude, a "higher power," and many other names well-documented and usually well-known by A.A. meeting-goers. Occasionally, a bold soul will refer to "My higher power, whom I choose to call God" or "My Higher Power Jesus." But the latter comment is apt to be heard only in the South.

Now let's assume you are a Jew, a Roman Catholic, a Protestant, or a member of a "non-denominational" Christian Church. You don't fit any of the foregoing atheist, gay, police, or doctor categories—none of them. You never heard of an "higher power." You are simply not stupid enough to pray to a radiator or a group or a lightbulb or Gertrude. In fact, as you look at the Twelve Steps and Twelve Traditions that can be found on the wall at most meetings, you see no mention of Gertrude or a radiator or Santa Claus or a lightbulb. You see the word "God." You see the phrase "as we understood Him." And you may begin to feel comfortable. As a believer, you think you are "home" at last. You are there with people in trouble, just like you are. You are there with people who seem to be saying that much of their trouble has to do with alcohol. You are there with people who seem friendly, cheerful, and at times extremely helpful. And you may begin to feel completely welcome.

Then you hear people talking about God. There is mention of an "higher power," but you don't really understand what that's all about because the phrase is not on the wall or in the Steps or the Traditions. Finally, you are there with people who tell you to "Keep coming back. It works." They are joined in a circle and are enthusiastic; and they usually end their meeting with the Lord's Prayer—a prayer that all but the Jew know fairly well, and which even the Jew may utter to be part of the affair. And you feel there is really hope. And there is!

However, a fuse is about to be lit. A blast will soon occur. The explosion may happen at your therapist's office, your

treatment center, your probation office, and very probably at an
A.A. meeting. Heretofore filled with hope and joy and peace and
comfort, you have just timidly shared that you went to a
Pentecostal church. Or you just boldly shared that you read the
Bible that morning. Or you just shared, with deep conviction, that
you claim in the name of Jesus Christ that you are healed of
alcoholism. Or you happily told one or more of these people how
you understand God and where *you* get your information (namely,
from religion, your church, or the Bible).

Boom!

The repercussion may be sudden or gradual. But the event
seems quite probable, based on the observations of those of us who
have attended hundreds, even thousands of meetings where the
condemnation and sarcasm have occurred. Someone may softly say
"A.A. is a spiritual program, not a religious program." Someone
else may share his or her "experience" a bit more boldly and say
that he or she used to believe in that "religious" stuff, but has now
come to learn and understand A.A.'s "spirituality." Someone else
may say he or she gets his religion in church and his spirituality
in A.A. Someone else may walk out on you, resentful that you
dared to mention a "religious" subject. Someone else may look
you directly in the eye and say, "We don't mention the Bible or
Jesus in A.A.—that violates A.A. Tradition." There are multiple
variations. But if you are a sick, confused, frightened, uninformed,
easily intimidated believer—as many of us are at the
beginning—you will never open your mouth again on that subject.
At best, if Christian, you'll probably opt to become a secret agent
A.A. Christian and keep your church and your Bible and your
Jesus Christ to yourself. At worst, you'll begin to adopt the
perplexing and confusing language and, before long, be repeating
it, intimidating with it, explaining it, and possibly even believing
it.

One thing is certain. It will be a rare day in June if anyone
ever tells you that early A.A. was part of "A First Century
Christian Fellowship." Or that A.A.'s co-founder Dr. Bob Smith
called every A.A. meeting a "Christian Fellowship." Or that every

early A.A. meeting opened with prayer, that the Bible was usually read, that newcomers surrendered to Jesus Christ as their Lord and Savior, and that early A.A. meetings studied Christian devotionals such as *The Upper Room*, and *My Utmost for His Highest* and *The Runner's Bible*. You may never hear that AAs were so fond of the Book of James in the Bible that many favored calling the fellowship the "James Club." Or that both A.A. founders said the underlying philosophy of A.A. came from Jesus's Sermon on the Mount in Matthew 5, 6, and 7. Or that Quiet Time (with Bible study, prayer, and listening for God's guidance) were "musts" in early A.A.—at the weekly meetings, at Dr. Bob Smith's home daily, and in the homes of the Akron Pioneers. Or that Christian literature was widely studied and circulated. Or that *all* of A.A.'s basic spiritual ideas came from the Bible.

As for God, A.A. co-founder Dr. Bob usually called God his "Heavenly Father." Bill Wilson often referred to Him as "God Almighty." And A.A.'s Big Book refers to "God," one way or another, more than 400 times—with capitalized letters of reverence and respect. Not merely for expedience. No radiators. No doorknobs. No lightbulbs. No chairs or Big Dippers. Just God, Jehovah, Almighty God, the one true and living God, as He is called in the Bible—the very Creator, Maker, Spirit, and Father. The God of our fathers (as Bill Wilson liked to call him) who is specified by name and with capitalized letters in A.A.'s basic text—*Alcoholics Anonymous*!

This present booklet is premised on the idea that there are many believers who are in A.A., who may come to A.A., who have left A.A., or who may simply be seeking the likes of the early AAs' program. And want to know: Can we still mention God, Jesus Christ, the Bible in A.A? Can we still pray and read the Bible and discuss Christian literature in A.A.? Can we still have meetings or groups whose members believe in God and say so? Can we still feel completely free to fellowship with other believers and share our experiences as to what God Almighty has done or can do for the alcoholic? Is there room in Twelve Step "anonymous" or "self-help" groups themselves today for coordinated study of A.A.'s Big Book, the Twelve Steps of recovery, and the Bible, as well as the biblical roots of A.A.?

The facts and a challenging answer are presented here. Conclusions are suggested. But the reader himself or herself—friend or foe—will be the one calling the shots as to what one can or should do or should not do with God Almighty, the Creator, in today's A.A. The aim is to shine a light on beclouded, misinterpreted, and misleading history—history that is scarcely known in A.A., in the churches, in the recovery community, in our government agencies, or by the general public today.

3

The Simple Program
As A.A. Pioneers Described It

"Your Heavenly Father will never let you down!" (A.A. co-founder Dr. Bob's personal story in *Alcoholics Anonymous*, 3rd ed., Alcoholics Anonymous World Services, Inc., 1976, p. 180).

At long last, exhaustive research has made plain exactly what the early A.A. program was like. You won't find the details or much reference to them in A.A. literature. You won't find many details or references in the text of A.A.'s Big Book today.

Yet the facts are simple and clear. A.A's program developed between 1935 and the Spring of 1939 in Akron, Ohio, primarily under the spiritual leadership of Dr. Bob. It was in Akron that the phenomenal successes were achieved in helping alcoholics. Seventy-five percent of those (*who really tried*) recovered from their alcoholism. It was from the Akron instruction by Dr. Bob that the pioneers began fanning out. Clarence Snyder in Cleveland. Bill Dotson in the midwest. Earl Treat in Chicago. Arch Trowbridge in Detroit. In fact, Cleveland A.A. grew from one group to thirty in a year; and it recorded a ninety-three percent success rate. Without much variation in detail, several of the pioneers described the spiritual program for us as follows.

19

- **Hospitalization or medical care, though quite brief, was very much a priority**. The newcomer was in danger of harming himself (there were only men in the program). He was much in danger of seizures and other early withdrawal problems. And he was sedated with paraldehyde, sometimes strapped down, and visited almost daily by Dr. Bob himself. The only reading material allowed in the hospital room was the Bible.

- **Visits by other members of the Akron group were made at the hospital**. Each newcomer was visited by several alcoholics together, and in varying stages of sobriety. Their mission was to tell him about their own drinking experiences, their downfall from alcoholism, their victory in the fellowship, and the program that had an answer which Dr. Bob would soon explain.

- **Surrender on one's knees was next**. After five to seven days of this detox period, Dr. Bob would make the final visit to the newcomer. Dr. Bob asked if the man believed in God (to which there was only one satisfactory answer). Then Dr. Bob asked him to get out of bed, get on his knees, give his life to Jesus Christ as Lord and Savior, and join Bob in prayer.

- **Then joining in fellowship**—fellowship with God and with other believers. Situations varied, depending upon marital status, job status, home life, and degree of sickness with the newcomer. But A.A. then was truly a "family" program in which wives and children participated. The following were some common elements: (1) A weekly meeting of the Christian fellowship on Wednesdays at the home of T. Henry and Clarace Williams, which consisted of about 50% Oxford Group people and 50% drunks and their families. There were no "drunkalogs." (2) A morning "Quiet Time" held at the home of Dr. Bob and

Anne Smith and conducted by Anne. (3) Individual Quiet Time in the pioneers' homes with Bible study, prayer, seeking guidance, and Christian literature. (4) Frequent fellowship in the homes, on the phone, and in social gatherings. (5) Surrender sessions for newcomers in which there was surrender to Christ, group prayer, and indoctrination as to simple Oxford Group principles such as the Four Absolutes—Honesty, Purity, Unselfishness, and Love. (6) Some form of life-changing work such as self-examination, confession, restitution, and prayer. And this often occurred in private with Dr. Bob himself.

- **Religious observances and fellowship were favored**. Dr. Bob and his wife Anne quickly became charter members of the Westside Presbyterian Church in Akron, and they saw to it that their two children received regular Sunday School training, just as Dr. Bob had in his youth. The end result was the incorporation in A.A.'s Big Book of suggestions *favoring religious affiliation, and* also *additional* spiritual growth through reading books suggested usually by Dr. Bob, and later by one's rabbi, minister, or priest.

- **There were two other features which assured biblical input**.

  — **First, the Bible itself was read and stressed**. It was called the primary source for information needed. There was prayer and listening for God's guidance. Then, with a topic having been selected at a Monday night leadership session, there was discussion led by Henrietta Seiberling, T. Henry Williams, or Dr. Bob. The format for discussion came from a page of *The Upper Room* (A Methodist Quarterly), *My Utmost for His Highest* by Oswald Chambers, *Victorious Living* by E. Stanley Jones, *The Runner's Bible* by Nora

Smith Holm, or the Bible itself. And the Bible
segments considered absolutely essential as guidance
for their principles were Jesus's Sermon on the Mount
(Matthew 5, 6, and 7), 1 Corinthians 13, and the Book
of James.

— **Second, and probably more important, was the
   daily morning quiet time at the Smith home**.
   Jokingly, pioneer AAs talked of coming to Anne
   Smith (Dr. Bob's wife) for "spiritual pablum." The
   Quiet Time meetings with Anne occurred in the early
   morning. They were of substantial length and involved
   Bible reading, prayer, listening for guidance, and
   discussion of some of the rich material Anne Smith
   would share from her spiritual journal. And it was
   these sessions which furnished, and played such a
   large part in, spiritual understanding and growth. For
   Anne thoroughly covered the Bible, suggested
   literature, and discussed all of the Oxford Group
   principles that later became embodied in A.A.'s
   Twelve Steps. Also, a good many practical ideas about
   love, prayer, God's guidance, daily surrender,
   Christian principles, and helping others both to come
   to Christ and to live Christian principles.

● **Finally, having recovered, the believers repeated the
   witnessing process.** Men with greater sobriety would take
   the newer members to the hospital to carry the message of
   hope and recovery to the hospitalized alcoholic patient.

Very simple ideas indeed:

There was recognition of defeat by the newcomer. A
determined call for help. Provision of medical care. Supportive
visits from those with more sobriety than the newcomer.
Information about alcoholism from Dr. Bob. Acceptance of Jesus

Christ as Lord and Savior on one's knees. Joining a fellowship where there was almost always Bible study, prayer, listening for guidance, journaling thoughts received, discussion of religious topics, and participation in a surrender session much like that in the Book of James. James 5:15-16 speaks of prayer by the elders for healing, petitioning in the name of the Lord, confessing one's faults, and praying for deliverance. Then there was a commitment to change one's life to that based on the will of God. Finally, a focus on the newcomer, and on fellowship. The rest of the program, whether conducted at home, on the telephone, at Anne Smith's quiet times, or in personal work with Dr. Bob, consisted simply of a spiritual growth process—seeking God's help, asking for His guidance, and agreeing to try to live in accordance with His will and Word.

4

The Real Foundations of
A.A.'s Pioneer Program

"Henrietta, the Lord has been so wonderful to me, curing me of this terrible disease, that I just want to keep talking about it and telling people." (Quote of Bill Wilson in the personal story of A.A. Number Three, *Alcoholics Anonymous*, 3rd ed., p. 191).

Bill Wilson was significantly vague about the specifics concerning the six major sources of early A.A.'s spiritual ideas. Furthermore, if one confines his or her reading to Bill's remarks, the reader might conclude that the Reverend Sam Shoemaker was the *only* significant spiritual source.

That is not the case; yet it is not a part of our journey to detail the other sources or even to document the facts about them. It is important, however, to know what they are. As stated, A.A. actually drew on *six major sources* for its spiritual ideas.

Bill Wilson stated many times and in many ways that A.A. was not invented—that nobody invented A.A.[1] He underlined that point by stating further that all of A.A.'s ideas were borrowed.[2] Unfortunately, save for lavish generalizations about Shoemaker's role, Bill left A.A.'s other, five, major spiritual sources in the

---

[1] See, for example: *As Bill Sees It*, p. 67.

[2] *A.A. Comes of Age*, pp. 231-32.

dust. The *basic* documentation for each of the six sources *can* be found in A.A.'s own literature; and the author has written extensively on the *specifics* of each of the six.

The six will be reviewed here only briefly and are as follows.

The Bible

First and foremost, A.A.'s basic ideas came from the Bible. The Bible—which early AAs affectionately called "The Good Book"—was the *main* source of A.A. principles and practices. Sam Shoemaker himself was known as a "Bible Christian." His focus—in books, pamphlets, sermons, and personal work—was definitely on the Bible.

As to A.A.'s Bible source, see A.A.'s own *DR. BOB And The Good Oldtimers*.[3] For a thorough discussion and detailing of what AAs specifically borrowed from the Bible, see Dick B., *The Good Book and The Big Book: A.A.'s Roots in the Bible*.[4]

Quiet Time and the Bible Devotionals

A second major source of A.A.'s biblical ideas was the daily use that early AAs made of Quiet Time. This was a period devoted to Bible study, prayer, listening for guidance from God, journaling, and using helpful Bible devotional books such as *The Upper Room*, *The Runner's Bible*, and *My Utmost for His Highest*. As to the importance of A.A.'s Quiet Time roots, again see *DR. BOB and the Good Oldtimers*.[5] For a thorough review of the specifics in the

---

[3] *DR. BOB and the Good Oldtimers* (New York: Alcoholics Anonymous World Services, Inc., 1980), pp. 96-97.

[4] Dick B., *The Good Book and The Big Book: A.A.'s Roots in the Bible*, Bridge Builders ed. (Kihei, HI: Paradise Research Publications, 1997).

[5] *DR. BOB*, pp. 71, 136, 139-40, 151, 178, 220, 310-11.

early AAs' meditation period, see Dick B., *Good Morning!: Quiet Time, Morning Watch, Meditation, and Early A.A.*[6]

The Teachings and Ideas of the Rev. Sam Shoemaker

The Sam Shoemaker source is the subject of several major works by the author.[7] The author's latest is the second edition of *New Light on Alcoholism: God, Sam Shoemaker, and A.A.*[8] This work establishes that almost 200 words and phrases in A.A. came directly from Sam Shoemaker's writings, sermons, and personal work with alcoholics. Wilson dubbed Sam a "co-founder" of A.A. And every recovery idea that is found in the Oxford Group, to which early AAs belonged, and of which Sam Shoemaker was an American leader, can also be found in Shoemaker's own writings. However, there were some major unique ideas that Shoemaker seems to have pumped into A.A.: (1) Man's separation and estrangement from God; (2) How to find God; (3) The turning point that was required; (4) The ingredients of A.A.'s spiritual awakening process: Conversion, prayer, fellowship, and witness; (5) Praying for God's will, not your own, listening for His voice, and obeying His commands; (6) The means of attaining a spiritual experience.

---

[6] Dick B., *Good Morning!: Quiet Time, Morning Watch, Meditation, and Early A.A.*, Bridge Builders ed. (Kihei, HI: Paradise Research Publications, 1998).

[7] See *Courage to Change: The Christian Roots of the Twelve-Step Movement*, Compiled and edited by Bill Pittman and Dick B. (Center City, MN: Hazelden, 1998); Dick B., *Turning Point: A History of Early A.A.'s Spiritual Roots and Successes* (San Rafael, CA: Paradise Research Publications, 1997).

[8] Dick B., *New Light on Alcoholism: God, Sam Shoemaker, and A.A.*, 2d ed. (Kihei, HI: Paradise Research Publications, Inc., 1999).

The Life-changing Program of the Oxford Group

The entire structure of A.A.'s Twelve Steps is based upon the
Oxford Group's "life-changing art."[9] Dr. Frank N. D. Buchman,
a Lutheran Minister, was the founder of the Oxford Group. Early
on, the Group was called "A First Century Christian
Fellowship."[10] And early A.A. was an integral part of that
fellowship.[11] In fact, Dr. Bob commonly called early Akron A.A.
a "Christian Fellowship."[12] The Akron group spoke of itself as
"the alcoholic squad of the Oxford Group."[13] For the history of
the Oxford Group, its life-changing program, and specific details
about its impact on the Twelve Steps and A.A., see Dick B., *The
Oxford Group & Alcoholics Anonymous: A Design for Living That
Works*.

Anne Smith's Journal: 1933-1939

It is safe to say that not one of the six major roots of early A.A.'s
spiritual ideas has been more ignored than the work Dr. Bob's

[9] See, for some of the earlier Oxford Group life-changing literature: A. J. Russell,
For Sinners Only (London: Hodder & Stoughton, 1932); Harold Begbie, *Life Changers*
(New York: G. P. Putnam's Sons, 1927); H. A. Walter *Soul-Surgery: Some Thoughts
on Incisive Personal Work*, 6th ed. (Oxford: at the University Press by John Johnson,
1940)—first published in 1919. Peter Howard (Frank Buchman's successor as leader of
the Oxford Group) wrote *Frank Buchman's Secret* (New York: Doubleday & Company,
Inc., 1961). Howard said at pp. 14-15: "Part of Frank Buchman's secret . . . was his
belief that he did nothing. God did everything if you allowed Him to do so. . . .
[Buchman said to a grateful Scottish coal miner:] "It's not my art. It's God's art."

[10] Dick B., *The Oxford Group & Alcoholics Anonymous: A Design for Living that
Works*, 2d ed. (Kihei, HI: Paradise Research Publications, Inc., 1998), pp. 83-87;
Samuel M. Shoemaker, Jr., *Twice Born Ministers* (New York: Fleming H. Revell
Company, 1929), pp. 23, 46, 90, 95, 101, 122, 147.

[11] *Pass It On*, p. 130.

[12] *DR. BOB*, pp. 118-19; Dick B., *The Oxford Group & Alcoholics Anonymous*, p.
85.

[13] *A.A. Comes of Age*, p. 39; *Pass It On*, pp. 197, 169, 171-72; Thomsen, *Bill W.*,
p. 239; *DR. BOB*, pp. 117, 156; Dick B., *The Akron Genesis of Alcoholics Anonymous*,
pp. 179-92.

wife, Anne Ripley Smith, did with early AAs and their families. Most important, perhaps, is the 64 page journal she kept from 1933 to 1939. In it she assembled and recorded the Biblical ideas, the Christian literature, the Shoemaker books, the Quiet Time practices, and the Oxford Group life-changing ideas, which she then *shared* with the pioneer AAs and their families. Her journal is *detailed*. Her ideas were *practical*. Her devotion and service to drunks was legendary and unselfish. It may well be that it was from Anne's sober teaching that the practical directions and ideas in the Big Book and Steps actually took form. As to Anne, see *The Language of the Heart*, pp. 356-57; *Pass It On*, p. 147; and Bob Smith and Sue Smith Windows, *Children of the Healer*.[14] For a detailed coverage and analysis of Anne's journal and ideas, see Dick B., *Anne Smith's Journal, 1933-1939: A.A.'s Principles of Success*.[15]

The Christian Literature Early AAs Read

Early AAs were readers.[16] They read the Bible.[17] They read books about the Bible; books about the life of Jesus Christ; and books about life-changing.[18] They read daily devotionals. They read books on prayer, healing, faith, religion, and the mind. And they certainly read books by the Rev. Sam Shoemaker and a host of other Oxford Group writers. All books dealt with the Bible and fleshed out the ideas from the Bible that were taking shape in

---

[14] Bob Smith and Sue Smith Windows, *Children of the Healer: The Story of Dr. Bob's Kids As Told to Christine Brewer* (Park Ridge, IL: Parkside Publishing Corporation, 1992).

[15] Dick B., *Anne Smith's Journal, 1933-1939: A.A.'s Principles of Success*, 3rd. ed. (Kihei, HI: Paradise Research Publications, Inc., 1998).

[16] See comments by Dr. Ernest Kurtz in the Foreword to the First Edition of Dick B., *Dr. Bob and His Library: A Major Source of A.A. Spiritual Ideas*, 3rd ed. (Kihei, HI: Paradise Research Publications, Inc., 1998).

[17] *DR. BOB*, pp. 151, 131.

[18] See Dick B., *Anne Smith's Journal, supra*.

A.A.'s recovery program.[19] For an accurate discussion of all the books that were read, studied, and recommended, see Dick B., *Dr and His Library, Anne Smith's Journal, The Books Early AAs Read for Spiritual Growth,* and *That Amazing Grace.*[20]

---

[19] *DR. BOB*, pp. 71, 96, 111, 131, 141, 150-51, 178, 220, 309-11.

[20] Dick B., *Dr. Bob and His Library*, 3rd ed., *supra*; *Anne Smith's Journal, 1933-1939*, 3rd ed., *supra,*; *That Amazing Grace: The Role of Clarence and Grace S. in Alcoholics Anonymous* (Kihei: HI: Paradise Research Publications, Inc., 1996); *The Books Early AAs Read for Spiritual Growth*, 7th ed. (Kihei, HI: Paradise Research Publications, Inc., 1998). See also, Bill Pittman, *AA The Way It Began* (Seattle: Glen Abbey Books, 1988).

Part Two

You Can Start a Good Book/Big Book Group in a Variety of Ways

- You can study the basic ideas AAs took from the Bible.

- You can learn the basic life-changing principles borrowed from the Oxford Group.

- You can obtain accurate evidence of what "Meditation" really meant.

- You can read what Dr. Bob's wife, Anne Smith, recorded and shared about the early program.

When Bill Wilson was asked by one of A.A.'s Cleveland pioneers *what this was that worked so many wonders*, Bill pointed to a picture of Jesus at Gethsemane that was over the mantel and said: *"There it is."* (See *Alcoholics Anonymous*, 3rd ed., pp. 216-17).

5

The Basics Early AAs Borrowed from the Bible

"... [W]e were convinced that the answer to our problems was in the Good Book. ... I didn't write the Twelve Steps. I had nothing to do with the writing of them. ... We got them, as I said, as a result of our study of the Good Book." (Quotations are from Dr. Bob's last major talk in December, 1948, *The Co-Founders of Alcoholics Anonymous*, Alcoholics Anonymous World Services, Inc., pp. 13-14).

It is well documented in the remarks of A.A. pioneers that early AAs read the Bible, studied the Bible, and were convinced that the answer to their problems was in the Bible, which they called the Good Book. Specific confirmation can be found in the statements and writings of Bill Wilson, Dr. Bob Smith, Anne Smith, Henrietta Seiberling, and T. Henry and Clarace Williams—all part of the earliest founding group and days of A.A. in Akron, Ohio. Further verification of the Bible's role exists in the writings of Bill Dotson (A.A. Number Three), Wally Gillam (who housed early AAs in his home), Bill Van Horn (a Pioneer Akron AA), Bob E. (who lived with the Smiths), Clarence Snyder (who got sober in February, 1938, and was sponsored by Dr. Bob), and a lone Easterner (John Fitz-Hugh Mayo), whom they called "Fitz."

You can find the Bible (albeit usually unmentioned as such) almost anywhere you look in the First Edition of *Alcoholics*

Anonymous. And in the personal stories in that edition (most of which have been edited or eliminated), there is specific and frequent mention of the Bible. In another chapter, we will set forth with particularity the various sources, including the Bible, from which particular Twelve Step ideas were borrowed. That treatment can provide a basis for studying the Twelve Steps and endeavoring to understand them better and from a biblical standpoint by looking at their roots. Yet many may simply want to know the basic ideas from the Bible, to which Dr. Bob was probably referring and which were the subject of studies by Bill Wilson, Dr. Bob, and other founders and pioneer alcoholics. So we highlight the points which early AAs actually borrowed from the Bible in connection with particular recovery ideas (principles that later were called Steps). Following are those points which can be study subjects.

- **They admitted they were licked and estranged from God, and that alcohol had become their master.**

  For I delight in the law of God after the inward man: But I see another law in my members, warring against the law of my mind, and bringing me into captivity to the law of sin which is in my members. O wretched man that I am! who shall deliver me from the body of this death? I thank God through Jesus Christ our Lord. So then with the mind I myself serve the law of God; and with the flesh the law of sin (Romans 7:22-25).

- **They came to God, asked for relief, and sought to do His will.**

  — Believed that God is and will deliver us when diligently sought.

    But without faith *it is* impossible to please *him*: for he that cometh to God must believe that he is, and *that* he is a rewarder of them that diligently seek him (Hebrews 11:6).

— Resolved to seek God's Kingdom and righteousness first.

But seek ye first the kingdom of God, and his righteousness; and all these things shall be added unto you (Matthew 6:33).

Ask, and it shall be given you; seek, and ye shall find; knock, and it shall be opened unto you. For every one that asketh receiveth; and he that seeketh findeth; and to him that knocketh it shall be opened (Matthew 7:7-8).

— Focused on doing God's will, not just their own will.

. . . Thy will be done in earth, as it is in heaven (Matthew 6:10).

. . . [N]evertheless not my will, but thine, be done (Luke 22:42).

Not every one that saith unto me, Lord, Lord, shall enter into the kingdom of heaven; but he that doeth the will of my Father which is in heaven (Matthew 7:21).

— Realized God wanted them to become His children and be born of His spirit.

Jesus answered and said unto him, Verily, verily, I say unto thee, Except a man be born again, he cannot see the kingdom of God. . . . I say unto thee, Except a man be born of water and of the Spirit, he cannot enter into the kingdom of God. That which is born of the flesh is flesh; and that which is born of the Spirit is spirit. Marvel not that I said unto thee, Ye must be born again (John 3:3, 5-7).

For God so loved the world, that he gave his only begotten Son, that whosoever believeth in him should

not perish, but have everlasting life. For God sent not
his Son into the world to condemn the world; but that
the world through him might be saved (John 3:16-17).

. . . Sirs, what must I do to be saved? And they said,
Believe on the Lord Jesus Christ, and thou shalt be
saved, and thy house (Acts 16:30-31).

That if thou shalt confess with thy mouth the Lord
Jesus, and shalt believe in thine heart that God hath
raised him from the dead, thou shalt be saved (Romans
10:9).

— As God's children, endeavored to trust in Him,
acknowledge His ways, and look to Him for direction.

Trust in the Lord with all thine heart; and lean not unto
thine own understanding. In all thy ways acknowledge
Him, and he shall direct thy paths (Proverbs 3:5-6).

— Saw they needed to study His Word to learn and know the
truth.

Study to shew thyself approved unto God, a workman
that needeth not to be ashamed, rightly dividing the
word of truth (2 Timothy 2:15).

Blessed *is* the man that walketh not in the counsel of
the ungodly, nor standeth in the way of sinners, nor
sitteth in the seat of the scornful. But his delight *is* in
the law of the Lord; and in his law doth he meditate
day and night. And he shall be like a tree planted by
the rivers of water, that bringeth forth his fruit in his
season; his leaf also shall not wither; and whatsoever
he doeth shall prosper (Psalm 1:1-3).

— Learned also that seeking God involved praying to Him.

Is any among you afflicted? let him pray. Is any merry? let him sing psalms. Is any sick among you? let him call for the elders of the church; and let them pray over him, anointing him with oil in the name of the Lord: And the prayer of faith shall save the sick . . . (James 5:13-15).

Give ear to my words, O Lord, consider my meditation. Hearken unto the voice of my cry my King, and my God: for unto thee will I pray. My voice shalt thou hear in the morning, O Lord; in the morning will I direct *my prayer* unto thee, and will look up (Psalm 5:1-3).

— Listening as well for His answers and guidance.

And the Lord came, and stood, and called as at other times, Samuel, Samuel. Then Samuel answered, Speak: for thy servant heareth (1 Samuel 3:10).

And he trembling and astonished said, Lord, what wilt thou have me to do? And the Lord *said* unto him, Arise, and go into the city, and it shall be told thee what thou must do (Acts 9:6).

— Most thought they should write down the thoughts they received in answer.

Take thee a roll of a book, and write therein all the words that I have spoken unto thee . . . (Jeremiah 36:2).

— The bottom line was obedience to what God said in His Word and by His *voice*.

Of his own will begat he us with the word of truth,
that we should be a kind of firstfruits of his creatures.
Wherefore, my beloved brethren, let every man be
swift to hear, slow to speak, slow to wrath: For the
wrath of man worketh not the righteousness of God.
Wherefore lay apart all filthiness and superfluity of
naughtiness, and receive with meekness the engrafted
word, which is able to save your souls. But be ye
doers of the word, and not hearers only, deceiving
your own selves (James 1:18-23).

- **They believed the Bible contained many clear statements as to what they were to obey.**

  — They were to obey Jesus' first, great commandment, which was to love God.

    Master, which *is* the great commandment in the law?
    Jesus said unto him, Though shalt love the Lord thy
    God with all thy heart, and with all thy soul, and with
    all thy mind. This is the first and great commandment
    (Matthew 22:37-38).

  — They were to fulfill the royal law of love.

    If ye fulfil the royal law according to the scripture,
    Thou shalt love thy neighbor as thyself, ye do well:
    But if ye have respect to persons, ye commit sin, and
    are convinced of the law as transgressors. For
    whosoever shall keep the whole law, and yet offend in
    one *point*, he is guilty of all (James 2:8-10).

  — They were to guard that erring member, the tongue.

    Even so the tongue is a little member, and boasteth
    great things. Behold, how great a matter a little fire
    kindleth. And the tongue *is* a fire, a world of iniquity:
    so is the tongue among our members, that it defileth

the whole body, and setteth on fire the course of
nature; and it is set on fire of hell. For every kind of
beasts, and of birds, and of serpents, and of things in
the sea, is tamed, and hath been tamed of mankind.
But the tongue can no man tame; *It is* an unruly evil,
full of deadly poison (James 3:5-8).

— They were to avoid envy, strife, and lying.

But if ye have bitter envying and strife in your hearts,
glory not, and lie not against the truth. This wisdom
descendeth not from above, but *is* earthly, sensual,
devilish. For where envying and strife *is*, there *is*
confusion and every evil work (James 3:14-16).

— They were to avoid lust, adultery, and pride.

From whence *come* wars and fightings among you?
come they not hence, *even* of your lusts that war in
your members? Ye lust, and have not: ye kill, and
desire to have, and cannot obtain: ye fight and war, yet
ye have not, because ye ask not. Ye ask, and receive
not, because ye ask amiss, that ye may consume it
upon your own lusts. Ye adulterers, and adulteresses,
know ye not that the friendship of the world is enmity
with God? whosoever therefore will be a friend of the
world is the enemy of God. Do you think that the
scripture saith in vain, The spirit that dwelleth in us
lusteth to envy? But he giveth more grace. Wherefore,
he saith, God resisteth the proud, but giveth grace unto
the humble (James 4:1-6).

— They were to avoid anger without cause.

Ye have heard it was said of them of old time, Thou
shalt not kill; and whosever shall kill shall be in danger
of the judgment: But I say unto you, That whosoever
is angry with his brother without a cause shall be in

danger of the judgment: and whosoever shall say to his brother, Raca, shall be in danger of the council: but whosoever shall say, Thou fool, shall be in danger of hell fire (Matthew 5:21-22).

— They were to stop fighting and turn the other cheek.

Ye have heard that it hath been said, An eye for an eye, and a tooth for a tooth: But I say unto you, That ye resist not evil; but whosoever shall smite thee on thy right cheek, turn to him the other also (Matthew 5:38-39).

— They were even to love their enemies.

Ye have heard that it hath been said, Thou shalt love thy neighbor, and hate thine enemy. But I say unto you, Love your enemies, bless them that curse you, do good to them that hate you, and pray for them which despitefully use you, and persecute you (Matthew 5:43-44);

— They were told they must choose between serving God or mammon.

No man can serve two masters: for either he will hate the one, and love the other; or else he will hold to the one and despise the other. Ye cannot serve God and mammon (Matthew 6:24).

— They were told to abide by the "golden rule" and that they would be known by their fruits.

If ye then, being evil, know how to give good gifts unto your children, how much more shall your Father which is in heaven give good things to them that ask him. Therefore all things whatsoever ye would that men do to you, do ye even so to them: for this is the law and the prophets (Matthew 7:11-12).

A good tree cannot bring forth evil fruit, neither can a corrupt tree bring forth good fruit. Every tree that bringeth not forth good fruit is hewn down, and cast into the fire. Wherefore by their fruits ye shall know them (Matthew 7:18-20).

- **For them, "sin" was not just transgression of the law. Sin meant anything that blocked them from God or from others. This kind of "sin" was identified by examining their own conduct, comparing it with the "yardsticks" containing what they believed to be the teachings of Jesus concerning absolute moral standards—absolute honesty, purity, unselfishness, and love. The self-examination and standards originated as follows.**

  — Self examination they found commanded in the Sermon on the Mount.

    Judge not, that ye be not judged. For with what judgment ye judge, ye shall be judged: and with what measure ye mete, it shall be measured to you again. And why beholdest thou the mote that is in thy brother's eye, but considerest not the beam that is in thine own eye? Or how wilt thou say to thy brother, Let me pull out the mote out of thine eye; and, behold, a beam *is* in thine eye? Thou hypocrite, first cast out the beam out of thine own eye; and then shalt thou see clearly to cast out the mote out of thy brother's eye (Matthew 7:1-5).

  — The standard of "absolute honesty" they found in the Gospels, the Sermon on the Mount in the Gospels, and elsewhere in the New Testament.

When he [the devil] speaketh a lie, he speaketh of his
own; for he is a liar and the father of it (John 8:44).

— So also "absolute purity."

And if thy right eye offend thee, pluck it out, and cast
it from thee: for it is profitable for thee that one of thy
members should perish, and not that thy whole body
should be cast into hell. And if thy right hand offend
thee, cut it off, and cast it from thee, for it is profitable
that one of thy members should perish, and not that thy
whole body should be cast into hell (Matthew 5:29-30).

— And "absolute unselfishness."

So likewise, whosoever he be of you that forsaketh not
all that he hath, he cannot be my disciple (Luke
14:33).

— And "absolute love."

A new commandment I give unto you. That ye love
one another; as I have loved you, that ye also love one
another (John 13:34).

● **The shortcomings and sins they unearthed were to be cast
out in a total life-change.**

— They were to confess to God and to another the
wrongdoing they had identified.

Confess your faults one to another, and pray for one
another that ye may be healed. The effectual fervent
prayer of a righteous man availeth much (James 5:16).

If we confess our sins, he is faithful and just to forgive
us our sins, and to cleanse us from all unrighteousness
(1 John 1:9).

— They were to become "convicted" of their sins and admit they had offended against God; that the faults were theirs and theirs only; and could be purged by God

Against thee, thee only have I sinned, and done *this* evil in thy sight. . . (Psalm 51:4).

Iniquities prevail against me: as *for* our transgressions, thou shalt purge them away (Psalm 65:3).

But God commendeth his love toward us, in that, while we were yet sinners, Christ died for us (Romans 5:8).

— They were to repent, seek, and receive remission of sins.

Then Peter said unto them, Repent, and be baptized every one of you in the name of Jesus Christ for the remission of sins, and ye shall receive the gift of the Holy Ghost (Acts 2:38).

Repent ye therefore, and be converted, that your sins may be blotted out, when the times of refreshing shall come from the presence of the Lord. . . . Unto you first God, having raised up his Son Jesus, sent him to bless you, in turning away every one of you from his iniquities (Acts 3:19, 26).

Submit yourselves therefore to God. Resist the devil, and he will flee from you. Draw nigh to God, and he will draw nigh to you. Cleanse *your* hands, *ye* sinners; and purify your hearts, *ye* double minded. . . . Humble yourselves in the sight of the Lord, and he shall lift you up (James 4:7-8, 10).

— This also required a transformation by renewal of the mind.

I beseech you therefore, brethren, by the mercies of God, that ye present your bodies a living sacrifice, holy, acceptable unto God, *which* is your reasonable service. And be not conformed to this world: but be ye transformed by the renewing of your mind, that ye may prove what *is* that good, and acceptable, and perfect, will of God (Romans 12:1-2).

Let love be without dissimulation. Abhor that which is evil; cleave to that which is good. *Be* kindly affectioned one to another with brotherly love; in honor preferring one another; Not slothful in business, fervent in spirit; serving the Lord; Rejoicing in hope; patient in tribulation; continuing instant in prayer; Distributing to the necessity of the saints; given to hospitality. Bless them which persecute you: bless and curse not. Rejoice with them that do rejoice and weep with them that weep. *Be* of the same mind one toward another. Mind not high things, but condescend to men of low estate. Be not wise in your own conceits. Recompense to no man evil for evil. Provide things honest in the sight of all men. If it be possible, as much as lieth in you, live peaceably with all men. Dearly beloved, avenge not yourselves, but *rather* give place unto wrath: for it is written, Vengeance is mine; I will repay, saith the Lord. Therefore if thine enemy hunger, feed him; if he thirst, give him drink: for in so doing thou shalt heap coals of fire on his head. Be not overcome of evil, but overcome evil with good (Romans 12:9-21).

Love worketh no ill to his neighbor: therefore love *is* the fulfilling of the law. And that, knowing the time, that now *it is* high time to awake out of sleep: for now *is* our salvation nearer than we believed. The night is far spent, the day is at hand: Let us therefore cast off the works of darkness, and let us put on the armour of light. Let us walk honestly, as in the day; not in rioting and drunkenness, not in chambering and wantonness,

not in strife and envying. But put ye on the Lord Jesus
Christ, and make not provision for the flesh, to *fulfill*
the lusts *thereof* (Romans 13:10-14).

- ## The result: a new man in Christ.

Therefore if any man *be* in Christ, *he is* a new creature: old
things are passed away; behold, all things are become new (2
Corinthians 5:17).

- ## The new life of godliness required restitution for harms caused.

Therefore if thou bring thy gift to the altar, and there
rememberest that thy brother hath ought against thee; Leave
there thy gift before the altar, and go thy way: first be
reconciled to thy brother, and then come and offer thy gift.
Agree with thine adversary quickly, whiles thou art in the way
with him; lest at any time the adversary deliver thee to the
judge, and the judge deliver thee to the officer, and thou be cast
into prison. Verily I say unto thee, Thou shalt by no means
come out thence, till thou hast paid the uttermost farthing
(Matthew 5:23-25).

I will arise and go to my father, and will say unto him, Father,
I have sinned against heaven, and before thee, And am no more
worthy to be called thy son: make me as one of thy hired
servants. And he arose, and came to his father. But when he
was yet a great way off, his father saw him, and had
compassion, and ran, and fell on his neck, and kissed him. And
the son said unto him, Father, I have sinned against heaven, and
in thy sight, and am no more worthy to be called thy son. But
the father said to his servants, Bring forth the best robe, and put
it on him; and put a ring on his hand, and shoes on *his* feet:
And bring hither the fatted calf, and kill *it*; and let us eat, and
be merry: For this my son was dead, and is alive again; he was
lost, and is found. And they began to be merry (Luke 15:18-
24).

And Zacchaeus stood, and said unto the Lord; Behold, Lord, the half of my goods I give to the poor; and if I have taken any thing from any man by false accusation, I restore *him* fourfold. And Jesus said unto him, This day is salvation come to this house, forsomuch as he also is a son of Abraham. For the Son of man is come to seek and to save that which was lost (Luke 19:8-10).

- **They realized their relationship with God was unearned and by Divine favor—they were saved by unmerited grace, not by works.**

For by grace are ye saved through faith: and that not of yourself; *it is* the gift of God. Not of works, lest any man should boast. For we are his workmanship, created in Christ Jesus unto good works, which God hath before that we should walk in them (Ephesians 3:8-10).

Grace be to you and peace from God the Father, and *from our* Lord Jesus Christ. Who gave himself for our sins that he might deliver us from this present evil world, according to the will of God and our father (Galatians 1:3-4).

For I am not ashamed of the gospel of Christ: for it is the power of God unto salvation in every one that believeth; to the Jew first, and also to the Greek. For therein is the righteousness of God revealed from faith to faith, as it is written, The just shall live by faith (Romans 1:16-17).

Jesus saith unto him. I am the way, the truth, and the life; no man cometh unto the Father but by me (John 13:6).

I have given them thy word. . . . Sanctify them through thy truth: thy word is truth (John 17:16-17).

Then said Jesus to those Jews which believed on him, If ye continue in my word, *then* are ye my disciples indeed. And ye shall know the truth, and the truth shall make you free. . . . If the Son therefore shall make you free, ye shall be free indeed (John 8:31, 32, 36).

If any man will do his will, he shall know of the doctrine, whether it be of God, or *whether* I speak of myself (John 7:17).

But be ye doers of the word, and not hearers only, deceiving your own selves (James 1:22).

Be ye also patient; stablish your hearts; for the coming of the Lord draweth nigh. Grudge not only against another, brethren, lest ye be condemned: behold, the judge standeth before the door (James 5:8-9).

Draw nigh to God, and he will draw nigh to you. Cleanse *your* hands *ye* sinners; and purify *your* hearts *ye* double minded (James 4:8).

- **They knew that after they were reborn, they would—by the gift of holy spirit—receive power, forgiveness, healing, and love because of Jesus Christ's accomplishments.**

For John truly baptized with water; but ye shall be baptized with the Holy Ghost not many days hence (Acts 1:5).

And behold, I send the promise of my Father upon you: but tarry ye in the city of Jerusalem until ye be endued with power from on high (Luke 24:49).

But ye shall receive power, after that the Holy Ghost is come upon you: and ye shall be witnesses unto me both in Jerusalem, and in all Judaea, and in Samaria, and unto the uttermost part of the earth (Acts 1:8).

For God hath not given us the spirit of fear; but of power, and of love, and of a sound mind (2 Timothy 1:7).

I write unto you, little children, because your sins are forgiven you for his name's sake (1 John 2:12).

Herein is love, not that we loved God, but that he loved us, and
sent his Son *to be* the propitiation for our sins (1 John 3:10).

And we have known and believed the love that God hath to us.
God is love; and he that dwelleth in love dwelleth in God, and
God in him (1 John 4:16).

There is no fear in love; but perfect love casteth out fear:
because fear hath torment. He that feareth is not made perfect
in love (1 John 4:18).

- **And they were to witness to what God had done for them.**

Having therefore obtained help of God, I continue unto this day,
witnessing both to small and great, saying none other things
than those which the prophets and Moses did say should come
(Acts 26:22).

And when he had called unto *him* his twelve disciples, he gave
them power *against* unclean spirits to cast them out, and to heal
all manner of sickness and all manner of disease (Matthew
10:1).

Jesus answered and said unto them, Go and shew John again
those things which *ye* do hear and see: The blind receive their
sight, and the lame walk, the lepers are cleansed, and the deaf
hear, the dead are raised up, and the poor have the gospel
preached to them (Matthew 11:4-5).

Afterward, he appeared unto the eleven as they sat at meat, and
upbraided them with their unbelief and hardness of heart,
because they believed not them which had seen him after he had
risen. And he said unto them, Go ye into all the world, and
preach the gospel to every creature. He that believeth and is
baptized shall be saved; but he that believeth not shall be
damned. And these signs shall follow them that believe; In my
name shall they cast out devils; they shall speak with new
tongues; They shall take up serpents and if they drink any
deadly thing, it shall not hurt them; they shall lay hands on the

sick, and they shall recover. . . . And they went forth, and
preached every where, the Lord working with *them*, and
confirming the word with signs following. Amen (Mark 16:14-
20).

- **Of utmost importance, they were to live love and serve.**

And this is his commandment, That we should believe on the
name of his Son Jesus Christ, and love one another, as he gave
us commandment (1 John 3:23).

My little children, let us not love in word, neither in tongue;
but in deed and in truth (1 John 3:18).

Beloved, let us love one another: for love is of God; and every
one that loveth is born of God, and knoweth God. He that
loveth not knoweth not God; for God is love (1 John 4:7-8).

Be ye therefore followers of God, as dear children: And walk
in love, as Christ also hath loved us, and hath given himself for
us an offering and a sacrifice to God for a sweetsmelling savour
(Ephesians 5:1-2).

And though I bestow all my goods to feed *the poor*, and though
I give my body to be burned, and have not charity (love), it
profiteth me nothing. Charity (love) suffereth long, and is kind;
charity envieth not; charity vaunteth not itself, is not puffed up,
Doth not behave itself unseemly, seeketh not her own, is not
easily provoked, thinketh no evil; Rejoiceth not in iniquity, but
rejoiceth in truth (1 Corinthians 13:3-6).

And whosoever of you will be the chiefest, shall be servant of
all. For even the Son of man came not to be ministered to, but
to minister, and to give his life a ransom for many (Mark
10:43-44).

Is it even possible to say that early AAs individually and as a
fellowship in Akron studied each of the foregoing verses? Is it

even remotely possible to say that they then sat down and worked out a program from the Bible?

Some of A.A.'s own literature seems to suggest this. But an entirely different process of assimilation was going on, whatever A.A.'s present literature, Dr. Bob's few comments, and Bill Wilson's silence may imply. First of all, the author's own thirteen titles show how the foregoing verses appeared over and over again in Oxford Group literature, in Sam Shoemaker's writings, in the Quiet Time devotionals AAs read, in the other Christian literature that was passed around and/or in Anne Smith's Journal. Second, there is no doubt whatever from the author's own research, interviews, and reading that the sober "founders" of A.A. did understand the life-changing program and interpret the Bible verses to support it by referring to the foregoing ideas and verses. Third, and who were they? Such "founders" as the Rev. Sam Shoemaker and his colleague Rev. Irving Harris; Oxford Group people such as Dr. Frank Buchman, Rowland Hazard, Shep Cornell, Hanford Twitchell, and Cebra Graves; Fitz and similar New York participants; sober Akron Oxford Group members Henrietta Seiberling, T. Henry Williams, and Clarace Williams; and most certainly Dr. Bob and his wife Anne.

All the foregoing A.A. ideas have been correlated to their biblical source verses above and documented in the author's titles. Citations showing where the verses were used in early A.A. literature were omitted here, but are thoroughly detailed in such titles as the author's *The Good Book and The Big Book: A.A.'s Roots in the Bible*.

In a talk at the Shrine Auditorium in Los Angeles to 4,500 alcoholics, their friends and relatives, Bill Wilson said Alcoholics Anonymous recommends a return to religion, resumption of church attendance. Bill emphasized that Divine Aid was A.A.'s greatest asset. In that same meeting, Bill's co-founder Dr. Bob said: "Read religious literature. Resume church attendance, cultivate the habit of prayer." And Dr. Bob particularly recommended reading the Bible. [The information in this paragraph was reported in *The TIDINGS*, March 26, 1943, p. 17 (a Roman Catholic newspaper)].

6

The Oxford Group Path
in Pioneer A.A.'s Steps

"They had the Bible, and they had the precepts of the Oxford Group. They also had their own instincts. They were working, or working out, the A.A. program—the Twelve Steps—without quite knowing how they were doing it" (*DR. BOB and the Good Oldtimers*, p. 96). "The principles of 'The Oxford Group' are the principles of the Bible. The group is not an organization, not a sect, not even a new method. The Group is a life—that life which is hid with Christ in God" (*The Principles of the Oxford Group*, by Sherwood Sunderland Day, The Oxford Group, p. 1).

Set forth below are some of the basic Oxford Group ideas that were transmitted to the A.A. Fellowship, its literature, and Steps. And these ideas can themselves be fruitful subjects for study in an A.A. Good Book/Big Book Group today.

Specific Oxford Group Ideas in the Twelve Steps

Step One

"O, God, manage me, because I cannot manage myself." This simple prayer was often mentioned by Frank Buchman, Sam Shoemaker, and Anne Smith. Its counter-part can be found in A.A.'s "Our lives had become unmanageable."

Step Two

Sam Shoemaker wrote of the need for "a Force outside himself, greater than himself" and "a vast Power outside themselves." He insisted that there be a willingness to believe, and that there be a belief in God. The willingness, he said, was wrapped up in the experiment of faith by which a person stepped out on his belief in God by obeying God and realizing, as Jesus taught in John 7:17, that the believing produced results.

Step Three

The Oxford Group laid the foundation for the A.A. idea that surrender starts with a *decision*. Using language in *Twice-Born Ministers* that was borrowed almost verbatim by A.A.'s Step Three, Shoemaker spoke of "the decision to cast my will and my life on God" (p.34). Then Shoemaker forecast and virtually framed the famous A.A. expression "God as we understood Him." He frequently spoke of "surrendering as much of yourself as you understand to as much of God as you understand" (*Children of the Second Birth*, pp. 27, 47). Using language similar to that in the original Third Step draft, Shoemaker had previously said: "She surrendered to God . . . and . . . turned over to Him her life for His direction" (*Children of the Second Birth*, p. 82).

Step Four

The language of Step Four is Oxford Group. In *Soul Surgery*, Oxford Group writer H. A. Walter pointed to Frank Buchman's insistence that each person "make the moral test" (pp. 43-44). Oxford Group mentor Henry Drummond wrote that man needs to "devote his soul to self-examination, to self-examination of the most solemn and searching kind" (*The Ideal Life*, p. 316). Frank Buchman said: "Moral recovery starts when everyone admits his own faults instead of spot-lighting the other fellow's" (*Remaking the World*, p. 46).

Step Five

Oxford Group writer Stephen Foot explained as to confession: "The first step for me was to be honest with God, the next to be honest with men" (*Life Began Yesterday*, p. 11). Howard Walter wrote: "Be ready to confess your own shortcomings honestly and humbly" (*Soul Surgery*, p. 57).

Step Six

In *The Venture of Belief*, Oxford Group activist Philip Marshall Brown wrote: "To summarize the various stages of spiritual adventure; first, the will to believe; second, the honest facing and sharing of all conscious sin; third, the complete surrender of self to God; and, fourth, the willingness to obey His will" (p. 36).

Step Seven

In *I Was a Pagan*, Bill Wilson's friend and Oxford Group co-worker Victor Kitchen wrote: "It takes the power of God to remove the desire for these indulgences" (p. 143). Kitchen also said: "I then and there admitted my inability to quit of my own will and asked God to take charge of the matter" (p. 74). He also said: "God . . . satisfied unsound desire by removing the desire itself" (p. 73).

Step Eight

"God cannot take over my life unless I am willing," said Cecil Rose in *When Man Listens* (p. 17). Oxford Group writer Jack Winslow said: "A further point in the moral challenge which the Oxford Group presents is that known as restitution, viz. putting right, as far as in our power, wrongs committed in the past" (*Why I Believe in the Oxford Group*, p. 31).

Step Nine

Cecil Rose said: "These first steps of restitution are absolutely necessary if I am to start the new life clear with God and other people. (*When Man Listens*, p. 20).

Step Ten

Oxford Group leader Sam Shoemaker said: "There is need for rededication day by day, hour by hour, by which progressively, in every Quiet Time, the contaminations of sin and self-will are further sloughed off, for they do have a way of collecting" (*The Conversion of the Church*, p. 79). And using language which A.A. seems to have adopted verbatim, Frank Buchman said: "What is the disease? Isn't it fear, dishonesty, resentment, selfishness?" (*Remaking the World*, p. 38).

Step Eleven

Oxford Group scholar Philip Marshall Brown wrote: "They tell of the strength of heart and mind, of the depth of knowledge of life, of the charity and love that are poured into human beings whenever they establish contact with God" (*The Venture of Belief*, p. 24). Stephen Foot said: (1) "Contact with God is the necessary fundamental condition, and that is made through prayer and listening. . . ." (2) "I will ask God to show me His purpose for my life and claim from Him the power to carry that purpose out" (*Life Began Yesterday*, pp. 13, 11). Victor Kitchen—Bill's Oxford Group friend—wrote: "I 'emerged' into God-consciousness" (*I Was a Pagan*, p. 43).

Step Twelve

The Oxford Group's earliest writer, H.A. Walter, stated in *Soul Surgery*: "The basis of conversion is the awakening of a new self, and the vital element in this new birth is the dawning of a new affection which dominates the heart" (p. 82). Sam Shoemaker said: "This experience, which I consider was my conversion, brought to me a new kind of life which was entirely new to me" (*Twice-Born Ministers*, p. 55). Long ago, Frank Buchman wrote: "The best way to keep an experience of Christ is to pass it on" (*Remaking the World*, p. x). As to practicing the principles taught in the Sermon on the Mount and elsewhere in the Bible, A. J. Russell, a leading writer for the Oxford Group, declared: "Moreover, it meant a relentless crusade to induce other men and women not only to believe in the possibility of living the victorious life, but to live it" (*For Sinners Only*, p. 62). Professor B. H. Streeter, an Oxford Group mentor, wrote in *The God Who Speaks*: "Christ does not merely teach men what to do, he gives them power to do it" (p. 151).

All the foregoing Oxford Group sources are fully discussed in, detailed by, and cited in full in the author's book, *The Oxford Group & Alcoholics Anonymous: A Design for Living that Works*. Bibliographic details can also be found in his *The Books Early AAs Read for Spiritual Growth*, 7th ed. Personally, I was astonished when I read the early Oxford Group books and talked to a dozen or so of the survivors. I could hear A.A. ideas, A.A. language, and A.A. techniques at every turn. Yet these were people who scarcely knew they had played a part in the founding of our fellowship.

7

Quiet Time, Devotionals, and the Guidance of God

"He must have devotions every morning—a 'quiet time' of prayer and some reading from the Bible and other religious literature. Unless this is faithfully followed, there is grave danger of backsliding" [From the report of A.A. trustee-to-be Frank Amos in 1938 on "the technique used and the system followed" [which] he described as the "Program" of the original alcoholic group in Akron and comprised some 50 men, two women former alcoholics—"all considered practically incurable by physicians—who have been reformed and so far have remained teetotalers."] (*DR. BOB and the Good Oldtimers*, pp. 130, 31).

You may study early A.A.'s Quiet Time source which, of course, included the guidance of God that they sought in developing their program. And you can find the origins, background, and Quiet Time practices of the Oxford Group and early A.A. in *Anne Smith's Journal, 1933-1939*; *The Oxford Group & Alcoholics Anonymous*; and *Good Morning! Quiet Time, Morning Watch, Meditation, and Early A.A.*[1]

There has been widespread recent publication of various meditation, "reflection," and "history" books. These either suggest meditation ideas or purport to describe the practices of early A.A. But not one even closely resembles the early A.A. situation.

---

[1] Dick B., *Good Morning!: Quiet Time, Morning Watch, Meditation, and Early A.A.*, 2d ed. (Kihei, HI: Paradise Research Publications, Inc., 1998).

Moreover, these, one page squibs, "a moment of silence," and what Sam Shoemaker called "half-baked prayers," have totally replaced the Bible-oriented Quiet Time of early A.A.

Present-day recovery meditation, reflection, or thought-for-the-day books and booklets omit several factors which were vital to the early A.A. Quiet Time. The most significant omission is that of a surrender *first* to Jesus Christ as Lord and Savior. Yet such a surrender was a "must" in the early program. In the East, Sam Shoemaker had people on their knees in surrender on the first meeting. So too with Dr. Bob in Akron. And, as far as Quiet Time itself was concerned, the reason was biblical. There was, and could be, no understanding or ability to understand the Bible, the prayers, or the voice of God without first being spirit-filled in a new birth which provided the *indwelling spirit of God*:

> But the natural man receiveth not the things of the Spirit of God: for they are foolishness unto him: neither can he know *them* because they are spiritually discerned. . . . For who hath known the mind of the Lord, that he may instruct him? But we have the mind of Christ (1 Corinthians 2:14, 16).[2]

---

[2] To illustrate the omission of a surrender to Christ as the *sine qua non* of hearing from God, see the third edition of *Alcoholics Anonymous* (pp. 86-87) which describes Divine guidance in terms of asking for inspiration, an intuitive thought or decision so that what used to be the hunch or the occasional inspiration becomes a working part of the mind. There is no mention of the surrender to Christ which was required in early A.A. To make matters worse, one popular guide to present-day attempts at early A.A. guidance, describes receiving Guidance from a Power; yet it makes no mention whatever of the requisite new birth (John 3:3-8), confession of Christ (Romans 10:9), or the consequent baptism with, and receipt of the gift of, the Holy Spirit (Acts 1:5-8, 2:38; 1 Corinthians 12:7-13; Ephesians 1:13, 2:18; Colossians 1:27; 1 Thessalonians 2:13). See *Back to Basics*, pp. 38-39, 48-49, 100-109, 119-127). Yet surrender to Christ was the essence of the Oxford Group's position, as well as the Bible's position. See Harry Almond, *Foundations for Faith*, 2d ed. (London: Grosvenor, 1980), pp. 14-25; A. J. Russell, *For Sinners Only* (New York: Harper & Brothers, 1932), pp. 184-98; B. H. Streeter, *The God Who Speaks* (London: Macmillan & Co., 1943); Samuel M. Shoemaker, Jr. *Religion That Works* (New York: Fleming H. Revell Company, 1928), pp. 9-80). *Conversion, not diversion* to the any god of today's A.A. was the absolute requirement as the foregoing Oxford Group writings and authorities make very very clear. *Ye must be born again, they all said.*

The early A.A. devotionals were peppered with verses of Scripture and suggestions for further Scripture study. Yet, in many of today's materials, there is reference to some "any god," suggestions that one need only "practice" more, and that the whole thing (meditation and receiving guidance) rests on "intuition."

Very simply, this was not the Quiet Time of early A.A. For that Quiet Time involved the Bible, Prayer, Listening, writing down thoughts, and often the use of devotionals such as *The Upper Room*, *My Utmost for His Highest*, *The Meaning of Prayer*, *Victorious Living*, or *The Runner's Bible*. Bible study was accompanied by many "helpful books" to aid understanding, such as the several commentaries on Jesus's sermon on the mount by Oswald Chambers, Glenn Clark, Emmet Fox, and E. Stanley Jones, and Henry Drummond's commentary, *The Greatest Thing in the World*, on 1 Corinthians 13.

In the foregoing context, then, one can study the basic ingredients of Quiet Time itself which involved *first* becoming born again of the spirit of God (See *Good Morning!*, pp. 53-62). The following, then, comprise the totality of practices:

- Surrender first to Jesus Christ (See Romans 10:9).

- "Clearing the receiver" by taking action to eliminate sin.

- A definite, adequate, early time.

- A quiet, peaceful, relaxed stance.

- Reading the Bible.

- Using Christian devotionals.

- Praying *to* God.

- Hearing *from* God.

- Writing down or "journaling" thoughts.

- "Checking" the guidance with Scripture or other believers to avoid self-deception.

- Obeying the "Voice of God."

Probably lacking an adequate understanding himself, or being reluctant to embrace this Oxford Group practice in full, Bill Wilson rejected the principle of "guidance" primarily because, he said, "to receive it accurately, considerable spiritual preparation was necessary" (*Pass It On*, p. 172).

There is also substantial evidence of Roman Catholic objections to the idea that a private individual receives messages from God (See *New Light on Alcoholism*, pp. 413-20). And Bill himself was moving toward greater and greater reliance on Roman Catholic views, asking Father Ed Dowling for specific suggestions, allowing Father John C. Ford's detailed editing of Bill's own *A.A. Comes of Age* and *Twelve Steps and Twelve Traditions*, and taking instruction from Bishop Fulton J. Sheen.

On the other hand, Protestant thinking, as embodied in Oxford Group ideas, relied heavily on guidance from God in the form of revelation in His Word and personal revelation given individually to man. (See B. H. Streeter, *The God Who Speaks*.)

Again a caution. The Biblical view of revelation for the Christian is based on the Christian's *receiving the gift of holy spirit* which *enables the communication with God to be received*. While that idea was part and parcel of early A.A., it is missing from the various approaches and explanations and practices emanating from the Eleventh Step today. There simply is no talk about revelation or the new man in Christ or salvation.

Since prayer and meditation were *vital* in early A.A. and are still highlighted throughout A.A.'s Big Book, a thorough understanding is called for. And no better source for such study can be found than the Bible itself, and then *The Upper Room*. Help in the quest can be found in the author's *Good Morning!*

You may find, as I did, that turning to God for help is a total winner. You may find, as I did, that a lot of time spent in reading His Word, praying, and seeking His guidance brings answers to your problems. You may find that one of the best messages you can transmit is the message that God has something to say to us!

8

Anne Smith's Specific Journal and Twelve Step Ideas

"Anne was the wife of Dr. Bob, co-founder of Alcoholics Anonymous. She was, quite literally, the mother of our first group, Akron Number One. . . . In the full sense of the word, she was one of the founders of Alcoholics Anonymous" (*The Language of the Heart: Bill W.'s Grapevine Writings*, 1988, pp. 353-54).

If Bill and Bob were developing the Twelve Step ideas primarily from the Bible and the Oxford Group program, Dr. Bob's wife Anne was certainly learning those ideas, teaching them, recording them, or all three. While we will not cover material already set forth in our sections about the Bible, the Oxford Group, and Shoemaker, we need to sketch out the Step ideas as Anne expressed them (Quotes are from *Anne Smith's Journal, 1933-1939*).

Let's start first, however, by declaring and accepting the importance of studying the journal which Dr. Bob's wife Anne kept from 1933-1939 and shared with early AAs and their families in the daily quiet times at the Smith home and also at other times. If you really want to know what early A.A. *was*, you will need to study Anne Smith's Journal. This material is a treasure that still remains officially *buried*! Following are some of Anne's major ideas and expressions concerning the Twelve Step ideas.

Step One. Anne twice specifically mentioned the "manage me" prayer that was popular with Buchman and Shoemaker ("O Lord manage me, for I cannot manage myself").

Step Two. Using language resembling that in A.A.'s Second Step, Anne said: "A stronger power than his was needed. God provided the power through Christ, so that we could find a new relationship with God."

Step Three. "Try to bring a person to a decision to 'surrender as much of himself as he knows to as much of God as he knows.' Stay with him until he makes a decision and says it out loud." She added, "Surrender is a complete handing over of our wills to God, a reckless abandon of ourselves, all that we have, all that we think, that we are, everything we hold dear, to God to do what he likes with. . . ."

Step Four. "It is absolutely necessary to face people with the moral test. . . . Criticism born of my own projection. Something wrong in me. Unless I can crystalize the criticism, I had better look for the mote in my eye. . . . Make the moral test. 4 Standards [the Four Absolutes]. . . . Why I had been absolutely honest but not living [it]. . . . Resentments to be faced and set right. . . . Fear and worry are atheism. . . . Just a glimpse of self-centered life."

Step Five. "Confess your faults one to another. . . . I must share to be honest with God, myself & others."

Step Six. "Be willing to ask God where I am failing and to admit sin."

Step Seven. [speaking of sins such as selfishness, dishonesty, and pride] "Christ can only remove them and replace with a new quality of life. Read Romans 12. . . . Do not pretend you can go on lifting yourself by your own boot straps. In all humility to God,

"What would thou have me to do?". . . . I'm wrong Father. . . show me the way."

Steps Eight and Nine. "Any restitution I won't make. . . . Resentments to be faced and set right. . . . Restitution to be made. . . . Help them make a list of things. . . . God can make me willing in the day of His power."

Step Ten. "Check your life constantly by the four absolutes." "Our lives will be one continuous surrender: surrender to God of every difficulty that confronts us, each temptation, each spiritual struggle, laying before Him either to take away or to show us in their proper spiritual proportions." "Be willing to ask God where I am failing and to admit sin."

Step Eleven. (1) *Prayer*: "Intercessory prayer—pray that Spirit may tell you what to pray for. . . . A way to find God's will not to change it." "Petitionary prayers. . . . These we submit not because we distrust His goodness or desire to bend His Will but because He is our Friend. . . . [Anne illustrated:] Correct me—direct—praise—adoration and thanksgiving. Romans II." (2) *Guidance*: "Guidance is the principle of the Bible, its very structure." "We must be in such relationship with God that He can guide us. . . . Specifically, guidance comes through intelligent knowledge of the Bible, through conscience, through circumstance. . . . guidance is thinking plus God." "I will lead you and guide you in all truth, and bring all thoughts to your remembrance (John)." (3) *Listening*: "Watch your thoughts. Your thoughts can come from three sources. 1. Subconscious. 2. The devil. 3. God." (4) *Bible study and reading*: "Let all your reading be guided. . . . Of course the Bible ought to be the main Source Book of all." (5) *Quiet Time*: "Effective Quiet Time: 1. Objective, God and obedience. 2. Attentive prayer and being willing to act immediately. 3. Stillness and surrender of all known sins." In addition, there are many, many specific comments about prayer, listening, reading, and so on that should be read to get the full flavor and depth of Anne's teaching.

Step Twelve. (1) *Having had a spiritual experience*: "A general experience of God is the first essential, the beginning. We can't give away what we haven't got. We must have a genuine contact with God in our present experience." (2) *Carrying the message*: "Giving Christianity away is the best way to keep it." "When we have that [a general experience of God], witnessing to it is natural, just as we want to share a beautiful sunset." (3) *Practicing the principles*: "Start the person on a new life with simple, concrete and definite suggestions, regarding Bible study, prayer, overcoming temptation and service to others." "God's answer to materialism is a basis of Christian living that lifts above material things." "Claim from God humility, patience, courage, faith and love."

The foregoing points are mere brief sketches of Anne's thorough treatment of the Twelve Step ideas. Any reader is in for a treat if he or she studies the entirety of *Anne Smith's Journal, 1933-1939*, as the author has set it forth in that title. I don't think there is any historical find that I have made that can and should be of greater significance in helping others, in understanding A.A. ideas, and in learning how our Fellowship began than the material found in the 64 pages of Anne's notes, which A.A. itself has never published.

Part Three

Sam Shoemaker, Bill's Acknowledged Mentor, and A.A.'s Six Basic Roots

"Every river has a wellspring at its source. AA is like that, too. In the beginning, there was a spring which poured out of a clergyman, Dr. Samuel Shoemaker. 'Way back in 1934 he began to teach us the principles and attitudes that afterward came to full flower in AA's Twelve Steps for recovery" (*The Language of the Heart*, p. 176).

"The basic principles of A.A., as they are known today, were borrowed mainly from the fields of religion and medicine, though some ideas upon which success finally depended were the result of noting the behavior and needs of the Fellowship itself" (*Twelve Steps and Twelve Traditions*, p. 16).

The six basic roots of Alcoholics Anonymous are:

- Bible Principles

- Quiet Time Practices

- Sam Shoemaker's Teachings

- The Oxford Group Life-changing Principles and Practices

- Anne Smith's Spiritual Guide

- Christian Literature Used for Study and Reference

9

Oxford Group Leader
Sam Shoemaker's Input

"Having now accounted for AA's Steps One and Twelve, it is natural that we should next ask, 'Where did the early AAs find the material for the remaining ten Steps? Where did we learn about moral inventory, amends for harm done, turning our wills and lives over to God? Where did we learn about meditation and prayer and all the rest of it?' The spiritual substance of our remaining ten Steps came straight from Dr. Bob's and my own earlier association with the Oxford Groups, as they were then led in America by that Episcopal rector, Dr. Samuel Shoemaker" (*The Language of the Heart: Bill W.'s Grapevine Writings*, The AA Grapevine, Inc., p. 298).

This chapter will present an in depth look at Sam Shoemaker's Twelve Step contributions as expressed in his own books and pamphlets. You can use it as a guide for real study of Sam's role.

- *Step One*: **We admitted we were powerless over alcohol—that our lives had become unmanageable.**

A.A.'s Biblical roots feed into this Step in three major ways—as to lack of power, as to an unmanageable life, and as to sin and alcoholism as the cause of the problem of powerlessness and unmanageability

Powerless!

In a 1931 title, Sam Shoemaker wrote about sin and the barrier it places between man and God—a block which man, by himself, is powerless to overcome. He said:

> It [sin] makes a gap between myself and the Ideal which I am *powerless* to bridge.[1] It distances me from the All-holy God. And I cannot climb or crawl back across that distance. . . . Only God, therefore, can deal with sin. He must contrive to do for us what *we have lost the power to do for ourselves* (emphasis added).[2]

The First Edition of A.A.'s Big Book states:

> *Lack of power*, that was our dilemma. We had to find a power by which we could live, and it had to be A Power Greater Than Ourselves. . . . And, it means, of course, that we are going to talk about God (p. 87, emphasis added).

---

[1] As often happens when the author is researching and revising, someone comes up with new material. A person in New Zealand wrote to call my attention to the language of Romans 5:6. The reader should remember that Shoemaker usually quoted King James or Moffatt's Translation. But as an interesting point, we will quote several versions of Romans 5:6: (1) "For when we were yet without strength, in due time, Christ died for the ungodly" (King James Version). (2) "For while we were still helpless, at the right time Christ died for the ungodly" (New American Standard Bible). (3) "You see, at just the right time, when we were *still powerless*, Christ died for the ungodly" (New International Version, emphasis added). (4) "When we were utterly helpless, Christ came at just the right time and died for us sinners" (New Living Translation). (5) "Christ died for us at a time when we were helpless and sinful" (Contemporary English Version). See *The Contemporary Parallel New Testament* (New York: Oxford University Press, 1997), pp. 1040-41. Compare the commentary *Recovery Devotional Bible: New International Version* (Grand Rapids, MI: Zondervan Publishing House, 1993), p. 1237.

[2] Samuel M. Shoemaker, *If I Be Lifted Up: Thoughts About the Cross* (New York: Fleming H. Revell Company, 1931), pp. 131, 133.

Shoemaker was not paddling the "powerless" canoe by himself. Sam's good Oxford Group friend Victor C. Kitchen (also a friend of Bill Wilson's) wrote the following in a 1934 title:

> This time, however, I decided to see if the *God* the Oxford Group had talked about *could and would* assist me. I asked His help rather than attempt the thing myself and something unusual happened. . . . I felt a strange sense of dependence on some *power that was utterly dependable—a power within yet coming from outside myself—a power far stronger than I was* (emphasis added).[3]

> With my new experience, however, the Holy Ghost or Spirit became a definite force flowing from God to me as electricity flows from a power house. . . . It was a force, moreover, which not only switched over my will and my affections but which I could actually feel within me as a sort of . . . power actually to *do* things—a force far stronger, far wiser, far more helpful and far more effective than any I myself had ever possessed.[4]

An unmanageable life

What about the unmanageable life? Here Shoemaker may have catalyzed in A.A. a prayer that had been bouncing around in the Oxford Group for years. In his well-known Oxford Group title, *For Sinners Only*, A. J. Russell described that prayer. Russell related Dr. Frank Buchman's story about "Victor," and how Victor had surrendered and had his life changed. Russell told at some length how Frank Buchman had converted Victor at a schoolboys' camp in the Himalayas. Russell recounted the following conversation between Buchman and Victor:

---

[3] Victor C. Kitchen, *I Was a Pagan* (New York: Harper & Brothers, 1934), p. 63. See Big Book, 1st ed., p. 72: "That probably no human power could have relieved our alcoholism. That God could and would if sought."

[4] Kitchen, *I Was a Pagan*, p. 78.

[Buchman said:] What we need is faith. When we are perfectly willing to forsake sin and follow Christ, then joy and release come. What we want to do is to get in touch with Him and turn our lives over to Him. Where should we go to do it? At once the lad replied: "There is only one place—on our knees." The lad prayed—one of those powerful, simple prayers which are so quickly heard by Him Who made the eye and the ear: "*O Lord, manage me, for I cannot manage myself*" (emphasis added).[5]

Variations of this "Victor story" were told again and again in Oxford Group writings.[6] To such an extent that Dr. Bob's wife, Anne Ripley Smith, several times suggested, in her spiritual journal, a prayer to God which used words identical to Buchman's unmanageability prayer to God.[7]

That "God, manage me" prayer had also reached Sam Shoemaker's Calvary Church in New York, where Bill Wilson received much Oxford Group indoctrination. Shoemaker's long-time associate and assistant minister related:

One of the very first individuals to catch fire proved to be a handsome, but poorly educated "east-sider" named Charlie, a young Italian. Very early every day he would deliver morning newspapers along Third Avenue and his route included Gramercy Park. Since the new rector of Calvary was an early riser, not much time elapsed before the man [Sam Shoemaker] and the newsboy met.

One morning, as the two chatted in the rectory hallway, "it" happened. No one knows what the rector said on that occasion but new life came to Charlie, and those who heard about Charlie's prayer could never forget it. It was a classic, simple

---

[5] A. J. Russell, *For Sinners Only* (New York: Harper & Brothers Publishers, 1932), p. 62.

[6] See Dick B., *The Oxford Group & Alcoholics Anonymous*, pp. 300-301.

[7] Dick B., *Anne Smith's Journal, 1933-1939: A.A.'s Principles of Success*, 3rd ed. (Kihei, HI: Paradise Research Publications, Inc. 1998), pp. 20-22.

plea in nine words: *"God, manage me, 'cause I can't manage myself"* (emphasis added).[8]

The Big Book's *First Edition* said:

(a) That we were alcoholic and *could not manage our own lives.* (b) That probably no human power could have relieved our alcoholism. (c) That *God could and would if sought* (p. 72, emphasis added).

Spiritual misery due to sin—being blocked from God

Powerless, said Shoemaker. An unmanageable life, he and his colleagues said. *Spiritual misery,* a topic Shoemaker discussed in his first significant title. The misery, said Shoemaker, was a *spiritual malady* caused by estrangement from God in people that were meant to be His companions.[9] And, for the first step toward a new or restored *relationship with God,* Shoemaker turned to God's Word!

In Romans 7:24-25, the Apostle Paul had written:

O wretched man that I am! who shall deliver me from the body of this death? I thank God through Jesus Christ our Lord. So then with the mind I myself serve the law of God; but with the flesh the law of sin.

Early on, Sam said:

William James has told us that people belong to one of two types, the once-born, or the twice-born types. . . . The twice-born type is aware of disunity, division, a rift at the centre of being, something in oneself that is out of gear and out of step

---

[8] Irving Harris, *The Breeze of the Spirit: Sam Shoemaker and the Story of Faith at Work* (New York: A Crossroad Book/The Seabury Press, 1978), p. 10.

[9] Samuel M. Shoemaker, *Realizing Religion* (New York: Association Press, 1923), pp. 4-5.

and needs righting. St. Paul is the great type of it, and the heart
of the need for second birth is his cry: "Wretched man that I
am! Who shall deliver me from the body of this death?"[10]

Later, Shoemaker wrote:

God is God, and self is not God—that is the heart of it. It is an
actual fact that we become God to ourselves unless we have
God to believe in: the final reference becomes ourselves. . . .
Ourselves are like our bodies, the inevitable instruments through
which we live and serve God. Put in their places, they become
servants of God; but riding on top of us, they become His
rivals. So inescapable are they that sometimes we want to cry
out with St. Paul, "Who shall deliver me from this dead body
of myself?"[11]

Not surprisingly, an early AA picked up Shoemaker's biblical
theme, consciously or by chance. In *Smile With Me, At Me*, that
A.A. pioneer wrote:

One morning, after a sleepless night worrying over what I could
do to straighten myself out, I went to my room alone—took my
Bible in hand and asked Him, the One Power, that I might open
to a good place to read—and I read. "For I delight in the law of
God after the inward man. But I see a different law in my
members, warring against the law of my mind and bringing me
into captivity under the law of sin which is my members.
Wretched man that I am! Who shall deliver me out of the body
of this death?" That was enough for me—I started to
understand. . . . From that day I gave and still give and always
will, time everyday to read the word of God and let Him do all
the caring. Who am I to try to run myself or anyone else (Big
Book, First Edition, p. 347).

---

[10] Samuel M. Shoemaker, *Religion That Works: Sermons of Practical Christian Life*
(New York: Fleming H. Revell Company, 1928), pp. 44-45.

[11] Samuel M. Shoemaker, *National Awakening* (New York: Harper & Brothers
Publishers, 1936), p. 48.

A wretched person, seemingly powerless over alcohol, with an unmanageable life—and suffering from spiritual misery. That's what many of us seem to have experienced when we entered the rooms of Alcoholics Anonymous. San Shoemaker saw that. Some listened to Sam. And most of the earliest people in our A.A. Fellowship usually started on the road to recovery by recognizing that they had lost, or needed to rediscover and establish, a relationship with God: They admitted defeat, through lack of power and an unmanageable life, and looked to God for power!

Wilson covered this religious territory with several well-chosen sentences:

[W]e have been not only mentally and physically ill, we have been *spiritually sick*. When the spiritual malady is overcome, we straighten out mentally and physically.[12]

Remember that we deal with alcohol—cunning, baffling, powerful! Without help it is too much for us. But there is One who has all power—that One is God. May you find Him now![13]

Of course, we have since found that these awful conditions of mind and body invariably bring on the third phase of our malady. This is the sickness of the spirit: a sickness for which there must necessarily be a spiritual remedy. We AAs recognize this in the first five words of Step Twelve of the recovery program. These words are: Having had a spiritual awakening . . . Here we name the remedy for our threefold sickness of body, mind, and soul. Here we declare the necessity for that all-important spiritual awakening.[14]

---

[12] Big Book, p. 64 (italics added; here and hereafter unless otherwise indicated, references are to the Third Edition of *Alcoholics Anonymous*).

[13] Big Book, pp. 58-59.

[14] *The Language of the Heart*, p. 297.

The real problem to be solved, the pioneers felt, was the absence of God. Many read The *Confessions of St. Augustine*, where Augustine wrote: "Thou madest us for Thyself, and our heart is restless until it repose in Thee."[15] Adding to Augustine's quote, Sam Shoemaker wrote:

> The emptiness, loneliness, homesickness, wistfulness, wonderment which all men feel at some time is a hollow place in the human soul that God is meant to fill.[16]

Dr. Carl Jung was later to explain it to Bill Wilson by quoting Psalm 42:1:

> As the hart panteth after the water brooks, so panteth my soul after thee, O God.

- *Step Two*: **Came to believe that a Power greater than ourselves could restore us to sanity.**

There are also three basic Biblical ideas that fed into this Step from A.A.'s root sources: (1) Belief in God—who was variously described as a "Power" and a "Power greater than ourselves." (2) Being willing to believe, act on God's known rules, and coming to believe as the result of the experiment. (3) Seeking God first.

Belief in God—the power greater than ourselves

In the Steps as Bill originally wrote them, "Step Two" read as follows: "Came to believe that *God* could restore us to sanity."[17] Bill later made much of the fact that he had been pressured away from "God" by his business partner in the Big Book venture (Hank

---

[15] *The Confessions of St. Augustine*, trans. by E. B. Pusey (New York: A Cardinal Edition, Pocket Books, 1952), p. 1.

[16] Shoemaker, *National Awakening*, p. 46.

[17] *Pass It On*, p. 198 (emphasis added).

Parkhurst) and by a "newcomer, dry barely three months" (Jimmy B.). These two, said Bill, [and perhaps some others], had objections to the frequent use of the word "God."[18] And the word "God" therefore disappeared from Step Two—in the multilith volume Bill circulated before publication, and in the First Edition of the Big Book.

More than twenty years later, after the death of A.A.'s co-founder, Dr. Bob, Bill Wilson wrote:

> In Step Two we decided to describe God as a "Power greater than ourselves." . . . God was certainly there in our Steps, but He was now expressed in terms that anybody—*anybody at all*—could accept and try.[19]

Indeed, God *was* there! *God*—the God of the Bible—was *certainly there*—still, however Bill Wilson chose to describe Him. How do we know that? Because, in part, of the number of times in the Big Book that Bill described God in biblical terms—Creator, Maker, Father, and Father of Lights. Some may wonder if they are supposed to think that *Creator* and *Maker* refer to a group, radiator, or a lightbulb, but common sense would call this nonsense or absurd—just as Sam Shoemaker did.

Also, on page 69 of the First Edition, Bill Wilson wrote a story about Fitz M. and described the question in capital letters: "WHO ARE YOU TO SAY THERE IS NO GOD?" The capitalized letters and sentence were so powerful that they caught the attention of Dr. Harry Emerson Fosdick, whom Bill had asked to endorse the Big Book. Fosdick wrote of A.A.: "The core of their whole procedure is religious." Fosdick then quoted the capitalized who-are-you phrase and added: "They agree that each man must have his own way of conceiving of God, but of God Himself they are utterly sure. . . ."[20] And for sure, even in the

---

[18] *Pass It On*, p. 199.

[19] *Alcoholics Anonymous Comes of Age*, p. 167.

[20] *A.A. Comes of Age*, p. 323.

Third Edition of the Big Book, the word "God," in biblical and, in varying forms of pronouns, is still there—used more than 400 times.[21]

Whence came the phrase—Power greater than ourselves? Did Sam Shoemaker's language contribute to the unusual phrase, "Power Greater Than Ourselves"—a phrase Bill substituted for "God"—Jehovah, the God Almighty to which the Bible refers? The answer seems to be "yes." Or, "Yes"—along with *other* Oxford Group sources.

First of all, Sam believed in, constantly wrote about, and regularly referred to, the Almighty God of the Bible. Second, Sam sometimes *did* refer to God as a "Power"—with a capital "P."[22] In fact, this occasional reference to God as a "Power" seemed to be a given in Oxford Group writings.[23] Finally, Sam also used words and phrases—referring to God Almighty—that called God a "Power" or "Force" *greater than ourselves*. For example, he said:

> . . . I asked him to commit himself this time to nothing, but only to accept in faith the great fact of salvation from God. I told him that I knew that if he would make that act in faith, he would find himself not the possessor of, but possessed by, a *Force outside himself, greater than himself*, independent of his moods and his sudden seizures of temptation (emphasis added).[24]

> They seemed to be *propelled by a vast Power outside themselves*. And I knew that I myself, and those whom I saw missing the way, needed to be got into touch with that Power.

---

[21] See discussion in Dick B., *The Good Book and The Big Book: A.A.'s Roots in the Bible*, 2d ed. (Kihei, HI: Paradise Research Publications, Inc. 1997), pp. 49-50.

[22] Samuel M. Shoemaker, *A Young Man's View of the Ministry* (New York: Association Press, 1923), p. 42; *Living Your Life Today* (New York: Fleming H. Revell Company, 1947), p. 13; *With the Holy Spirit and with Fire* (New York: Harper & Brothers, Publishers, 1960), p. 27.

[23] See Dick B., *The Oxford Group & Alcoholics Anonymous*, pp. 303-04, 341, 344.

[24] Shoemaker, *If I Be Lifted Up*, p. 176.

. . . [A]nd I went into the profession whose business it is to keep people from missing the track in life, by showing them The Way (emphasis added).[25]

Willingness to believe—to take action and find God and the power

Sam's contribution to the "Came to believe" idea in Step Two is a bit harder to discern than the words "powerless" and "unmanageable" in Step One. But Sam's foot print is nonetheless there in Step Two. It is embedded in the "do and know" philosophy of Shoemaker and A.A. ("act as if"), as distinguished from some of the "*believe*, do, and know" ideas in the Bible.[26]

Sam once began a discussion with the Book of James ideas set forth below:

Wherefore lay apart all filthiness and superfluity of naughtiness and receive with meekness the engrafted word [of God], which is able to save your souls. But be ye doers of the word, and not hearers only, deceiving your own selves (James 1:21-22).

---

[25] Shoemaker, *A Young Man's View of the Ministry*, p. 42. Shoemaker was referring to Jesus' statement in John 14:6: ". . . I am the way, the truth, and the life: no man cometh unto the Father, but by me."

[26] John 20:28: "Jesus saith unto him, Thomas, because thou has seen me, thou has believed: blessed are they that have not seen, and *yet* have believed;" John 20:31: "But these [things that are written in the Word of God] are written that ye might believe that Jesus is the Christ, the Son of God; and that believing ye might have life through his name;" Mark 16:15-18, 20: "And he [Jesus] said unto them, Go ye into all the world, and preach the gospel to every creature. He that believeth and is baptized shall be saved. . . . And these signs shall follow them that believe; In my name shall they cast out devils; they shall speak with new tongues; [if] They shall take up serpents; and if they drink any deadly thing, it shall not hurt them; they shall lay hands on the sick, and they shall recover. . . . And they went forth, and preached every where, the Lord working with *them*, and confirming the word with signs following. Amen."

And Sam then wrote:

> Begin at a different angle altogether. St. James has said it, "Act
> on the Word!" Begin, not with the part of religion which is at
> present beyond our grasp, like immortality, but with that part of
> it that is within our reach. The first thing that must come is a
> living, working experience of Christ. . . . [The person
> addressed] must be honest with those to whom he had written
> so bravely, leaving them "hearers" of his word only, and tell
> them he had been only a "hearer" himself, and not a doer—a
> person who listened to these great ideas of courage and hope,
> but who had not really acted on them. That meant facing a real
> dishonesty in himself and admitting it to others.[27]

To Sam, finding God meant active obedience to, and cooperation
with, God's will.[28] It meant that a person might well be a "doer
of the Word," without a *reality of experience*. To Sam, the
problem was not knowing the Word and sincerely trying to apply
it; it was the failure to follow through, and carry things forward,
in an *experiment of faith* that would produce a "reality, of
experience, and therefore of assurance and joy in believing."[29]
      You will not find the language of James 1:21-22 in the Second
Step itself. But you will find A.A.'s interest in the Book of James
spelled out several times in Big Book quotes: (1) "Faith without
works is dead" (James 2:20; Big Book, 3rd ed., pp. 14, 76, 88);
(2) "He humbly offered himself to his Maker—then he knew"
(James 4:10—"Humble yourselves in the sight of the Lord, and he
shall lift you up"; Big Book, 3rd ed., p. 57); and (3) "When we
drew near to Him He disclosed Himself to us!" (James
4:8—"Draw nigh to God, and he will draw nigh to you"; Big
Book, 3rd ed., p. 57).

---

[27] Samuel M. Shoemaker, *The Gospel According to You* (New York: Fleming H.
Revell, 1934), pp. 46-47.

[28] Shoemaker, *The Gospel According to You*, p. 46.

[29] Shoemaker, *The Gospel According to You*, p. 46.

These Book of James verses involved *action* principles. And they appeared in A.A. in the *action* sections of Big Book discussions. But the entire idea of "coming to believe" that is spelled out in the Big Book rests on the Oxford Group's life-changing *action* program, particularly as Shoemaker laid it out to Wilson. Shoemaker called it the *experiment of faith*. It rested on three Bible verses, to which Shoemaker referred again and again in his writings. They all amounted, in Shoemaker's view, to the ongoing *obedience* to God's Word that would produce an experience, a finding, and a knowledge of God.

As stated, any action begins with belief that *God is*: To come to God, you must start with a belief that God IS. Hebrews 11:6 states:

> But without faith *it is* impossible to please *him*: for he that cometh to God must believe that he is, and *that* he is a rewarder of them that diligently seek him.

Shoemaker referred to this verse frequently.[30] Then, challenging his readers, he said:

> Religion is a risk. The romance of religion is the romance of a risk. . . . Faith is not sight: it is a high gamble. There are only two alternatives here. *God is, or He isn't.* You leap one way or the other. It is a risk to take to bet everything you have on God. So is it a risk not to [emphasis added].[31]

Lo, and behold! Bill Wilson wrote:

> When we became alcoholics, crushed by a self-imposed crisis we could not postpone or evade, we had to fearlessly face the proposition that either God is everything or else He is nothing.

---

[30] Shoemaker, *Religion That Works*, p. 88; *The Gospel According to You*, p. 47; *National Awakening*, p. 40.

[31] Shoemaker, *Confident Faith*, p. 187; *Extraordinary Living for Ordinary Men* (Grand Rapids, MI: Zondervan Publishing House, 1965), pp. 20-21.

God either is, or He isn't. What was our choice to be? (Big Book, 3rd ed., p. 53).

Seeking God first

God is not lost. Man has the free will and the recurrent capacity to rely on himself, rather than upon the Creator. Man becomes *estranged from God.* From the separation comes fear. And self-reliance, ego-centricity, and self-centeredness fail. Shoemaker had much to say on this subject:

> Let us face at the outset how many Christians are not victorious, but defeated. Defeated by circumstances, defeated by other peoples' natures and wrong-doings, defeated by the down-drag of the flesh, defeated by loss, by pain, by suffering, by worry. Instead of saying with confidence, "This is the victory that overcometh the world, even our faith", they have to say in honesty, "This is the defeat that has been caused by the world, even our self-centeredness." That is the opposite of faith. Unbelief is not the opposite of faith; self-centeredness is—being centered in self rather than in God.[32]

> God is God. It is the Fact of all facts. We shall learn it through faith, or we shall learn it through tribulation. But God is God.[33]

> "Having on the breastplate of righteousness—wearing integrity as your coat of mail." That means to me the inward certainty of

---

[32] Shoemaker, *Extraordinary Living*, p. 91. See Big Book, 3rd ed., p. 62: "Selfishness—self-centeredness! That, we think, is the root of our troubles;" p. 68: "self-reliance failed us. . . . For we are now on a different basis; the basis of trusting and relying upon God. We trust infinite God rather than our finite selves."

[33] Samuel M. Shoemaker, *Christ and This Crisis* (New York: Fleming H. Revell Company, 1943), p. 71. See Big Book, 3rd ed., p. 62: "First of all, we had to quit playing God. It didn't work. Next, we decided that hereafter in this drama of life, God was going to be our Director."

being single-minded.[34] It does not mean the certainty of continuous perfection, for none of us has that; but we can have a mind single towards God, which is undiscouraged and undeterred by its own failures, simply because its final refuge and strength are in God, not in self.[35]

"Give in, admit that I am God." I see in these words, too, not only the truth of our capacity for God and of our estrangement from Him, but a vigorous emphasis upon God's lordship over every man. God is God, and self is not God—that is the heart of it.[36]

Sin is not mixing up the relationship between men only; it is the estrangement of lives from God.[37]

God in mercy strip us this day of the last vestiges of self-reliance, and help us to begin life anew trusting to nothing but His grace! . . . We said that what God did for us on the Cross is the cure and corrective for the gospel of "self-help," so common to-day even amongst believers, which centers in the effort of the human will toward self-improvement.[38]

---

[34] See Matthew 6:22 (from Jesus's sermon on the mount): "The light of the body is the eye: if therefore thine eye be single, thy whole body shall be full of light;" Matthew 6:24: "No man can serve two masters. . . . Ye cannot serve God and mammon;" James 1:8: "A double minded man *is* unstable in all his ways."

[35] Samuel M. Shoemaker, *God's Control* (New York: Fleming H. Revell, 1939), p. 30. See Big Book, 3rd ed., p. 62: "Neither could we reduce our self-centeredness much by wishing or trying on our own power. We had to have God's help."

[36] Shoemaker, *National Awakening*, p. 48. See Big Book, 3rd ed., pp. 61-63: "Our actor is self-centered—ego centric. . . . Above everything, we alcoholics must be rid of this selfishness. We must or it kills us! God makes that possible. . . . He is the Principal; we are his agents. He is the Father, and we are His children. Most good ideas are simple, and this concept was the keystone of the new and triumphant arch through which we passed to freedom. . . . We were reborn."

[37] Shoemaker, *A Young Man's View of the Ministry*, p. 27; Big Book, 3rd ed., p. 59: "May you find Him now!"

[38] Shoemaker, *If I Be Lifted Up*, pp. 166-67. See Big Book, 3rd ed., p. 60: ". . . any life run on self-will can hardly be a success."

The second thing [in a faith in God which includes an experiment] is utter preoccupation with God's plan. "Seek ye first the Kingdom of God, and his righteousness."[39] Personal considerations are out: what happens to us in the bargain is irrelevant. Ordinarily we think that if we look after our needs, God will take care of His plan. The truth is that if we look after God's plan, He takes care of our needs.[40]

And the presence of the "seek God first" idea in early A.A. is quite evident:

(Dr. Bob was always positive about his faith, Clarence said. If someone asked him a question about the program, his usual response was: "What does it say in the Good Book?" Suppose he was asked, "What's all this 'First Things First'?" Dr. Bob would be ready with the appropriate quotation: "Seek ye first the kingdom of God and His righteousness, and all these things shall be added unto you.")[41]

"FIRST THINGS FIRST" (Big Book, First Edition, p. 149)

That God could and would if sought (Big Book, First Edition, p. 72).

Be obedient to God: Do His Will and You Will Know (John 7:17).

According to one Oxford Group writer, Sam Shoemaker's favorite verse was John 7:17.[42] The verse reads:

---

[39] Matthew 6:33 (from the Sermon on the Mount).

[40] Shoemaker, *National Awakening*, pp. 41-42. See Big Book, 3rd ed., p. 60: "God could and would if He were sought."

[41] *DR. BOB and the Good Oldtimers* (New York: Alcoholics Anonymous World Services, Inc., 144). For further verification, see Dick B., *That Amazing Grace: The Role of Clarence and Grace S. in Alcoholics Anonymous* (San Rafael, CA: Paradise Research Publications, 1996), pp. 30, 38.

[42] Russell, *For Sinners Only*, p. 177.

If any man will do his will, he shall know of the doctrine whether it be of God, or *whether* I [Jesus] speak of myself.

If repetition indicates what Sam favored, then John 7:17 wins the prize. The author found Sam quoting and illustrating how he understood this verse many, many times.[43]

From John 7:17, Sam spun out the concept of *willingness*, which became a part of A.A. language in the Second, Sixth, Seventh, and Eighth Step discussions.[44] Sam said:

It [a friend's not being willing to do what God said] points to the truth that no man can see the will of God who is not willing to see it. One of Drummond's favourite verses in this connection was John 7:17: "If any man *willeth* to do his will, he shall know." And wrapped up in this little verse there lies more empirical spiritual experience than almost anywhere else I know.[45]

---

[43] Shoemaker, *A Young Man's View of the Ministry*, p. 41; *Religion That Works*, pp. 36, 46, 58; *How You Can Help Other People* (New York: E. P. Dutton & Co., 1946), p. 61; *Living Your Life Today* (New York: Fleming H. Revell, 1947), pp. 102, 103, 104, 109; *The Church Alive* (New York: E. P. Dutton & Co, 1950), pp. 119, 150; *The Experiment of Faith* (New York: Harper & Brothers, 1957), p. 36; *The Adventure of Living Under New Management* (Grand Rapids, MI: Zondervan Publishing House, 1966), p. 46; *Steps of a Modern Disciple* (Atlanta, GA: Lay Renewal Publications, 1972), p. 30; *How To Find God* (New York: Faith at Work, n.d.), p. 6.

[44] See Big Book, 3rd ed.: "Do I now believe, or am I even willing to believe. . . As soon as a man can say that he does believe, or is willing to believe, we emphatically assure him that he is on his way" (p. 47); "If we still cling to something we will not let go, we ask God to help us be willing" (p. 76); "My creator, I am now willing that you should have all of me, good and bad" (p. 76); "We have a list of all persons we have harmed and to whom we are willing to make amends. . . . We attempt to sweep away the debris which has accumulated out of our effort to live on self-will and run the show ourselves. If we haven't the will to do this, we ask until it comes" (p. 76).

[45] Shoemaker, *Religion That Works*, p. 58. See also how Professor Philip Marshall Brown, who was friend to Shoemaker, Rowland Hazard, and Bill Wilson, elaborated on the "willingness" idea in the title to which Shoemaker wrote the Introduction. Philip Marshall Brown, *The Venture of Belief* (New York: Fleming H. Revell, 1935), p. 29: "the abasement of intellectual pride, the humble acknowledgment of a sense of need, the deliberate determination to find a rational adjustment to this universe, and the willingness to obey the Will of God." See also pp. 27, 36.

How, then, according to Sam Shoemaker, can you "come to believe?" The answer is to do as much of God's will as is put before you. Then you will know from the experiment and resultant experience that what you did was God's will because it worked![46] Sam wrote:

> The soundest approach I know to religious discovery is found in St. John's Gospel, chapter 7, verse 17; "If any man willeth to do his will, he shall know of the doctrine." We are busy getting "willing to do His will," and that means changing many of our ways. The verse says clearly that this is the order: moral change, then intellectual perception. "Blessed are the pure in heart, for they shall see God."[47]

From Shoemaker's "do and know" teachings from John 7:17, Bill Wilson seemed to fashion his "second step" for the agnostics and atheists. Bill wrote in the Third Edition:

> It was only a matter of being willing to believe in a Power greater than myself. Nothing more was required of me to make my beginning. I saw that growth could start from that point. Upon a foundation of complete willingness I might build what I saw in my friend (p. 12).

> My friend promised when these things were done [the steps Ebby Thacher had suggested and that Bill took in Towns Hospital] I would enter upon a new relationship with my Creator; that I would have the elements of a way of living which answered all my problems. Belief in the power of God, plus enough willingness, honesty and humility to establish and maintain the new order of things, were the essential requirements (pp. 13-14).

---

[46] See Big Book, p. 88: ". . . humbly saying to ourselves many times each day 'Thy will be done'. . . . It works—it really does."

[47] Shoemaker, *The Experiment of Faith*, p. 36.

We [of agnostic temperament] found that as soon as we were able to lay aside prejudice and express even a willingness to believe in a power greater than ourselves, we commenced to get results, even though it was impossible for any of us to fully define or comprehend that Power, which is God (p. 46).

That is how Bill Wilson, who (early on) called himself a "conservative atheist," came to believe, he said.[48] Note: He honestly admitted he was "licked," and that alcohol was his master.[49] He was willing to believe in God.[50] He then took the next step—the surrender we will discuss with reference to Step Three. And he and those who followed, such as Fitz M., had then come to believe and believed.[51] Bill was convinced that action on a solid belief brought about the experience of God—and from which the famous "spiritual experience" idea of early A.A. emerged. That idea was, for AAs, to become the spiritual solution to the spiritual malady—estrangement from God, being blocked from God, and relying upon self as God. Bill did the surrendering, and God did the healing. Came to believe! A Shoemaker idea from the beginning.

- *Step Three*: **Made a decision to turn our will and our lives over to the care of God** *as we understood Him*.

There are several concepts which follow the admission of powerlessness and an unmanageable life, coupled with a belief in

---

[48] See Bill's specific characterization of himself as a "conservative atheist" in manuscripts the author found at Stepping Stones. Dick B., *Turning Point: A History of Early A.A.'s Spiritual Roots and Successes* (San Rafael, CA: Paradise Research Publications, 1997), pp. 96, 112, 172.

[49] See Big Book, 3rd ed., p. 8: "Alcohol was my master."

[50] See Big Book, 3rd ed., p. 12: "Upon a foundation of complete willingness I might build what I saw in my friend [Ebby Thacher]. Would I have it? Of course I would! Thus was I convinced that God is concerned with us humans when we want Him enough. . . . There had been a humble willingness to have Him with me—and He came."

[51] See Big Book, 3rd ed., p. 57: "Circumstances made him willing to believe. He humbly offered himself to his Maker—then he knew."

God, a willingness to seek Him first, and an understanding that action is the prerequisite to finding God and the power of God. The concepts are: (1) The turning point. (2) A decision to trust God. (3) The actual surrender to God or conversion.

Though it is not a part of the language of the Twelve Steps themselves, A.A.'s "surrender" idea immediately precedes them. And every AA is familiar with the following:

> But there is One who has all power—that One is God. May you find Him now! Half measures availed us nothing. We stood at the *turning point*. We asked His protection and care with complete abandon. Here are the steps we took, which are suggested as a program of recovery (Big Book, 3rd ed., p. 59, emphasis added).

In an interesting summary of the ideas of the Oxford Group which the author found among Shoemaker's papers at the Episcopal Archives in Texas, there is the following about the surrender:

> There was nothing actually new to be learned from the experience when related. "I just gave my life over to God", or "I surrendered to Christ."[52]

The idea that this act of self-surrender was the *turning point* was borrowed from the following statement by Professor William James—a statement which Sam Shoemaker quoted over and over, beginning with his first significant book:

> William James speaks with great emphasis upon this crisis of self-surrender. He says that it is "the throwing of our conscious selves on the mercy of the powers which, whatever they may be, are more ideal than we are actually, and make for our redemption. . . . *Self-surrender* has always been and always must be regarded as *the vital turning point* of the religious life,

---

[52] Page 3, Document titled "Oxford Movement," Archives of the Episcopal Church, Record Group UP 229, Box 3 (94.68).

so far as the religious life is spiritual and no affair of outer works and ritual and sacraments. One may say that the whole development of Christianity in inwardness has consisted in little more than the greater and greater emphasis attached to this *crisis of self-surrender*" (emphasis added).[53]

For Sam, self-surrender unquestionably involved being "born again." He often spoke of the necessity for the new birth. For example, in *National Awakening*, he wrote:

Except a man be born again, he cannot see the kingdom of God. . . . A man is born again when the control of his life, its center and its direction pass from himself to God (p. 57).[54]

Shoemaker did nod to the importance, in assuring salvation, of the verses in Romans 10:9-10:

That if thou shalt confess with thy mouth the Lord Jesus, and shalt believe in thine heart that God hath raised him from the dead, thou shalt be saved. For with the heart man believeth unto righteousness; and with the mouth confession is made unto salvation.[55]

But Shoemaker's major contribution to A.A.'s "process" of finding and establishing a relationship with God is embraced in this statement:

---

[53] Shoemaker, *Realizing Religion*, p. 30. See also Shoemaker, *A Young Man's View of the Ministry*, p. 55; *Religion That Works*, p. 48; *Children of the Second Birth*, p. 16; *God's Control*, p. 138; and so on.

[54] See John 3:3: Jesus answered and said unto him, Verily, verily, I say unto thee, Except a man be born again, he cannot see the kingdom of God; John 3:5: Jesus answered, Verily, verily, I say unto thee, Except a man be born of water and *of* the Spirit, he cannot enter the kingdom of God; John 3:7: Marvel not that I said unto thee, Ye must be born again.

[55] Shoemaker, *If I Be Lifted Up*, p. 83.

Surrender is not conversion, we cannot convert ourselves; but
it is the first step in the process.[56]

As we move along, we can see that, confused and/or confusing
though their premises might have been theologically, Shoemaker
and the Oxford Group saw the life-change as something that *began*
with a surrender. Though *man* made the surrender, it necessarily
involved God's part. And, the Oxford Group thought, several steps
were necessary to completion of a life-change. These steps
primarily involved the so-called 5 C's (Confidence, Confession,
Conviction, Conversion, and Continuance).[57] Shoemaker rightly
attributed these to Dr. Frank Buchman.[58] And they represented
the "usual stages of development," the process of "cooperating
with God and doing the work which of all work He most wants
done."[59] Then, believed Shoemaker, success, through Him, does
come, and lives are changed.

The life change process—the new birth—began with a decision.
A.A. adopted this idea in the Third Step. And the reader should
know that there are three very specific Shoemaker ideas in the
Third Step language: (1) The *Decision.* (2) To *Surrender*—the act
of "turning it over," as AAs often say—the act of surrendering
one's life to God's care and direction. (3) *To God as you
understand Him.*

The foregoing three ideas, accompanied by Third Step
language which is similar, if not identical, to Shoemaker's, bear
Sam's sure markings. And Shoemaker wrote on each of the
foregoing three points:

1. *Make a Decision: "There must be decision.* Much
    spiritual aspiration vaporizes into wasted emotion
    because it is not tied down to a decision. . . . [T]his

---

[56] Shoemaker, *Confident Faith*, p. 41.

[57] Shoemaker, *Realizing Religion*, pp. 79-80.

[58] Shoemaker, *Realizing Religion*, p. 80, n. 9.

[59] Shoemaker, *Realizing Religion*, pp. 78-79.

is an act, not a desire—a final and irrevocable act."[60] *"Decision. . . .* We must help people to make an act of self-surrender to Christ, which renounces all known sins, accepts Him as Saviour, and begins Christian life in earnest."[61] "He made his decision. . . . 'I came to Jesus.'"[62] "Upheaval?—yes, a complete personal revolution; but no emotion and fireworks in it, the whole thing centering in the giving of his will to God. And what happens next, so that this one decision becomes the gateway to permanent living in Christ and building His Kingdom?"[63]

2. *Surrender to God*: "He went into his room, *knelt by his bed*, and gave his life in surrender to God."[64] "She surrendered to God her groundless fears, and with them *turned over her life for His direction*."[65] "Before the week-end was over, he had made the *greatest decision of his life*, to *surrender himself unconditionally and for always to the will of God*."[66] "That night I decided to 'launch out into the deep:' and with the *decision to cast my will and my life on God*, there came an indescribable sense of relief, of burdens dropping away."[67]

"We felt we had come somewhere within hearing-distance of His [Jesus Christ's] tremendous surrender, 'Let this cup pass. . . . *Nevertheless, not my will, but*

---

[60] Shoemaker, *Revive Thy Church Beginning with Me*, p. 25.

[61] Shoemaker, *The Church Alive*, p. 41.

[62] Shoemaker, *Children of the Second Birth*, p. 125.

[63] Shoemaker, *National Awakening*, pp. 52-53.

[64] Shoemaker, *Children of the Second Birth*, p. 175 (emphasis added).

[65] Shoemaker, *Children of the Second Birth*, p. 82 (emphasis added).

[66] Shoemaker, *Children of the Second Birth*, pp. 61-62 (emphasis added).

[67] Shoemaker, *Twice-Born Ministers*, p. 134 (emphasis added).

thine be done' And that night, right in the middle of
the service of Holy Communion just at the great
moment when he took the cup into his hands to 'drink
this in remembrance that Christ died for thee,' he gave
all that was left of his heart to Christ in full and final
surrender. It shook him to the very depths of his
soul."[68]

3. *To God as you understand Him*: "So they prayed
    together, opening their minds *to as much of God as he
    understood*, removing first the hindrance of self-will,
    allowing the Spirit to focus an impression upon the
    mind, like light upon a camera."[69] "So he said that
    he would "surrender as much of himself as he could,
    to as much of Christ as he understood."[70]

    "The finding of God, moreover, is a progressive
    discovery; and there is so much more for all of us to
    learn about Him. . . . Nevertheless, there are people
    in the world who are sure about God, and we all want
    to become some of those people if we can. And there
    stands in the Word of God His ancient promise, "and
    ye shall seek me and find me, when ye shall search
    for me with all your hearts.'"[71] "Begin honestly
    where you are. Horace Bushnell once said, 'Pray to
    the dim God, confessing the dimness for honesty's
    sake.' I was with a man who prayed his first real
    prayer in these words: 'O God, if there be a God, help
    me now because I need it.' God sent him help. He
    found faith. He found God. . . . God will come

---

[68] Shoemaker, *Children of the Second Birth*, pp. 182-83.

[69] Shoemaker, *Children of the Second Birth*, p. 47 (emphasis added).

[70] Shoemaker, *Children of the Second Birth*, p. 25 (emphasis added).

[71] Shoemaker, *How to Find God*, p. 1. From Jeremiah 29:13: "And ye shall seek me,
and find *me*, when ye shall search for me with all your heart."

through to you and make Himself known."[72] ". . .
[A]ny honest person can begin the spiritual experiment
by *surrendering "as much of himself as he can, to as
much of Christ as he understands.'*"[73]

- *Step Four*: **Made a searching and fearless moral
inventory of ourselves.**

There has been much misunderstanding of the Fourth Step process
because of lack of knowledge of its origins. It required honest
effort. It was concerned with "morality"—moral standards, not
merely "truth." It meant self-examination—taking stock of one's
own moral shortcomings or sins, as they were originally
understood to be.

A.A. adopted two different ideas connected with the Oxford
Group's "self-examination" step. One idea had to do with making
an *inventory of one's own shortcomings*. The other had to do with
recognizing the immorality of those flaws which blocked one from
God and other people and fell short of the standards believed to
have been set by Jesus in his Sermon on the Mount. Unfortunately,
today most AAs are totally unfamiliar with their own early tests or
yardsticks for measuring immorality. Hence they frequently do not
understand Bill Wilson's use of the word *moral* or what he meant
by that term.[74]

Wherever Bill Wilson *first* started—and it *was with the "Four
Absolutes" that he did first start*—Wilson adopted several important

---

[72] Shoemaker, *How to Find God*, p. 6

[73] Shoemaker, *Extraordinary Living for Ordinary Men*, p. 76 (emphasis added).

[74] An example is the definition of *moral* used by Joe and Charlie (of Big Book
Seminar experience) in their discussion of the Fourth Step. They erroneously, we
believe, *equate moral with truthful*. See Joe McQ., *The Steps We Took* (Little Rock:
August House Publishers, Inc., 1990), p. 58; *A Program for You: A Guide to the Big
Book's Design for Living* (Center City, MN: Hazelden, 1991), p. 89—"a truthful
inventory is the same as a moral inventory."

Oxford Group ideas.[75] The first was that (whether they be called "sins," "shortcomings," "character defects," "wrongs," or simply falling short of Jesus's standards of perfection) man was engaged in behavior that *blocked* him from God and from his fellow men.[76] The second was that the behavior or "sins" had to do with "immorality" and man's breach of "*moral*" standards. Man needed to make the "moral test."[77] Third, in order to have the "blocks" removed, man had to *search* honestly and fearlessly *for them*.[78] He would, said the Oxford Group, find them in himself; they would be the common manifestations of self-centeredness.[79] Finally, man must therefore begin with self-searching, self-examination, and, in short, with a good hard look at himself.[80]

---

[75] *Pass It On*, pp. 127-28: Bill said, "Little was heard of theology, but we heard plenty of absolute honesty, absolute purity, absolute unselfishness, and absolute love. Confession, restitution, and direct guidance of God underlined every conversation. They were talking about morality and spirituality, about God-centeredness versus self-centeredness. . . . They felt that when people commenced to adhere to these high moral standards, then God could enter and direct their lives."

[76] *Alcoholics Anonymous*, 3rd ed., pp. 64, 66, 71, 72; Russell, *For Sinners Only*, 61, 319.

[77] *Alcoholics Anonymous*, 3rd ed. Bill Wilson not only spoke of a moral inventory; he spoke of "whatever self-will has blocked you off from Him [God] . . . and an inventory of your grosser handicaps." See H. A. Walter, *Soul Surgery*, pp. 43-44, for the "moral test."

[78] *Alcoholics Anonymous*, 3rd ed. Bill said: "We went back through our lives. Nothing counted but thoroughness and honesty" (p. 65). In *Remaking the World*, Dr. Frank Buchman said: "Moral recovery starts when everyone admits his own faults instead of spot-lighting the other fellow's" (p. 46).

[79] Alcoholics Anonymous, 3rd ed. Bill said: "Being convinced that self, manifested in various ways, was what had defeated us, we considered its common manifestations" (p. 64). In *I Was a Pagan*, Victor Kitchen wrote: "And whether insidious or gross, this selfishness had as surely shut me off from a true consciousness of God. . . . How, then, does one reverse this process? How did I accomplish self-deflation instead of continuing the advancement of self interest?" (pp. 46-47).

[80] *Alcoholics Anonymous*, 3rd ed. Bill said: "We took stock honestly. First, we searched out the flaws in our make-up which caused our failure. Being convinced that self, manifested in various ways, was what had defeated us, we considered its common manifestations" (p. 64). In *Remaking the World*, Dr. Buchman wrote: "What is our real

(continued...)

And, as we will see in a moment, he was to *write down his findings*.

Sam Shoemaker spoke eloquently on all these ideas:

> He gave me the *four absolute principles of Christ*: honesty, purity, unselfishness and love, and asked me how my life stacked up beside them (emphasis added).[81]

> We must get to the point whether the man is "willing to do his will" in all areas. Take *the four standards of Christ*: absolute honesty, absolute purity, absolute unselfishness, and absolute love. When people's lives are wrong, they are usually wrong on one or more of these standards (emphasis added).[82]

> For if we truly define *sin* as "anything that *walls us off* from God, or from other people," then . . . (emphasis added).[83]

> Whatever *keeps us from* a living, loving relation with other people—or from a vital and open relationship with God—is sin (emphasis added).[84]

> There is a *moral obligation* to be as intelligent as you can. Turn over the possibilities in your mind. *Face all the facts you can find, honestly and fearlessly.*[85]

> Christ put it in a nutshell when He said, "Thou hypocrite, cast out first the beam out of thine own eye, and then shalt thou see

---

[80] (...continued)
problem? . . . The symptoms may differ. . . . The disease remains the same. . . . What is the disease? Isn't it fear, dishonesty, resentment, selfishness? We talk about freedom and liberty, but we are slaves to ourselves" (p. 38).

[81] Shoemaker, *Twice-Born Ministers*, p. 150.

[82] Shoemaker, *The Church Can Save the World*, p. 110.

[83] Shoemaker, *Twice-Born Ministers*, p. 177.

[84] Shoemaker, *How to Become a Christian*, p. 56.

[85] Shoemaker, *Religion That Works*, p. 58 (emphasis added).

clearly to pull out the mote that is in thy brother's eye." . . .
Begin with yourself.[86]

The fact is that I sin. I deliberately sin. With my eyes open, with
my mind perfectly aware of God's opposition to what I am
about to do, with a will unstruggling against evil but consciously
choosing it instead, I have many a time and oft chosen my way
as against God's. And that means that there are *moral lapses in
me for which I can never hope to atone.*[87]

They taught me that the proving-ground of religious sincerity
was *moral earnestness*: only by this should I find God, and
know His will for my life (emphasis added).[88]

So don't run. Stand by. Grasp the nettle. Face the music. Begin
with the facts.[89]

Then we thought we would take off the glasses, and begin to
think about the fellow who was looking through them. As we
talked, conviction developed that he was up against certain quite
clearly defined sins in his own life.[90]

For most men the world is centered in self, which is misery.[91]

You and God are reconciled the moment you surrender. You
know it. The shackles fall away. Self recedes, God looms up.
Self-will seems the blackest sin of all, rebellion against God the
only hell.[92]

---

[86] Shoemaker, *God's Control*, p. 63; Matthew 7:3-5 (part of Jesus's sermon on the mount).

[87] Shoemaker, *If I Be Lifted Up*, p. 131 (emphasis added).

[88] Shoemaker, *Twice-Born Ministers*, pp. 50-51.

[89] Shoemaker, *The Gospel According to You*, pp. 30-31.

[90] Shoemaker, *The Conversion of the Church*, p. 30.

[91] Shoemaker, *Realizing Religion*, p. 11.

[92] Shoemaker, *Realizing Religion*, p. 31.

Doing the will of God means total emancipation from selfish consideration so far as that is possible on earth. . . . One is perhaps never quite free from mixed motives; but even the presence of mixed motives has not completely done away with moral law nor has it tilted the Ten Commandments. It is well to remember that selfishness, like all evil, is ingenious.[93]

God help us all today to come to a divine distrust of ourselves, to turn our look in the one necessary direction, to put pride and self-sufficiency behind us, and to "give in" to Him with all our hearts. Let us pray: O God, Help us to look deeply enough into ourselves, and into life, to find Thee: and grant us to know that all stumbling-blocks to faith and consecration are in ourselves. . . . Through Jesus Christ our Lord. Amen.[94]

"Sam, don't you enjoy your sins?" "Yes," I said, "I do, but I'll tell you something else I enjoy even more, and that is getting rid of them, so that God can really use me." He told me of some of his personal needs. Next week he came back, and I asked him whether he had had a Quiet Time about the four standards: absolute honesty, purity, unselfishness, and love. He said he had, and produced a piece of yellow fool's-cap from his pocket, neatly divided into four quarters, one for each standard, on which *he had written down all the places where he felt he had fallen down.*[95]

It would be a very good thing if you took a piece of foolscap paper and wrote down the sins you feel guilty of. . . . One of the simplest and best rules for self-examination that I know of is to use the Four Standards, which Dr. Robert E. Speer said represented the summary of the Sermon on the Mount—Absolute Honesty, Absolute Purity, Absolute

---

[93] Samuel M. Shoemaker, *My Life-Work and My Will* (Pamphlet prepared for Conference to consider the Christian Ministry, Concord, New Hampshire, January 3-6, 1930), p. 6.

[94] *Calvary Church Sermons*, "The Way to Find God," Preached by the Rev. S. M. Shoemaker, June 30, 1935, p. 226.

[95] Shoemaker, *The Church Can Save the World*, p. 119 (emphasis added).

Unselfishness, and Absolute Love. Review your life in their light. *Put down everything that doesn't measure up. Be ruthlessly, realistically honest.*[96]

- *Step Five*: **Admitted to God, to ourselves, and to another human being the exact nature of our wrongs.**

Shoemaker wrote:

The thing to do next is to face your sins. Where are you cutting corners? . . . I found it necessary to go to someone I could trust, and make a clean breast of my sins.[97]

Many quite respectable people have hidden things in their past and their present that need to come out in confidence with some one. A sin often does not appear in all its "exceeding sinfulness" until it is brought to light with another; and it almost always seems more hopelessly unforgivable, and the person who committed it more utterly irredeemable, when it remains unshared. The only release and hope for many bound and imprisoned and defeated people lies in frank sharing. It is not only costly to share our problems, or even our comfortable sins, but it is costly to share the worst thing we ever did, the deepest sin in our life, the besetting temptation that dogs us.[98]

If the person is honest with himself and with God, he will be honest also with us and be ready to take the next step, which is a decision to surrender these sins, with himself, wholly to God (emphasis added).[99]

I am equally convinced that the Protestant notion of "confession to God only" ignores the deep spiritual and psychological fact that we almost always need a human hearer and witness to

---

[96] Shoemaker, *How to Become a Christian*, pp. 56-57.

[97] Shoemaker, *Confident Faith*, p. 41.

[98] Shoemaker, *The Church Can Save the World*, p. 110.

[99] Shoemaker, *The Church Can Save the World*, p. 112.

validate our confession to God and make it *real to us*. Of course confession, in the absolute sense, is to God alone: but where there is a human listener, confession is found to be both more difficult and more efficacious. . . . [I]t is a very costly thing to say these things out in the presence even of a human being we can trust; and, as a matter of fact, this is extraordinarily effective in making the first break to get away from sins.[100]

It is my conviction, and that of the Oxford Group with which I am associated, that detailed sharing should be made with one person only.[101]

You will never do effective work with individuals unless you have first fully caught their attention and made them want what you have; and unless next you have learned the secrets of their lives, and they have told you what kind of people they are underneath where most people do not see them.[102]

Yes, sharing is just simple honesty with those who deserve to know the truth. We all need to share. When we say we do not need it, we are displaying a perhaps unconscious pride which makes us the neediest of all people. We ought to find a person whom we can fully trust, who is spiritually sound and mature, and with such a person in full confidence to talk out our sins and problems through to the bottom. That will not only help in solving the immediate difficulty, but it may make the first real assault on our pride, which is often so subtle that we do not know we have it.[103]

It is commonly acknowledged that A.A.'s Fifth Step had its biblical origins in James 5:16:

---

[100] Shoemaker, *The Conversion of the Church*, p. 36.

[101] Shoemaker, *The Conversion of the Church*, p. 37.

[102] Shoemaker, *The Conversion of the Church*, p. 77.

[103] Shoemaker, *The Gospel According to You*, p. 150.

Confess *your* faults one to another, and pray one for another, that ye may be healed. The effectual fervent prayer of a righteous man availeth much.[104]

Sam wrote:

We must find out how to go the rest of the way with our conversion. . . . It must start, as my minister friend stated, by the sharing of these sins with another Christian who has found his way a bit farther than we have. That has a Scriptural basis: "Confess your sins one to another, and pray for one another that ye may healed." I would remind those of the Catholic inclination that it does not say, "Confess your sins to a priest:" and I would remind those of the Protestant persuasion that it does not say, "Confess your sins to God only." It says very plainly, "Confess your sins one to another."[105]

- *Step Six*: **Were entirely ready to have God remove all these defects of character.**

Step Six is A.A.'s "Conviction" Step—a remnant of the Oxford Group's third of the five C's. Sam wrote plenty on this concept and was later to explain:

We must remove the blocks. We may make casual acquaintances with many people, but if we are to enter into long-time relationships with them, we must come to an understanding. In forming a lasting relationship with the Greatest of all persons, we are obliged to look into ourselves and see what there is which is inconsistent with our friendship with Him. We shall soon discover that if there be uncleanness in any relation, or hatred and bitterness, or selfishness and dishonesty, this will affect the Great Relationship adversely. . . . A quickened sense of sin—of particular sins that need to be put away, and of the

---

[104] *Pass It On*, p. 128; Dick B., *The Good Book and The Big Book*, 2d ed., p. 154

[105] Shoemaker, *The Conversion of the Church*, p. 35.

state of sin which is ever recurrent in our human experience—is our first and greatest need.[106]

St. Paul's conversion conformed to many others: namely in the need which preceded it, the divided life, sharpening into a sense of sin and the need for forgiveness. And in the willing surrender of the self to God and His mercy and His plan, as represented in the words, "What shall I do, Lord" [Acts 22:10]?[107]

Most of the misery of this world lies in divided hearts. We want to make the best of two worlds. We want God, but we want other things too. The sense of conflict, the sense of sin, is really a well-placed danger signal, telling us that we are headed for trouble, perhaps nervous breakdown, because we are still two or more selves.[108]

He must be willing to give up the sins which beset, and to accept in full God's plan for his life.[109]

I talked this week with a man who told me he was more miserable than ever he had been in his life. He knows, too, that he is miserable for want of God. . . . Let him once face all that is prodigal in him, all that is estranged from God, and offensive to God. Let him come back in honest penitence to God, like the son in the story, and all that misery will be left behind.[110]

Miss Olive M. Jones (an educator of world-wide repute) became president of the National Education Association in 1923. And then she joined Sam Shoemaker at Calvary Church. She became superintendent of Calvary Church School and director of Calvary House, which was the location of America's Oxford Group headquarters and of many of its New York area meetings.

---

[106] Shoemaker, *They're on the Way*, pp. 154-55.

[107] Shoemaker, *Confident Faith*, p. 115.

[108] Shoemaker, *The Gospel According to You*, p. 112.

[109] Shoemaker, *Confident Faith*, p. 117.

[110] Shoemaker, *The Gospel According to You*, p. 113.

Miss Jones later authored *Inspired Children*, with Sam Shoemaker writing the Foreword.[111] She included, in the foregoing title, this definition of Conviction:

> *Conviction*, by which we come to a conscious realization of our sins which shut God away from us (p. 135).

Both Dr. Bob's wife Anne Ripley Smith and Bill Wilson's wife Lois Burnham Wilson spoke of *conviction*. Lois used the Oxford Group expression "convicted."[112] Anne wrote at much more length about "conviction" in her spiritual journal:

> [Specifically discussing the Oxford Group's "The Five C's"] 3. Conviction. . . . Stay with him until he makes a decision and says it out loud.

> Many people go into tirades about sin in the national life, but refuse to deal with it in their own life. Challenge them as to how much they really care about such situations.

> Obedience is one of the key-words of the Christian life. Refusal to obey blocks the channel, and prevents further word from God.

> Barriers to a full surrender. 1. Is there anything I won't give up? 2. Is there any apology I won't make. . . . 13. Ideas about self—holding on to my own judgment of things, people, common sense and reason.

> Be willing to ask God where I am failing and to admit sin.

> Our first need is an emetic, not a narcotic. This emetic is facing the barrier, that is, our specific sins which are keeping us from

---

[111] Olive M. Jones, *Inspired Children* (New York: Harper & Brothers Publishers, 1933).

[112] See Dick B., *The Akron Genesis of Alcoholics Anonymous*, pp. 154-55.

Christ and from this complete and utter giving of ourselves to Christ.[113]

It seems apparent that Shoemaker and the early AAs believed: First, man has to give up (surrender) sins, not that God first takes them away. Man surrenders; and God imparts spirit. Man changes his mind; and God changes man. Man sees the error of his ways; and then, by reason of what Jesus Christ accomplished, man is forgiven by the miracle of the new birth. Frank Buchman put it this way: Sin is the disease (the problem). Jesus Christ is cure (the solution). And the result is a miracle.[114]

AAs today often get caught up in the idea that they actually must "give their wills to God" and *then* that they are able to, and do in fact, *take* their wills "back again." In so declaring, they lose sight of the free will God has given them, and also of the "conviction" idea. The first aspect of the Oxford Group-Shoemaker life-change or transformation was that man himself had to become "convicted" or "convinced" that the old ideas and old ways were non-productive and contrary to the will of God.[115] Repentance was a change of mind. That was a biblical idea, a Shoemaker idea, and a Bill Wilson idea—whatever the theology.

The Sixth Step involved specific biblical ideas: "Against thee, thee only have I sinned, and done *this* evil in thy sight" (Psalm 51:4); "Iniquities prevail against me: as *for* our transgressions, thou shalt purge them away" (Psalm 65:3).[116]

---

[113] See Dick B., *Anne Smith's Journal*, 3rd ed., pp. 42-45.

[114] *Foundations for Faith*, 2d ed., Compiled by Harry J. Almond (London: Grosvenor Books, 1980), pp. 9-29.

[115] H. A. Walter, *Soul Surgery: Some Thoughts on Incisive Personal Work*, 6th ed. (London: Blandford Press, n.d.), p. 64: "CONVICTION. . . . Is the recognition that sin—in the graphic, personal terms Dr. Joseph Parker used to employ—is *striking God in the face.*" See Big Book, 3rd ed., p. 58: "Some of us have tried to hold on to our old ideas and the result was nil until we let go absolutely."

[116] Walter, *Soul Surgery*, 6th ed., pp. 64, 68; and see Dick B., *The Good Book and The Big Book*, 2d ed., pp. 154-56.

The individual examines himself or herself. This is done under
the confidential impetus and witnessing by one whose life has
already been "changed." So A.A.'s Fourth and Fifth Steps really
comprehend "Confidence" and "Confession," to use the Oxford
Group/Shoemaker parlance. Shoemaker explained how
"conviction" follows on the heels of "confession.":

> I have found a way to draw confession from others. It is to
> confess first myself. . . . By "conviction" two things are meant:
> conviction first of sin, and then a growing assurance that Christ
> can meet the need.[117]

- *Step Seven*: **Humbly asked Him to remove our shortcomings.**

Though he probably was not speaking for Dr. Bob (since Dr. Bob
said he had nothing to do with the writing of the Twelve Steps),
Bill Wilson has been quoted as follows:

> Bill Wilson said that he built the four absolutes of the Oxford
> Group—absolute truth, absolute love, absolute unselfishness,
> and absolute purity—into the Sixth and Seventh Steps of the
> Program.[118]

> Absolutes in themselves are not necessarily destructive. Every
> sound theological system contains them. When we say that our
> destiny is to grow in the likeness and image of God, we are
> stating a healthy relation between a relative and an absolute state
> of affairs. Therefore when writing the Twelve Steps, it was
> necessary to include some sort of absolute value or else they
> wouldn't have been theologically sound. . . . However, we
> couldn't make them as promising and as misleading as we found

---

[117] Shoemaker, *Realizing Religion*, pp. 80-81.

[118] Ernest Kurtz, *Not-God: A History of Alcoholics Anonymous*, Expanded ed. (Center
City, MN: Hazelden, 1991), p. 242.

them in the Oxford Group emphasis. So in Steps Six and Seven, and *in the use of the word God, we did include them.*[119]

There are several difficulties with these statements by Wilson, though it would not be appropriate to analyze them at length in this particular title.

Suffice it to observe here:

1. One would be hard-pressed to find the Four Absolutes *in* Steps Six and Seven because Wilson's statements ignored or intentionally omitted the role of the Five C.'s in the "conversion" process Wilson had necessarily learned from his "sponsor" Ebby Thacher.[120] Which Bill had inevitably heard taught by Sam Shoemaker.[121] And which he most assuredly must have heard as he listened to Anne Smith explain during Bill's pioneer days in Akron.[122]

2. One could say that the principles of honesty, unselfishness, and love *can* be found in the Big Book many times; and that the elimination of their possible opposites—lying, self-centeredness (pride), and hate—are probably three of the four shortcomings or "sins" covered by the Fourth Step self-examination. But one would be hard-put to find "absolute purity" in the Big Book. This—as distinguished from the position taken by early Akron A.A.[123]

---

[119] Kurtz, *Not-God*, pp. 242-43.

[120] As to Ebby's familiarity with the principles, see Mel B., *Ebby: The Man Who Sponsored Bill W.* (Center City, MN: Hazelden, 1998), pp. 58-62, 69, 73.

[121] See Shoemaker, *Realizing Religion*, pp. 79-80.

[122] See Dick B., *Anne Smith's Journal*, pp. 18-28, 30-33, 60-66; *The Oxford Group and Alcoholics Anonymous*, pp. 178-79.

[123] Bill weaseled out of this problem in several ways. First, he wrote, "God alone can judge our sex situation" (Big Book, 3rd ed., p. 69). That can hardly be said to be true if you read the sermon on the mount which Bill said contained the underlying philosophy
(continued...)

3. When Wilson used the word "We" in his Steps, he was hardly speaking for anyone. The fact is that he said he wrote the Twelve Steps in half an hour by himself, and that he expanded them from the original six steps, which did not *per se* include any particular Oxford Group "Absolute" other than honesty.[124]

4. Wilson's criticisms of the Oxford Group's Four Absolute emphasis by calling it "misleading" was hardly justified. The remark demonstrates that Wilson did not understand or perhaps even wish to understand the Four Absolutes as targets, or their origins in the teachings of Jesus Christ. Instead, he seemingly tried to accuse the Oxford Group of demanding "perfection" while courting favor with what he

---

[123] (...continued)
of A.A. "Blessed *are* the pure in heart: for they shall see God," said Jesus as quoted in Matthew 5:8. "Ye have heard that it was said by them of old time, Thou shalt not commit adultery: But I say unto you, That whosoever looketh on a woman to lust after her hath committed adultery with her already in his heart." Second, Bill laid a trip on the Oxford Group by saying (for himself, and certainly not Dr. Bob): "The principles of honesty, purity, unselfishness, and love are as much a goal for A.A. members and are as much practiced by them as by any other group of people; yet we found that when the word 'absolute' was put in front of these attributes, they either turned people away by the hundreds or gave a temporary spiritual inflation resulting in collapse" (*Pass It On*, p. 72). Third, he ignored the clearcut practices of the successful program in Akron, as reported by Frank Amos: "Not only must he [the alcoholic] want to stop drinking permanently, he must remove from his life other sins such as hatred, *adultery*, and others which frequently accompany alcoholism. *Unless he will do this absolutely, Smith and his associates refuse to work with him* (*DR. BOB*, p. 131, emphasis ours). It is no secret that Bill Wilson was, as one writer put it, a "compulsive womanizer" during his sober decades in A.A. in the forties, fifties, and sixties. Such blatant conduct provides little support for Wilson's writings about why "absolute" purity needed to be abandoned as a "yardstick" or "standard" to shoot at. See Nan Robertson, *Getting Better Inside Alcoholics Anonymous* (New York: Fawcett Crest, 1988), pp. 23-24, 27-28, 70.

[124] *Pass It On*, p. 172; Dick B., *The Oxford Group and Alcoholics Anonymous*, pp. 237-46, 308-11.

thought was the A.A. conduct pointed toward "progress."[125]

5. The problem with Steps Six and Seven is that, together, *they* do not demonstrate any particular theological soundness such as Wilson mentions, other than an expressed desire to eliminate shortcomings, coupled with a humble recognition that God has a part in that change. From a biblical standpoint, from the Oxford Group viewpoint, and from Sam's standpoint, God sets absolute standards; and he did so in his revelations to Jesus in the Sermon on the Mount.[126]

God is not a vacuum cleaner. Any "removal" comes ultimately, only because of God's grace—what has already been accomplished by Jesus Christ for those who believe on him. By confessing Jesus as Lord and believing that God raised Jesus from the dead, man receives a new nature.[127] Any "removal" is simply the receipt—by the mercy and grace of God—of forgiveness, healing, deliverance, love, power, and a sound mind.[128] The transformation does not accomplish the elimination

---

[125] See Big Book, 3rd ed. p. 60; Robert E. Speer, *The Principles of Jesus: Applied to Some Questions of To-day* (New York: Association Press, 1902), pp. 33-36; Henry B. Wright, *The Will of God and a Man's Lifework* (New York: Association Press, 1924), pp. 167-218; Dick B., *The Oxford Group & Alcoholics Anonymous*, pp. 242-45.

[126] See the comments of Dr. Robert E. Speer, *The Principles of Jesus: Applied to Some Questions of Today* (New York: Association Press, 1902), pp. 33-36. Speer was the origin of the four absolute standards. And Speer opened his discussion of them in this fashion at page 33: "Jesus did not attempt to issue a code of laws to guide human conduct. He put men in possession of great moral principles which they would have to apply themselves. . . . And these standards were absolute, the more boldly absolute because Jesus intentionally framed His teaching in direct opposition to the casuistical method of the scribes. . . . He cut off escapes and pretexts, and taught that standards are standards." See also, Dick B., *The Oxford Group & Alcoholics Anonymous*, 2d ed., pp. 237-46.

[127] 2 Corinthians 5:17; Romans 10:9.

[128] Acts 4:7-12; 2 Timothy 1:7; 2 Peter 2:24.

of free will, or of man's basic "old man" nature, or of the efforts of the Devil to lure bad or sinful decisions and choices into action again.[129] The contrast between what God gives, and what man is offered, can be found in the book that was a favorite in A.A.—the Book of James.[130]

Man "surrenders"—to use the Oxford Group term.[131] *God* enables man to have a new birth—to receive a new nature.[132] Then man has a choice—to use the power of God to do the will of God, or to return to his old ways, despite the power of God that he gained through being born again of God's spirit.[133]

Now what did Sam Shoemaker have to say that can be related to Step Seven as Bill himself, and alone, actually wrote it? Let's return again to Shoemaker's protege Miss Olive M. Jones and her definition of "Conversion":

---

[129] See Ephesians 4:22-24: "That ye put off concerning the former conversation the old man, which is corrupt according to the deceitful lusts; And be renewed in the spirit of your mind; And that ye put on the new man, which after God is created in righteousness and true holiness;" Philippians 2:5: "Let this mind be in you, which was also in Christ Jesus;" Colossians 3:9-10: "Lie not one to another, seeing that ye have put off the old man with his deeds; And have put on the new *man*, which is renewed in knowledge after the image of him that created him;" Romans 12:2: "And be not conformed to this world: but be ye transformed by the renewing of your mind, that ye may prove what *is* that good, and acceptable, and perfect, will of God;" 1 Peter 5:8: "Be sober, be vigilant; because your adversary the devil, as a roaring lion, walketh about, seeking whom he may devour."

[130] James 1:17-19: "Every good gift and every perfect gift is from above, and cometh down from the Father of lights, with whom is no variableness, neither shadow of turning. Of his own will begat he us with the word of truth. . . . Wherefore, my beloved brethren, let every man be swift to hear, slow to speak, slow to wrath." James 3:14-17: "But if ye have bitter envying and strife in your hearts, glory not, and lie not against the truth. This wisdom descendeth not from above, but *is* earthly, sensual, devilish. . . . But the wisdom that is from above is first pure, then peaceable, gentle, *and easy* to be intreated, full of mercy and good fruits, without partiality, and without hypocrisy."

[131] See, for a better biblical understanding, Romans 10:9.

[132] Galatians 3:13-16; Ephesians 1:13-14; 2:1-9; 1 Peter 1:23.

[133] 2 Peter 2:20-22.

Conversion, which means simply a changed life. "Ye must be born again," said Christ.[134]

The conversion or new birth or changed life is only the beginning. Man receives a new nature which is the spirit of God and the spiritual power to change things.

Did Shoemaker say that? Let us look at these remarks by Sam:

> There are a good many people who know that they need to be converted: but they have such an august conception of conversion that they have not learned that they may have a part in their own conversion. It is true that only the Spirit of God converts any man: it is His direct action on the soul that alone converts. But we may draw near and put ourselves in position to be converted by the simple act of self-surrender. . . . The act of surrender should mean the assumption upon ourselves of God's will for us, and should open our minds completely to His will.[135]

> But clearly the sharing of needs is not enough. There must be a decision in which the will gathers up the facts which the mind has collected, and the aspiration of the heart has felt, and packs them into a moral choice. This is the act of self-surrender which is man's part in his own conversion, the step which puts him in a position to receive the grace of God which alone converts.[136]

> Surrender is a handle by which an ordinary person may lay hold of the experience of conversion. It is the first step, the step of the will. In order to make surrender the decision of the whole life, and not merely the emotion of a moment, it needs to be filled with practical content: we must help people to see just what they are surrendering to God, their fears, their sins, most of all their *wills*, putting God's will once and for all ahead of every other thing. When these items are cleared through talking

---

[134] Jones, *Inspired Children*, p. 136.

[135] Shoemaker, *The Conversion of the Church*, pp. 40-41

[136] Shoemaker, *The Conversion of the Church*, p. 77.

and sharing, they can be lumped together, and with the self flung out in abandon upon the mercy and power of God.[137]

The world does not need an awakening any more than the church does. It was to an educated religious gentleman that Jesus said, "Ye must be born again." That imperative is a judgment against those who withstand conversion. . . . The new life begins by utter self-dedication to the will of God. . . . Conversion is the beginning, not the ending, of an experience of God. That experience continues when we use all the means Jesus put at our disposal for continuation—prayer, the Scriptures, the Church and the Sacraments, Christian fellowship and worship.[138]

We believe entirely that conversion is the experience which initiates the new life. But we are not fools enough to think that the beginning is the end! All subsequent life is a development of the relationship with God which conversion opened.[139]

Now, the place where our wills pass out of our own hands and into God's hands is the place of surrender: and surrender is our answer to this command from God: "Give in." . . . Cooperation will come later—gladder, freer cooperation than every you knew you could have with God: but it begins with surrender.[140]

We shall begin knowing the need of a new birth when we begin knowing that it is the sins of people like you and me that have made this world the hell it is today. . . . Tell them of these things [of the need for being born again] and, with them as witness, give these sins and our old selves with them, to God. You say that you can do this alone with God; and I ask you, Have you succeeded in doing so? I said I was going to do that for years, but it never happened until I let a human witness

---

[137] Shoemaker, *The Conversion of the Church*, p. 78.

[138] Shoemaker, *Religion That Works*, p. 14.

[139] Shoemaker, *Children of the Second Birth*, p. 16.

[140] Shoemaker, *National Awakening*, p. 51.

come in on my decision. That is the "how" of getting rid of sin if you are in earnest about doing it at all: face it, share it, surrender it. Hate it, forsake it, confess it, and restore for it. [141]

With the foregoing as a backdrop, we can understand Shoemaker's influence on the Seventh Step better if we take a look at the "Seventh Step Prayer" in the Big Book:

My Creator, I am now willing that you should have all of me, good and bad. I pray that you now remove from me every single defect of character which stands in the way of my usefulness to you and my fellows. Grant me strength, as I go out from here, to do your bidding. Amen (p. 76).

Shoemaker seems to have written about all the elements Bill mentioned in his Seventh Step language and in his Seventh Step Prayer. You can see "humility" in the self-surrender and in the gratitude which should follow from being lifted up by God. [142] And Shoemaker said:

Let us this morning "lift up our eyes unto the hills," and consider several of the high places of the spirit . . . *faith* . . . *love*. . . . And humility—the high place of *humility*. . . . The truest humility in the world is that of the man who has been lifted up by God, carried above his sins, given peace for his pain and joy for his crying; and who, standing on the strong rock, thinks not of the security of his own position but of the mercy of God for putting him there. . . . There are human door-mats who feign humility but do not have it. . . . Let them experience a great deliverance, or really know the salvation of God in their souls, and their humility will grow out of their sense of obligation and gratitude. [143]

---

[141] Shoemaker, *National Awakening*, p. 58.

[142] See James 4:10.

[143] Shoemaker, *Religion That Works*, pp. 122-23.

What about *removal*? In the Sixth Step discussion above, we quoted Shoemaker to the effect that *we* must remove the blocks. However good or bad the theology, the Oxford Group writings and Dr. Bob's wife did speak of the *removal* of defects.[144] But it is hard for the author to think in any other terms than the following as Shoemaker presented the life-changing path:

We decide to surrender and become God's kids. *We* spot the flaws. *We* confess the flaws. *We* make up our mind to forsake the flaws. The accomplishments of Jesus Christ *save* us from the consequences of the flaws, as far as punishment or condemnation by God are concerned.[145] But an effective relationship with God and with others requires that the power of God, received by His grace, be utilized through *our* putting on the mind of Christ, *our* putting off the old man, and *our* following in the footsteps of Christ as portrayed in the Good Book.[146]

First comes God's power and love and forgiveness.[147] Then comes the walk of love and practice which His grace and mercy made available to us.[148] And, then, often come further flaws, with still more opportunity for us to seek God's forgiveness since

----

[144] See Kitchen, *I Was a Pagan*, p. 143: "It takes the power of God to *remove* these fears and mental conditions;" p. 74: "God simply lifted that desire entirely out of my life. . .;" p. 180: "Finally Christ taught me, through His beatitudes, that I could not enter the kingdom of heaven until, through recognizing my own poverty of spirit, I let God remove the obstacles that kept His love from flowing in. . . . So it is—when I will let Him—that God is shaping me towards the Christ-like character."

[145] Romans 8:1.

[146] 1 Peter 2:21: "For even hereunto were ye called: because Christ also suffered for us, leaving us an example, that ye should follow in his steps." See Charles M. Sheldon, *In His Steps* (Nashville, TN: Broadman Press, 1935). Sheldon's famous book was a part of Dr. Bob's library.

[147] 1 John 4:10: "Herein is love, not that we loved God, but that he loved us; and sent his Son *to be* the propitiation for our sins."

[148] 1 John 4:11-13: "Beloved, if God so loved us, we ought also to love one another. No man hath seen God at any time. If we love one another, God dwelleth in us, and his love is perfected in us. Hereby know we that we dwell in him, and he in us, because he hath given us of his Spirit."

even our new sins have been paid for.[149] It's not the other way around. Shoemaker put it this way:

> A further surrender is needed when and whenever there is found to be something in us which offends Christ, or walls us from another. We shall need, in this sense, to keep surrendering so long as we live. But I should also like to say that something happens the first time the soul says "Yes" to God with its whole force, that never wholly disappears. As terrible sin does something to the human heart which may be forgiven but leaves its trace, so, thank God, does tremendous surrender leave such an eradicable mark. . . . I believe that with a God of love, there is no limit to the number of times we may come back to him in surrender, provided only we mean it and are penitent for the past.

- *Step Eight*: **Made a list of all persons we had harmed, and became willing to make amends to them all.**

There was no Eighth Step in the original A.A. program. Bill simply added this idea to the restitution requirement for recovery. But there are evidences of Shoemaker's influence on Bill's decision to make the Step Eight addition:

The List of Harms

Bill Wilson wrote: "We *have* a list of all persons we have harmed. . . . We made it when we took inventory" (Big Book, p. 76, emphasis added). Shoemaker had written:

> For most people there is wrapped up in the decision to surrender to God the *necessity to right all wrongs with men*, and

---

[149] 1 John 1:8-10: "If we say that we have no sin, we deceive ourselves, and the truth is not in us. If we confess our sins, he is faithful and just to forgive us *our* sins, and to cleans us from all unrightheousness. If we say that we have not sinned, we make him a liar, and his word is not in us."

it generally means a specific wrong of act or attitude toward somebody in particular. This is the hurdle of *restitution* (emphasis added).[150]

I asked him whether he had had a Quiet Time about the *four standards*: absolute honesty, purity, unselfishness, and love. He said *he had, and produced a piece of yellow fool's-cap from his pocket*, neatly divided into four quarters, one for each standard, on which *he had written down all the places where he had fallen down on them*. The paper was quite full. . . . We had a Quiet Time, and more guidance came to Him. There were *various people he must make restitution to*, and others he must help (emphasis added).[151]

Straightening out the Damage

Wilson wrote: "Now we go out to our fellows and repair the damage done in the past. We attempt to sweep away the debris which has accumulated out of our effort to live on self-will and run the show ourselves" (Big Book, p. 76). Shoemaker had written:

I want to remind you that our experience of God is all bound up inextricably with our human relationships. "If a man love not his brother whom he hath seen, how can he love God whom he hath not seen?"[152] . . . *It is idle for us to try to be in touch with God, or keep in touch with Him, so long as there are human relationships which must be righted* at the same time (emphasis added).[153]

I am certain that the most important factor in continuance, second only to prayer, is in a series of new relationships. First

---

[150] Shoemaker, *The Gospel According to You*, p. 87.

[151] Shoemaker, *The Church Can Save the World*, pp. 119-20.

[152] See 1 John 4:20.

[153] Shoemaker, *The Conversion of the Church*, pp. 47-48

with the family. Here, for instance, is a clergyman who has seen the failure of his ministry and *faced his sins, and made a new start with God.* The family ought to be the first people to see a change in him. *He may make a blanket-apology to the entire family for impatience, for temper, for wanting his own way, for wanting to play Providence to them all.* There may be specific wrongs to be shared with individuals. Probably heretofore he has been confessing their sins to them: now he confesses his own (emphasis added).[154]

Asking God for Help in Getting Started

There is possibly no more misunderstood and misused word in A.A. language and chatter than "willingness." You hear people talking about willingness. Then about willingness to become willing. Then about praying for the willingness to be willing. And so on.

Wilson's own language need not have given rise to such nonsense. He wrote, concerning the road to amends: "We have a list of all persons we have harmed and to whom we are willing to make amends. . . . If we haven't the will to do this, we ask until it comes" (Big Book, p. 76). Simply put, this means: Get going! As Shoemaker often put it in Pittsburgh, "Get changed. Get together. Get going." If there is reluctance, ask God for help in getting started. Shoemaker taught:

We want to know that God can and does speak directly to the human heart. The reason why some of us believe in guidance, at least in theory, is that the Old and New Testaments are full of instances of it, specific as you please. . . . There are, of course, conditions of guidance. *We must have a surrendered will, as we have said, which wants God's will more than its own, and is ready to do what one is told, no matter whether it be to one's taste or not.* . . . The positive attitude here seems to me to be, instead of thinking about whether we or humanity in

---

[154] Shoemaker, *The Conversion of the Church*, pp. 41-42.

general are capable of receiving guidance, to remember the
omnipotence of God, and His power to send us light if He wills
to. . . . Guidance comes rather to active than to passive people:
it comes when the guidedly active person stops for a fresh
lesson from God; the more obedience, the more guidance—not
as a quantitative *quid pro quo*, but as a spiritual law. . . .
Guidance always comes with an authority all its own. This
varies in intensity; for guidance is sometimes the motion of a
consecrated human mind mobilized to do the will of God. . . .
But nothing makes up for our private time alone with the living
God. *There He may give us the conviction of sin that clears us
of a stoppage and sends us to someone with restoration and
apology* (emphasis added).[155]

- *Step Nine*: **Made direct amends to such people wherever
  possible, except when to do so would injure them or
  others.**

There were several Bible verses relied upon in early A.A. for the
importance of making restitution. These included Numbers 5:6-7;
Luke, chapter 15; and Luke 19:1-10. All were cited by A. J.
Russell in *For Sinners Only*.[156] But the most commonly quoted
verses can be found in Jesus' Sermon on the Mount:

But I say unto you, That whosoever is angry with his brother
without a cause shall be in danger of the judgment: and
whosoever shall say to his brother, Raca, shall be in danger of
the council: but whosoever shall say, Thou fool, shall be in
danger of hell fire. Therefore if thou bring thy gift to the altar,
and there rememberest that thy brother hath ought against thee;
Leave there thy gift before the altar, and go thy way; first be

---

[155] Shoemaker, *The Conversion of the Church*, pp. 50-51, 61.

[156] Russell, *For Sinners Only*, pp. 119, 129, 135. See discussions in Dick B., *The
Good Book and The Big Book*, pp. 159-160; and *The Oxford Group & Alcoholics
Anonymous*, 2d ed, pp. 206-11.

reconciled to thy brother, and then come and offer thy gift (Matthew 5:22-24).[157]

It is not necessary to quote the Big Book's extended discussion of making amends and restitution. But the following remarks by Shoemaker put force behind A.A.'s amends step (Step Nine):

"If a man love not his brother whom he hath seen, how can he love God whom he hath not seen?" "If thou bring thy gift to the altar, and there rememberest that thy brother hath ought against thee, first go and be reconciled unto thy brother, and then come and offer thy gift."[158]

It is my own conviction that the truest counter-part of the Cross is the sharing of our sins. I know people, and so do you, who wear their lives out in human service, but that kind of love and laying down their lives is not in them. They will work their fingers out, but no one ever got a real word of apology or admission of need or failure out of them. . . . [T]he last stand of self, in the righteous as in the sinner, is pride. We want some inner citadel, shut away from the influence of man or God, where we may cherish fine ideas about ourselves, nurse our hurt feelings which usually only hurt pride, and make up to ourselves for the inadequate appreciation of an unjust world. . . . We can talk about humility as much as we like, and pray for it: but we shall not have it until our pride licks the dust.[159]

The other person may have been primarily responsible for the trouble, but if our resentment, anger, self-pity was wrong, let us share that.[160]

---

[157] Shoemaker, *The Conversion of the Church*, pp. 47-48; *The Gospel According to You*, pp. 146-51; *Confident Faith*, p. 33; Dick B., *The Good Book and The Big Book*, 2d ed., p. 159; *The Oxford Group & Alcoholics Anonymous*, 2d ed., pp. 209-11.

[158] Shoemaker, *The Conversion of the Church*, p. 47.

[159] Shoemaker, *The Gospel According to You*, pp. 146-48.

[160] Shoemaker, *The Gospel According to You*, p. 149.

I know heaps of nominal Christians who wonder why they do not have divine guidance, and the joy of real faith; but over in the corner of their minds and memories, motionless but not dead, is an old resistance against someone. Vaguely we know we are in for a difficult letter, or visit. But we put it off. . . . What reception we find in the other person is not our responsibility—only that we go to him in love and in honesty and clear any wrong on our side.[161]

We need to know how to recognize sin, how to get it shared, surrendered, forgiven, *restored for*, and then used to help others in like case (emphasis added).[162]

What convinces the average person is results: they don't want theories, they want samples. . . . When a home, like the one I am thinking of, has gone through the breakup of separation, has been reunited because the husband has profoundly changed, repented of his part of the sin, made full restitution to his wife, and been guided to begin life anew with her—when through this restored home influences have been sent out into a community that have resulted in numbers of changed lives and other restored homes, there you have a demonstration unit that talks louder than a hundred sermons about the home.[163]

When a person is honest, spiritual diagnosis comes like welcome light. But we have asked much of him, indeed we have asked everything, for God will have nothing less. He sees in the distance a discipline over indulgence that may cost more than he wants to pay. He sees himself being rooted out of comfortable old ruts, like blaming other people for the condition of the country, instead of taking responsibility himself. He sees not only costly apologies and restitutions at once if he is going to be absolutely honest and absolutely loving, but he sees a lifetime

---

[161] Shoemaker, *The Gospel According to You*, p. 87.

[162] Shoemaker, *The Church Can Save the World*, p. 153.

[163] Shoemaker, *The Church Can Save the World*, p. 129.

of living in the light instead of keeping part of himself in the dark.[164]

Notice what Bill Wilson wrote in his specific instructions for taking the Ninth Step:

> Probably there still are some misgivings. As we look over the list of business acquaintances and friends we have hurt, we may feel diffident about going to some of them on a spiritual basis. . . . At the moment we are trying to put our lives in order. But this is not an end in itself. Our real purpose is to fit ourselves to be of maximum service to God and the people about us (Big Book, pp. 76-77).

> . . . [W]e ask that we be given strength and direction to do the right thing, no matter what the personal consequences may be (Big Book, p. 79).

> Yes, there is a long period of reconstruction ahead. We must take the lead. A remorseful mumbling that we are sorry won't fill the bill at all. We ought to sit down with the family and frankly analyze the past as we now see it, being very careful not to criticize them. Their defects may be glaring, but the chances are that our own actions are partly responsible (Big Book, p. 83).

A better understanding of Shoemaker's ideas and of the Big Book itself could help to eliminate so much of the nonsensical talk in A.A. meetings about "writing a letter to a dead person," "making amends to myself," "putting myself at the top of the amends list," and "volunteering to do good works because the person wronged is now dead." With one exception, the author was given such ideas by his own first sponsor, and heard them many times thereafter.

---

[164] Shoemaker, *The Church Can Save the World*, pp. 112-13.

- *Step Ten*: **Continued to take personal inventory and when we were wrong promptly admitted it.**

If one understands the structure of Wilson's Twelve Steps and the nature of the Oxford Group's "Continuance" idea (Continuance being one of the Five C's), an understanding of Shoemaker's impact on the Tenth Step is easy.

Bill Wilson commenced his Tenth Step language with the word *Continued* (Big Book, p. 59). In the instructions for taking the Tenth Step, note how many times Wilson used the word *continue*:

> This thought brings us to *Step Ten*, which suggests we *continue* to take personal inventory and *continue* to set right any new mistakes. . . . This is not an overnight matter. It should *continue* for our lifetime. *Continue* to watch for selfishness, dishonesty, resentment, and fear (Big Book, p. 84, emphasis added).

We believe this language makes clear that the person who took the first nine steps of A.A. is to *continue* doing what was learned in those previous Steps. That person is to continue the process. Bill lays out (in Step Ten), in outline form, a "mini" and "daily" and "prompt" taking of the same steps that were previously learned: (1) Continue to watch for the Step Four problems—resentment, fear, self-seeking, and dishonesty. (2) Continue the Step Five discussion of these defects or harms with someone—immediately. (3) Continue to call God off the bench, as in Steps Six and Seven. (4) Continue to make amends promptly—as learned and undertaken in Steps Eight and Nine. And then, work with others and practice love and tolerance—Step Twelve being thrown in for good measure.

It hardly seems necessary to repeat the material Shoemaker infused into the first nine steps. But it is appropriate to point to Shoemaker's espousal of *Continuance* in the life-changing process:

> It may help to keep our object in view if we choose five words which will cover the usual stages of development [the Five C's]:

Confidence; Confession; Conviction; Conversion; Conservation [later changed to "Continuance"][165]

Conversion is the beginning, not the ending, of an experience of God. That experience continues when we use all the means Jesus Christ put at our disposal for continuation—prayer, the Scriptures, the Church and Sacraments, Christian fellowship, and worship.[166]

We believe entirely that conversion is the experience which initiates the new life. But we are not fools enough to think that the beginning is the end! All subsequent life is a development of the relationship with God which conversion opened.[167]

There is need for rededication day by day, hour by hour, by which progressively, in every Quiet Time, the contaminations of sin and self-will are further sloughed off. . . . We shall need, in this sense, to keep surrendering as long as we live.[168]

In discussing the spiritual disease, Dr. Frank Buchman used language almost identical to that Wilson used in his Step Ten and Step Eleven instructions. Buchman said:

What is the disease? Isn't it fear, dishonesty, resentment, selfishness?[169]

---

[165] Shoemaker, *Realizing Religion*, pp. 79-80. In a footnote on page 80, Shoemaker said, "For these words I am indebted to Frank N. D. Buchman." See Harold Begbie, *Life Changers*, who says that Frank Buchman wrote down "Confidence, Confession, Conviction, Conversion, Continuance" (p. 169). In *Twice-Born Ministers*, Shoemaker used the different word and said: "All the values of *continuance* would be thus conserved" (p. 168, emphasis added).

[166] Shoemaker, *Religion That Works*, p. 14.

[167] Shoemaker, *Children of the Second Birth*, p. 16.

[168] Shoemaker, *The Conversion of the Church*, p. 79.

[169] Buchman, *Remaking the World*, p. 38.

Not only did Shoemaker frequently refer to Buchman, the Oxford Group, and the spiritual malady, he wrote at length on the problems of fear, dishonesty, resentment, and selfishness. And those writings will be covered elsewhere in this title. However, just as Bill Wilson spoke, in Tenth Step instructions, of "love and tolerance" as the code, so did Shoemaker speak of Professor Henry Drummond—the great evangelist, writer, and Bible student (a favorite of Dr. Bob's):

> "If a man has not the love of God shed abroad in his heart, he has never been regenerated," cried Moody, whose greatest praise of Drummond was that he "lived continually in the thirteenth chapter of First Corinthians." . . . [T]he great saving souls of history, and the very saints of our own day, have been those who believed that any success without love was failure, and any failure without love was success in disguise—for "love never faileth." [170]

Concluding his first major piece of writing with a discussion of "Continuance," Shoemaker wrote:

> Lastly, they want means to live this life of grace. . . . Let us not forget the words of the shrewd and great-hearted Paul, that we should give "not the gospel of God only, but also our own souls," sharing our best, and not hiding our worst—humble, earnest, frank, glad, and above all loving. It is the greatest work in the world. [171]

Love and tolerance were not only Wilson's code; they were the essence of 1 Corinthians 13 and Drummond's writing about that chapter in Henry Drummond's *The Greatest Thing in the World.*

---

[170] Shoemaker, *Realizing Religion*, p. 50. See 1 Corinthians 13:8: "Charity [love] never faileth."

[171] Shoemaker, *Realizing Religion*, pp. 82-83.

- *Step Eleven*: **Sought through prayer and meditation to improve our conscious contact with God *as we understood Him*, praying only for knowledge of His will for us and the power to carry that out.**

The heart of A.A.'s Eleventh Step, as it reads today, is *prayer and meditation*. Prayer and meditation as practiced in early A.A. were part and parcel of *Quiet Time*. And Quiet Time involved: (1) *Bible study*, (2) *Prayer*, (3) *Listening* for thoughts from God, (4) *Writing* the thoughts down, (5) Using *Bible devotionals and other Christian reading* when considered necessary or helpful. The author has discussed each of these roots at great length in other titles.[172]

Since Shoemaker subscribed to all the material covered in our other titles, it is not necessary to cover those matters at length. But it *is* important to note the following points.

How Bill Organized the Eleventh Step

Bill Wilson essentially divided the Eleventh Step process into four groupings: (1) What one does *on retiring* in reviewing his or her day and how well the "continuance" in the Tenth Step was practiced. (2) What one does *on awakening* by way of seeking God's further guidance. (3) What one does *to grow* in spiritual understanding by way of church services, devotional time, prayer, and the use of helpful books. (4) What one does *all through the day* in order to abide by God's will and seek His guidance—avoiding anxiety, doubt, and frustration. And we have covered in our other titles the Biblical ideas, the Oxford Group roots, and the Quiet Time practices that were observed in connection with these four groups of practices.

---

[172] See Dick B., *The Good Book and The Big Book*, 2d ed., pp. 162-70; *The Oxford Group & Alcoholics Anonymous*, 2d ed., pp. 246-69, 319-22; *Good Morning!: Quiet Time, Morning Watch, Meditation, and Early A.A.*, 2d ed.

What AAs Themselves Published about Quiet Time

Though lacking in details, A.A.'s *own* literature—and the remarks of its founders and their families—speak loudly on the importance of Quiet Time in early A.A.:

"The A.A. members of that time did not consider meetings necessary to maintain sobriety. They were simply 'desirable.' Morning devotion and 'quiet time,' however, were musts"[173]

"He [the A.A. member of that time] must have devotions every morning—a 'quiet time' of prayer and some reading from the Bible and other religious literature. Unless this is faithfully followed, there is grave danger of backsliding."[174]

. . . [T]hey were convinced that the answer to their problems was in the Good Book.[175]

We already had the basic ideas [said Dr. Bob], though not in terse and tangible form. We got them . . . as a result of our study of the Good Book.[176]

Each morning [during Bill's stay with Dr. Bob and Anne in the summer of 1935], there was a devotion, he [Bill Wilson] recalled. After a long silence, in which they awaited inspiration and guidance, Anne would read from the Bible. "James was our favorite," he said. "Reading from her chair in the corner, she would softly conclude, 'Faith without works is dead.'"[177]

Sue [Dr. Bob's daughter] also remembered the quiet time in the mornings—how they sat around reading the Bible. Later, they also used *The Upper Room*, a Methodist publication that

---

[173] *DR. BOB and the Good Oldtimers*, p. 136.

[174] *DR. BOB*, p. 131.

[175] *DR. BOB*, p. 96.

[176] *DR. BOB*, p. 97.

[177] *DR. BOB*, p. 71.

provided a daily inspirational message, interdenominational in its approach.[178]

Emphasis was placed on prayer and on seeking guidance from God in all matters. The movement [the Oxford Group, of which A.A. was then an integral part] also relied on study of the Scriptures and developed some of its own literature as well.[179]

Usually, the person who led the Wednesday meeting took something from *The Upper Room* [the Methodist periodical mentioned earlier] or some other literature as a subject. Sometimes, they selected a theme such as "My Utmost Effort" or "My Highest Goal." There would be a quiet time. Then different people would tell something out of their own experience. . . . [After the meeting, when someone went upstairs to "surrender":] This was in the form of a prayer group. Several of the boys would pray together, and the new man would make his own prayer, asking God to talk alcohol out of his life. . . . During the prayer, he usually made a declaration of his willingness to turn his life over to God. . . . [At the meetings:] The leader would open with a prayer, then read Scripture, Clarence recalled. Then he would spend 20 to 30 minutes giving witness—that is, telling about his past life. Then it would open for witness from the floor. . . . After the meeting closed with the Lord's Prayer, all the men beat it out to the kitchen for coffee, and most of the women sat around talking to each other.[180]

What Sam Said about Quiet Time

We will hit the high points on what Shoemaker and his books could have taught Wilson about Quiet Time; and also probably a good many others in early Akron A.A., where the Fellowship was founded:

---

[178] *DR. BOB*, p. 71.

[179] *DR. BOB*, p. 54.

[180] DR. BOB, pp. 139-41.

We have had altogether too much indefinite exhortation to pray and *read our Bibles*, and too little definite information as to how to do either (emphasis added).[181]

The chief thing that I want to emphasize about our use of the Bible is not so much the way each of us shall pursue our study of it, as the setting apart of a definite time each morning for this, together with prayer. . . . And, therefore, the best time of the day is the first hour of it. . . . This practice of the "Morning Watch" is the most fruitful personal habit of religion for those who use it. . . . [T]he results will justify the effort; and granted the desire and determination to use this time daily, with the Bible open before you, you will soon make a better method of study for yourself that will suit you better than anything which this book might recommend (emphasis added).[182]

I want to give a few practical suggestions which one might follow. One should have the best, that is the most accurate translation obtainable. . . . It is good to have a marked copy where you make plenty of entries, and for this you want a wide margin, and also a fresh copy. . . . Study one book at a time. . . . Read what is there, not your own ideas into it. . . . Read, as President Wilson urged the solders, "Long passages that will really be the road to the heart of it," sometimes a whole book at a sitting. One may read topically. . . . Read and know the Bible, and all else, including public worship, will fall into its place.[183]

Whatever be one's theories about prayer, two things stand: man will pray as long as God and he exist, and the spiritual life cannot be lived without it. . . . But it is an art—the art of discerning God's will—and one must learn it. . . . And we are praying best when we come quite empty of request, to bathe

---

[181] Shoemaker, *Realizing Religion*, p. 58.

[182] Shoemaker, *Realizing Religion*, pp. 60-61.

[183] Shoemaker, *Realizing Religion*, pp. 61-62.

ourselves in his presence, and to "wait upon Him" with an open mind, concerned far more with His message to us than with anything we can say to Him. And as one grows into the longing love of God for men, intercession becomes more and more a necessity. . . . The prayer of confession and for forgiveness is perhaps the deepest, best prayer of all, and the one which we shall need most often if God gives us an acute sense of sin (emphasis added).[184]

I plead again for the *keeping of the "Morning Watch"*—coming fresh to God with the day's plans unmade, submitting first our spirits and then our duties to Him for the shedding of His white light upon both.[185]

Something happened to the quality of my time of prayer when I moved up out of the old conception of a "Morning Watch" (which had a way of slipping round till evening), to the conception of a "Quiet Time." . . . Listening became the dominant note. Not the exclusive note: for there was Bible study first, taking a book and studying it straight through; and there was also ordinary prayer, confession, petition, thanksgiving, intercession. But the bulk of the time is listening.[186]

We are building a solid spiritual roadway under people's feet. . . . And there are four *next steps which they will need if they are to keep travelling*. The first is their daily *Quiet Time*. . . . They will need constant help, suggestions about *how to study the Bible*, where and what to read in it. For most the Gospels will come first . . . (emphasis added).[187]

A full-orbed *Quiet Time means Bible study, prayer, ample time to wait upon God in quiet, writing down what is given to us,*

---

[184] Shoemaker, *Realizing Religion*, pp. 63-64.
[185] Shoemaker, *Realizing Religion*, pp. 65-66.
[186] Shoemaker, *The Conversion of the Church*, p. 60.
[187] Shoemaker, *The Conversion of the Church*, p. 79.

and perhaps the sharing of what has come to us with those who
are closest to us . . . (emphasis added).[188]

Read before you pray. Read the Bible systematically. You may
find *helpful* the serial books of devotion called Forward Day by
Day, or the Upper Room or E. Stanley Jones' "Abundant
Living." Use any devotional book that helps you. This draws
your mind toward God, and makes you ready to pray (emphasis
added).[189]

*Let great prayers help you to pray. Make frequent use of books
of prayer.*[190]

The Bible Verses Sam Used to Show the Way

Wilson's biographer spoke of the great influence Shoemaker had
on Bill's prayer life.[191] The name of the game, said Shoemaker,
was to find God's will and obey it. It was not to inform God of
our will and wonder why things did not come off very well. Bill's
Third Step discussion had much to say about how one fails at
playing God. His Eleventh Step discussion had much to say about
how well things go when one seeks God's will, asks the strength
to carry it out, and obeys it.

Shoemaker repeated five verses over and over in his writings.
These verses illustrated his teaching on how to learn God's
particular or private will for a person. These verses certainly did
not exclude reliance upon the Bible; for, as Shoemaker often said,

---

[188] Shoemaker, *The Conversion of the Church*, p. 80.

[189] Shoemaker, *How to Find God*, p. 15. See also Dick B., *Good Morning!*, pp. 72-75.

[190] Shoemaker, *How to Find God*, p. 16.

[191] Robert Thomsen, *Bill W.* (New York: Harper & Row Publishers, 1975), p. 229: "Perhaps the most important contribution Sam Shoemaker made to Bill's life was in giving him a new interpretation of prayer."

the Bible contains the general will of God.[192] But the following verses were cited to show the importance of *listening* for God's particular will, for His guidance, and for His direction, *and obeying*:

Be still, and know that I *am* God (Psalm 46:10).[193]

Speak, Lord, for thy servant heareth (1 Samuel 3:9).[194]

Lord, what wilt thou have me to do? (Acts 9:6).[195]

What shall I do, Lord? (Acts 22:10).[196]

. . . [N]evertheless not my will, but thine, be done. (Luke 22:42).[197]

- *Step Twelve*: **Having had a spiritual awakening as the result of these steps, we tried to carry this message to alcoholics, and to practice these principles in all our affairs.**

---

[192] Shoemaker, *A Young Man's View of the Ministry*, p. 78; *My Life-Work and My Will*, pamphlet, circa 1930, p. 3.

[193] Shoemaker, *National Awakening*, pp. 45-54. Shoemaker used the Moffatt Translation which was "Give in . . . [A]dmit that I am God." See also *Calvary Church Sermons*, "The Way to Find God," Preached by the Rev. S. M. Shoemaker, June 30, 1935, pp. 220-26.

[194] Shoemaker, *Children of the Second Birth*, p. 16, *National Awakening*, pp. 78, 83, 86, 88; *The Church Can Save the World*, p. 30; *God's Control*, pp. 115-16

[195] Shoemaker, *A Young Man's View of the Ministry*, pp. 80, 86; *Religion That Works*, p. 65; *My Life-Work and My Will*, p. 5; *How to Find God*, p. 10.

[196] Shoemaker, *Confident Faith*, pp. 107, 110, 115; *Extraordinary Living for Ordinary Men*, pp. 42, 46, 48.

[197] Shoemaker, *A Young Man's View of the Ministry*, p. 70; *Children of the Second Birth*, pp. 58, 182; *If I Be Lifted Up*, p. 93; *How to Find God*, p. 10; *Extraordinary Living For Ordinary Men*, pp. 43, 130.

In many ways, the influence of Sam Shoemaker on the Twelve Steps is nowhere more evident than it is in Step Twelve. You may have some difficulty seeing that influence because of the variety of words Bill used to describe three simple ideas: First, because you have taken the Steps, you have established a relationship with God. Second, having established that relationship, you are to carry to others the message of what that relationship and the consequent availability of the power of God have done for you. Third, you must then endeavor to *live in a right* relationship with God and others. The "right" way to act was found in the design for living (in the spiritual principles)—that was laid out for, and learned by, you in taking the preceding Eleven Steps.

Unfortunately, for a variety of reasons, the three simple Twelfth Step ideas have been so mangled by the onrush of the "higher power," the "universality" aim, the psychological terms, and the "non-belief" or "unbelief" theories that are in present-day A.A. and recovery literature that many may deny the three ideas themselves. In fact, many have.

"Not-God" is not only the title, but also the noticeable theme, of one major history of A.A. Also, in a very real way, of rational recovery thinking.[198] As can readily be seen from the quote in the footnote and a significant rational recovery title, at least one rational recovery leader accuses A.A. of what he calls a "bait-and-switch game." He declares present-day-A.A. directly attacks atheists, agnostics, skeptics, "disbelievers," and those whose religious views do not include a rescuing deity.[199] Would that this were the case, we opine. For the author would side with Dr. Bob—who specifically said (in 1938!)—that he felt sorry for such

---

[198] See Kurtz, *Not-God*; Jack Trimpey, *The Small Book*, Rev. ed. (New York: Delacorte Press, 1992), p. 37: ". . . [L]ittle attention [in the Big Book] is paid to the intellectual violence done to troubled people who do not endorse God, Jesus, the Bible, Christianity, or religion in general. One purpose of *The Small Book* is to vindicate those individuals . . ."

[199] Trimpey, *The Small Book*, p. 37.

people, assuring them that their Heavenly Father would never let them down.[200]

The difficulty with those who attack today's A.A. as being hostile to skeptics, agnostics, and atheists is that such writers are just plain out of the loop. They don't seem to have attended A.A. meetings recently. Meetings where some vague higher power is called the "goddess," the "group," a "lightbulb," and a "doorknob." The author has! Or meetings where someone boldly asserts: "You don't have to believe *anything.*" The author has! Nor have such writers apparently read A.A.'s latest "Conference Approved" literature. Literature such as "*a Newcomer asks...,*" which states: "This A.A. General Service Conference-Approved literature." That particular piece—*a Newcomer asks*—and plenty of others in a similar vein, claims:

> However, everyone defines this power as he or she wishes. Many people call *it* God, others think *it* is the A.A. group, still others don't believe in *it* at all. *There is room in A.A. for people of all shades of belief and nonbelief.*

While the author does not agree with this kind of material and strongly believes Dr. Bob would, if he could, turn over in his grave if he read it, such talk is the stuff that pours out of the publishing arm of today's A.A. And the "rational recovery" people don't seem to realize they are pedaling rumor, not fact. They don't appear, either, to have visited a treatment center program in recent days. Some rational recovery proponents contend AAs do *not* espouse a "Higher Power" which can be a wrench, a tree, music, the AA group, etc. This simply demonstrates they haven't even read A.A.'s own recently published *Daily Reflections.*[201]

---

[200] Big Book, 3rd ed., p. 181.

[201] *Daily Reflections: A Book of Reflections by A.A. Members for A.A. Members* (New York: Alcoholics Anonymous World Services, Inc., 1990). The "new" A.A. "Higher Power" includes "Him, or Her, or It" (p. 334); "G.O.D. . . . which I define as 'Good
(continued...)

The A.A. of today is very plainly not an A.A. which tells people in its literature (other than by retaining Dr. Bob's story at the back of its text) that their "Heavenly Father will never let them down."

One rational recovery advocate says A.A. does intellectual violence to troubled people who do *not* endorse God, Jesus, the Bible, Christianity, or religion in general. But we would ask: Where in the world has such a writer—or any of the others who argue that A.A. is Christian—been when the fellowship was passing out the "any god" ideas, a small part of which we have quoted here? Where have such writers or others been while *"Self-help" has been the designated and accepted label for A.A. and other Twelve Step groups*, as they are frequently labeled in bookstores, book covers, professional writings, and many government materials.[202] The very *self-help* idea that Sam Shoemaker criticized *before* A.A. was founded.[203]

---

[201] (...continued)
Orderly Direction'" (p. 79); "In desperation I chose a table, a tree, then my A.A. group, as my Higher Power" (p. 175). For documentation of more of the same, see Dick B., *Turning Point: A History of Early A.A.'s Spiritual Roots and Successes* (San Rafael, CA: Paradise Research Publications, 1997), pp. 161-62; *The Oxford Group & Alcoholics Anonymous*, pp. 157-58; Clarence Snyder, *My Higher Power-The Lightbulb* (Altamonte Springs, FL: Stephen F. Foreman, 1985).

[202] See *The Self-Help Sourcebook: Your Guide to Community and Online Support Groups*, 6th ed. (New Jersey: American Self-Help Clearinghouse, 1998); Al J. Mooney, Arlene Eisenberg, Howard Eisenberg, *The Recovery Book* (New York: Workman Publishing, 1992), Glossary, pp. 574, 576-77; Herbert Fingarette, *Heavy Drinking: The Myth of Alcoholism as a Disease* (Berkeley: University of California Press, 1988), p. 87; Mim J. Landry, *Overview of Addiction Treatment Effectiveness*, Revised February, 1997 (Rockville, MD: SAMHSA, Office of Applied Studies, 1997), p. 26, where Landry speaks of "Twelve-Step, self-help meetings (such as AA, Narcotics Anonymous, and Cocaine Anonymous) on and off premises."

[203] See Samuel M. Shoemaker, Jr., *If I Be Lifted Up* (New York: Fleming H. Revell Company, 1931), p. 167: "We said that what God did for us on the Cross is a fountain of inexhaustible blessing and power, and that faith in the Cross is the cure and corrective for the gospel of 'self-help,' so common to-day even amongst believers, which centers in the effort of the human will toward self-improvement."

Heaven knows what the "awakening," the "message," and the "principles" *are* today. You can hear just about any idea you want on those three subjects in many A.A. meetings today.

Sometimes the *awakening* is a feeling! Sometimes, an awareness. Sometimes, a personality change! Sometimes, a relationship with God. Sometimes, "God-consciousness"—though rarely is the latter mentioned today.

The *message* is not even defined in the Big Book itself. And the *principles* have ranged from the principles of the Steps to the principles of the Twelve Traditions (which weren't written until years after the Big Book was first published). And sometimes the principles are whatever a speaker chooses to call them. The author has heard most of this over and over in meetings! And if you don't go to meetings of Twelve Step programs, you are not in the game.

In fairness to Sam Shoemaker and early A.A. history, we will stick with the First Edition of the Big Book in this section. We will point to the three categories of Twelfth Step ideas. And we will deal with Sam's teachings on those subjects—teachings which Bill himself said inspired A.A.'s spiritual ideas. Though Bill never specified or elaborated upon the inspiration!

Again, the three Twelfth Step ideas are: (1) Having achieved a relationship with God which results from taking the Steps. (2) You are to carry a message about what God has done for you as the result of trusting God, cleaning house, and helping others. (3) You are to practice spiritual principles which harmonize your life with a right relationship with God. Principles which challenge you, from the A.A. viewpoint, to keep progressing in your efforts toward "doing the will of the Father."[204]

---

[204] See Matthew 7:21 (part of the Sermon on the Mount, upon whose philosophy A.A. was said by its founders to have been based).

Consciousness of Your Relationship with God

Here are some of the concepts Bill Wilson used, in the Big Book's First Edition, to describe the *result* of taking the Twelve Step path to a relationship with God:

- A relationship with God, the Creator (pp. 35-36, 39, 84, 178).
- A spiritual experience (pp. 35, 37-38, 69, 72).
- Consciousness of the presence of God (pp. 23, 63, 69, 75).
- Finding a new Power, peace, happiness, and sense of direction within (p. 63).
- God's coming into our lives (pp. 22, 24, 75).
- Being "reborn" (p. 75).

Incidentally, every one of these ideas can still be found in the Big Book's Third Edition, published in 1976. The emphasis has shifted, just as it shifted when Bill's original draft manuscripts were subjected to the criticisms and perhaps intimidations of his New York atheist cohorts.

What did Sam have to say on these subjects? Well, he wrote about them with much frequency. And when Bill decided to call a "spiritual experience" a "spiritual awakening," Bill still had a ready source for the new phrase—"spiritual awakening"—in both the writings of the Oxford Group and in those of Sam Shoemaker.[205] Here you will find precisely what Shoemaker wrote on the first of Bill's three Twelfth Step subjects:

- Establishing a relationship with God (*e.g.*, Shoemaker, *Children of the Second Birth*, pp. 16, 53; *Confident Faith*, pp. 87, 104; *If I Be Lifted Up*, p. 161; *National Awakening*, p. 13; *The Experiment of Faith*, p. 10).

---

[205] Buchman, *Remaking the World*, pp. 19, 24, 35, 54; Shoemaker, *The Conversion of the Church*, p. 124; *National Awakening*, p. 3; *By the Power of God*, pp. 133-54.

- A spiritual experience (*e.g.*, Shoemaker, *Twice-Born Ministers*, p. 61).

- Consciousness of the presence of God (*e.g.*, Shoemaker, *Twice-Born Ministers*, p. 123; *Confident Faith*, pp. 57, 189-90; *By the Power of God*, p. 69).

- God's coming into our lives (*e.g.*, Shoemaker, *National Awakening*, pp. 23-33).

- "Ye shall have power, after that the Holy Ghost is come upon you. . . ." (*e.g.*, *Sam Shoemaker, at his best*, p. 113; *Extraordinary Living for Ordinary Men*, p. 143; *cf.*, *If I Be Lifted Up*, pp. 125, 178).

- Ye must be born again (*e.g.*, Shoemaker, *Religion That Works*, p. 14; *Children of the Second Birth*, p. 32 (p. 25—"I do feel reborn, born of the Spirit"); *Twice-Born Ministers*, p. 56 (p. 10—"rebirth"); *Confident Faith*, pp. 137, 140; *National Awakening*, pp. 55-66; *By the Power of God*, p. 28).

Carrying the Message of What God Has Done for You

If there was one subject on which the Bible, the Oxford Group, Sam Shoemaker, and early AAs could be found in agreement, that subject had to do with *witnessing*—sharing, evangelizing, *giving it away to keep it*. Here is what each source had to say:

- *The Bible*: "Go ye therefore, and teach all nations. . . . Teaching them to observe all things whatsoever I have commanded you. . . ." (Matthew 28:19-20); "And he said unto them, Go ye into all the world, and preach the gospel to every creature" (Mark 16:15); "But ye shall receive power, after that the Holy Ghost is come upon you: and ye shall be witnesses unto me both in Jerusalem, and in all

Judaea, and in Samaria, and unto the uttermost part of the earth" (Acts 1:8); "And with great power gave the apostles witness of the resurrection of the Lord Jesus: and great grace was upon them all" (Acts 4:33); "For so hath the Lord commanded us, *saying*, I have set thee to be a light of the Gentiles, that thou shouldest be for salvation unto the ends of the earth" (Acts 13:47); "Having therefore obtained help of God, I continue unto this day, witnessing both to small and great, saying none other things than those which the prophets and Moses did say should come. That Christ should suffer *and* that he should be the first that should rise from the dead, and should shew light unto the people and to the Gentiles" (Acts 26:22-23).

• *Frank Buchman for the Oxford Group*: "The best way to keep an experience of Christ is to pass it on" (Buchman, *Remaking the World*, p. x).

• *Sam Shoemaker*: "I told him that the only way to keep religion is to give it away. . . . Give what you can right away; it will increase as you give it" (Shoemaker, *One Boy's Influence*, p. 15); "Get them into the stream of God's will and God's grace, till they ask Him to use them to reconcile others. They will not keep this unless they give it away" (Shoemaker, *The Church Alive*, p. 139); "The best way to keep what you have is to give it away, and no substitute has ever been found for personal Christian witness" (Shoemaker, *They're on the Way*, p. 159).

• *Bill Wilson*: "He [Wilson] suddenly realized that in order to save himself he must carry his message to another alcoholic" (Big Book, p. xvi); "It is important for him to realize that your attempt to pass this on to him plays a vital part in your own recovery" (Big Book, p. 94);

"Helping others is the foundation stone of your recovery" (Big Book, p. 97).

- *Dr. Bob*: "I think the kind of service that really counts is giving of yourself, and that almost invariably requires effort and time. It isn't a matter of just putting a little quiet money in the dish. . . . I don't believe that type of giving would ever keep anyone sober. But giving of our own effort and strength and time is quite a different matter (*The Co-Founders of Alcoholics Anonymous: Biographical Sketches Their Last Major Talks*, pp. 16-17).

Bill Wilson devoted the Big Book's largest chapter (on a single portion of the Twelve Steps) to the subject of "Working with Others." AAs are thoroughly familiar with the expression "Twelfth Step" work. And Dr. Bob, having personally helped more than 5000 alcoholics, was called the "Prince of Twelfth Steppers."[206]

The Bible called such workers (when they carried the good news of what Jesus Christ had accomplished) "ambassadors for Christ."[207] The Oxford Group called such people "life-changers."[208] Sam Shoemaker sometimes called them "fishers of men."[209] And A.A. spoke of their carrying the message to the alcoholic who still suffers.

Probably the most confusing issue for someone in A.A. today is: "*What is the message?*" A.A. has, in its present-day publications—formally and clearly abandoned the Bible, Jesus

---

[206] "Between 1940 and 1950, in the company of that marvelous nun, Sister Ignatia, he [Dr. Bob] had treated 5,000 drunks at St. Thomas Hospital in Akron. . . . So Dr. Bob became the prince of all twelfth-steppers. Perhaps nobody will ever do such a job again." See *The Co-Founders of Alcoholics Anonymous: Biographical Sketches, Their Last Major Talks* (New York: Alcoholics Anonymous World Services, Inc., 1972, 1975), p. 27.

[207] 2 Corinthians 5:20.

[208] See Harold Begbie, *Life Changers* (London: Mills & Boon Limited, 1923).

[209] See Matthew 4:19: "And he [Jesus] saith unto them [Simon and Andrew, his brothers, who "were fishers"]. Follow me, and I will make you fishers of men."

Christ, and—to a great extent—the God Almighty *in* the Bible.[210]
Yet in early A.A., the message about God was quite simple and
quite clear.

Bill Wilson's friend and "sponsor" Ebby Thacher simply said
to Bill: *God had done for him what he could not do for himself*
(Big Book, First Edition, pp. 20-21). Bill said:

> That floored me. It began to look as though religious people
> were right after all. Here was something at work in a human
> heart which had done the impossible. My ideas about miracles
> were drastically revised right then. Never mind the musty past;
> here sat a miracle directly across the kitchen table. He shouted
> great tidings (Big Book, First Edition, p. 21).

Dr. Bob insisted that the newcomer profess a belief in God and
then surrender to God.[211] In that surrender, the newcomer
accepted Jesus Christ as his personal Lord and Savior.[212] He got
born again.[213] Bill got born again.[214] Dr. Bob had been born
again for many years.[215] And those who followed during the
pioneer days were led to Christ and, of course, born again.[216]
Most in today's A.A. will consider this a misstatement, a mystery,
or surprising news.

The records are there—though not readily available. They
show: (1) What Bill Wilson did at the Calvary Rescue Mission
altar in New York—which prompted him to write in two different

---

[210] Kurtz, *Not-God*, p. 50.

[211] Dick B., *That Amazing Grace*, p. 26.

[212] Dick B., *That Amazing Grace*, p. 27.

[213] Dick B., *The Akron Genesis of Alcoholics Anonymous*, pp. 194-97.

[214] Dick B., *Turning Point*, pp. 95-96.

[215] See Dick B., *Dr. Bob and His Library: A Major A.A. Spiritual Source*, 3rd ed.
(Kihei, HI: Paradise Research Publications, Inc., 1998), pp. 2-3, 111-19.

[216] See Dick B., *The Akron Genesis of Alcoholics Anonymous*, pp. 192-97; *That
Amazing Grace*, pp. 26-27, 33-34, 52, 66-67, 68, 74, 89, 92-93; Clarence S., *Going
Through the Steps* (Altamonte Springs, FL: Stephen F. Foreman, 1985), pp. 2-3, 6.

manuscripts: "For sure I was born again."[217] (2) Dr. Bob's status as a born again Christian from his youth at St. Johnsbury Congregational Church and his confessions at Christian Endeavor.[218] (3) What two different old-timers specifically said about the Akron A.A. "surrenders" in the hospital or at the home of T. Henry Williams.[219] (4) That all the pioneers belonged to "A First Century Christian Fellowship."[220] (5) That Dr. Bob called A.A. a "Christian Fellowship."[221] (6) That John D. Rockefeller, Jr.'s colleague observed that early A.A. was like "first century Christianity" and very successful in Akron.[222]

The message was: "God could and would if sought."[223] (2) "God is doing for us what we could not do for ourselves."[224] (3) Others can get well by establishing a "relationship with God."[225]

Here's what Sam Shoemaker had to say about the message and message carrying:

The deepest thing in the Christian religion is not anything that we can do for God, it is what God has already done for us.[226]

Do not marvel at what God has done *through* you, for you may wind up merely marvelling at you: but marvel at what God has done *for* you, for He has had compassion on you and is saving you unto eternal life.[227]

[217] Dick B. *The Akron Genesis of Alcoholics Anonymous*, pp. 326-28.

[218] Dick B., *Dr. Bob and His Library*, *supra*, pp. 2-3, 111-19.

[219] Dick B., *The Akron Genesis of Alcoholics Anonymous*, pp. 194-97; *That Amazing Grace*, pp. 27, 52, 68-69.

[220] Dick B., *The Akron Genesis of Alcoholics Anonymous*, pp. 156, 175.

[221] Dick B., *The Akron Genesis of Alcoholics Anonymous*, pp. 187-88.

[222] *DR. BOB and the Good Oldtimers*, pp. 128-29, 136; *Pass It On*, pp. 131, 135.

[223] Big Book, 1st ed., p. 72.

[224] Big Book, 1st ed., p. 98.

[225] Big Book, 1st ed., p. 39.

[226] Shoemaker, *If I Be Lifted Up*, p. 161.

[227] Shoemaker, *If I Be Lifted Up*, p. 34.

Men run from your arguments about God, they will not listen
to your elaborate explanations; but when you tell them what life
was without God, and then tell them what it is with Him, their
hearts, as John Wesley said, are "strangely warmed," and their
minds also are strangely persuaded. . . . Then Jesus gave them
His answer to John. . . . He just gathered up in a cascade of
living words the living deeds He and they had been seeing, and
said, "Go your way, and tell John what things ye have seen and
heard; how that the blind see, the lame walk, the lepers are
cleansed, the deaf hear, the dead are raised, to the poor the
gospel is preached." It was proof by evidence. They had seen
these people themselves.[228]

Practicing the Christian Principles

We repeat: Bill Wilson and Dr. Bob Smith both said that the
Sermon on the Mount contained the underlying philosophy of
Alcoholics Anonymous. Jesus's Sermon on the Mount was filled
with principles and standards. Many felt the Four Absolutes came
directly from the Sermon on the Mount. As we will see in a
moment, Sam Shoemaker certainly did.

Bill Wilson and Dr. Bob both subscribed to the importance of
1 Corinthians 13 in their deliberations over how to frame the
recovery program. And 1 Corinthians 13 is filled with statements
as to what the love of God means. Early AAs read Henry
Drummond's *The Greatest Thing in the World*—a study of 1
Corinthians 13. And Sam Shoemaker frequently referred to those
principles.[229]

Finally, the Book of James was not only a favorite among the
early AAs; some actually favored calling the new fellowship the
James Club. James also was filled with Christian principles. Sam
Shoemaker wrote an entire chapter based on the idea in James: Be
ye doers of the Word, not hearers only. So early AAs had before
them a full platter of important Christian principles which they

---

[228] Shoemaker, *National Awakening*, p. 28.

[229] See, for example, Shoemaker, *Realizing Religion*, p. 50.

used to frame their steps and by which they also attempted to live their lives.

Briefly, let's look at a few of the things Sam Shoemaker had to say about: (1) The Four Absolutes, (2) The Sermon on the Mount (Matthew, Chapters Five to Seven), (3) 1 Corinthians 13, and (4) The Book of James. Also, about the principles in them.

- *The Four Absolutes*: "Dr. Robert E. Speer, in one of his books, had said that the essence of the ethics of the Sermon on the Mount was the Four Absolutes: Honesty, Purity, Unselfishness, and Love" (as quoted by Helen Shoemaker in *I Stand by the Door*, p. 24); "He gave me the four absolute principles of Christ: honesty, purity, unselfishness and love, and asked me how my life stacked up beside them" (Sam Shoemaker, *Twice-Born Ministers*, p. 150); "Though I had been converted to Christ many years before, they made me face up for the first time to His fourfold challenge of absolute honesty, purity, unselfishness and love" (Sam Shoemaker, *Twice-Born Ministers*, p. 91).

- *The Sermon on the Mount*: ". . . sullen and stubborn rebellions which lie at the bottom of men's hearts . . . the obdurate unbelief that any practical man can take the Sermon on the Mount seriously in twentieth-century economics. . . . The average person in the pews has never been told how to make Christian experience a fact instead of an aspiration" (Shoemaker, *Children of the Second Birth*, pp. 87-88); "'Seek ye first the kingdom . . . and all these things shall be added' became living to me as part of my own experience" (Shoemaker, *Twice-Born Ministers*, p. 56); "It will be a great day for the Christian cause when the world begins to realize that 'Thy will be done' does not belong on tombstones, but ought to be graven into the lives of eager men and women who have enlisted in God's warfare beyond return and recall" (Shoemaker, *Children of the Second Birth*, p. 187); "We have gone sound asleep over the Sermon on the Mount" (Shoemaker, *Realizing Religion*, p. 51); "Not every one that saith unto me, Lord, Lord, shall enter into the kingdom of heaven; but he that doeth the will of my Father who is in heaven" (Shoemaker, *Religion That Works*, p. 65); "We have said, 'Of course,' to the Sermon on the Mount, till its terrible demands roll off us like so much water from a roof. Sometimes I see a safe and complacent Christian carrying a Bible in his hand: and I wonder the dynamite in that old Book doesn't go off in his hands, and blow his safety to pieces" (Shoemaker, *Religion That Works*, p. 83); "Pentecost was more than a promise to obey the Sermon on the Mount. . . . [W]e shall not get past the rather matter-of-fact and spiritless Christianity so prevalent to-day until we learn to believe that the Holy Spirit still guides and empowers" (Shoemaker, *A Young Man's View of the Ministry*, p. 26);[230] "It is plain that the first thing America needs is to stop sentimentalizing over the Ten Commandments and the Sermon on the Mount, and face honestly the difference between ourselves and those essential laws" (Shoemaker, *God and America*, p. 21).

Shoemaker covered many verses from the Sermon on the Mount in detail. You have seen and will see some of these as we move along, including the following: Matthew 5:8 ("Blessed are the pure in heart . . .");[231] Matthew 5:14 ("Ye are the light of the world . . .");[232] Matthew 5:15 ("Neither do men light a candle, and put it under a bushel, but on a candlestick . . .");[233] Matthew 5:23 ("Therefore

---

[230] See Acts chapter 2 for the account of Pentecost.
[231] E.g., see Shoemaker, *The Experiment of Faith*, p. 36.
[232] E.g., see Shoemaker, *Freedom and Faith*, pp. 121-22.
[233] E.g., see Shoemaker, *The Gospel According to You*, p. 66.

if thou bring thy gift to the altar . . .");[234] Matthew
5:43 (". . . Thou shalt love thy neighbor . . .");[235]
Matthew 6:9 ("Our Father . . .");[236] Matthew 6:10
("Thy will be done");[237] Matthew 6:23 ("If therefore
the light that is in thee be darkness . . .");[238] Matthew
6:33 ("But seek ye first the kingdom of God . . .");[239]
Matthew 7:3 ("And why beholdest thou the mote that is in
thy brother's eye . . .");[240] Matthew 7:7 ("Ask, and it
shall be given you . . .");[241] Matthew 7:21 ("Not everyone
that saith unto me, Lord, Lord . . .").[242]

- *1 Corinthians 13*: "Love never faileth" (Shoemaker,
  Children of the Second Birth, p. 159); ". . . Moody [the
  great evangelist], whose greatest praise of Drummond
  [Henry Drummond] was that he "lived continually in the
  thirteenth chapter of First Corinthians. . . . [T]he great
  saving souls of history, and the very saints of our own
  day, have been those who believed that any success
  without love was failure, and any failure with love was
  success in disguise—for 'love never faileth.'" (Shoemaker,
  Realizing Religion, p. 50); "I should like always to live in
  the high places of *love*. Love that allows nobody to stand
  outside its view, builds no artificial fences between people,
  sees men's hearts and not their clothes or their colour, and
  looks on them somewhat as God looks on them. Love that

---

[234] E.g., see Shoemaker, *The Conversion of the Church*, pp. 47-48; *The Gospel According to You*, p. 149..

[235] E.g., see Cecile Cox Offill, . . . *And Thy Neighbor As Thyself*, pp. 11-18.

[236] E.g., see Shoemaker, *Confident Faith*, pp. 64, 74.

[237] E.g., see Shoemaker, *Children of the Second Birth*, pp. 175-87.

[238] E.g., see Shoemaker, *The Gospel According to You*, p. 56.

[239] E.g., see Shoemaker, *National Awakening*, p. 41.

[240] E.g., see Shoemaker, *God's Control*, p. 69.

[241] E.g., see Shoemaker, *The Experiment of Faith*, p. 36.

[242] E.g., see Shoemaker, *A Young Man's View of the Ministry*, p. 86.

is never uncomfortable in the presence of incompatibles, but with ingenuity brings together into fellowship divers kinds of people who would usually not understand each other, love which is a great reconciler of those whom the crusty custom of the world has divided. Love that rejoices in the success of those who are our rivals, is fair to the truth of those who are our critics, is patient of those who wilfully misunderstand us. Love that is brave enough to call sin sin, and to conclude all men under sin: and then to refuse to believe that there is a soul anywhere that cannot be saved. Love for those that irritate us, foolishly take our time, needlessly harry us about trifles, are stupid about taking a hint. Love that always sees people and situations as they lie in the mind of God, big with potentiality, no matter what the situation be" (Shoemaker, *Religion That Works*, p. 122).[243]

- *The Book of James*: ". . . [C]an you visualize our people, as Franklin urged, 'humbly applying to the *Father of Lights* to illuminate our understandings?'" (Shoemaker, *Freedom and Faith*, pp. 70, 71);[244] "Be ye doers of the word, and not hearers only, deceiving your own selves" (Shoemaker, *The Gospel According to You*, p. 44);[245] "And when I find people who have all their lives been

---

[243] From 1 Corinthians 13:4-7 (Moffatt's Translation) come the following: "Love is very patient, very kind. Love knows no jealousy; love makes no parade; gives itself no airs, is never rude, never selfish, never irritated, *never resentful*; love is never glad when others go wrong, love is gladdened by goodness, always slow to expose, always eager to believe the best, always hopeful, always patient." Shoemaker often recommended the Moffatt Translation for better understanding.

[244] James 1:17: "Father of lights."

[245] James 1:22.

coming to church, and have never mastered a quick tongue
. . ." (Shoemaker, *Religion That Works*, p. 50);[246] "It
must start, as my minister friend stated, by the sharing of
these sins with another Christian who has found his way
a bit farther than we have. That has a Scriptural basis:
"Confess your sins one to another, and pray for one
another that ye may be healed" (Shoemaker, *The
Conversion of the Church*, p. 35);[247] "Faith without
works is dead" (Shoemaker, *National Awakening*, p.
13).[248]

Sam Shoemaker was a powerful man. I've spent a lot of time with
people who knew him well in the days when A.A. was ripening.
Jim Newton said Sam was a crackerjack life-changer. Parks
Shipley said Sam had almost everyone on his knees at the very
first meeting. Julia Harris spoke of Sam's good looks and
wonderful writing skills. Norman Vincent Peale told me Sam was
a wonderful communicator. Norman Vincent Peale's son-in-law
Rev. Paul Everett said Sam would toss aside a person's credentials
and say, I don't care who you are or what you are; I want to know
what's in your heart. The *golf club crowd* of Sam's Pittsburgh
days are still around. They met with me in a garden party and told
how Sam had steam-rolled them into Bible study, Quiet Time,
prayer, and witnessing. Sam's daughter Nickie told me she had
heard her dad say so many times: God has a plan. Find it. Fit
yourself into it. And Sam's associate Irving Harris said that Sam's
sermons were filled with Bible, How to obtain faith, and How to
pray.

In an early book that is filled with expressions seemingly
adopted by AAs, Sam asked and then preached on this subject:

---

[246] James 1:26: "If any man among you seem to be religious, and bridleth not his
tongue, but deceiveth his own heart, this man's religion *is* vain." Also James, Chapter
Three.

[247] James 5:16 - specifically cited by Shoemaker.

[248] James 2:20.

What if I had But One Sermon to Preach? He pointed to John 17:3 as the subject:

> This is life eternal, that they should know thee the only true God, and him whom thou didst send, even Jesus Christ.

Just think what's happened to that in today's self-help meetings. I like to say in talks to AAs that alcoholics may be sick, but they are not stupid. Neither was Bill Wilson. The things Bill heard over and over from Shoemaker had to do with eternal life, knowing the only true God, and knowing Jesus Christ whom God sent. Bill used to talk about those things. And there was *no* talk in 1943 about lightbulbs, radiators, chairs, Gertrude, or a group! The talk concerned God Almighty, coming to him through Christ as Bill did at Shoemaker's Calvary Rescue Mission, and establishing a personal relationship with God and His son Jesus Christ.

10

Putting the Steps and Their Sources Together

"A.A. was not invented! Its basics were brought to us through the experience and wisdom of many great friends. We simply borrowed and adapted their ideas" (*As Bill Sees It*, Alcoholics Anonymous World Services, Inc., p.67)

Having considered or studied each of the six major spiritual sources of A.A., you may then want to take a look at what was borrowed from the sources, and how the borrowed ideas were fashioned into the Twelve Step picture.

Step One and Deflation at Depth

[Step One: We admitted we were powerless over alcohol—that our lives had become unmanageable.][1]

A.A.'s medical mentor, Dr. William D. Silkworth, chief psychiatrist at Towns Hospital in New York, and the man who treated Bill Wilson as Bill sought and attained recovery, said:

---

[1] In this chapter and elsewhere in our book, *The Twelve Steps of Alcoholics Anonymous* are reprinted with permission of Alcoholics Anonymous World Services, Inc.

Men and women drink essentially because they like the effect
produced by alcohol. The sensation is so elusive that, while they
admit it is injurious, they cannot after a time differentiate the
true from the false. To them, their alcoholic life seems the only
normal one. They are *restless, irritable and discontented*, unless
they can again experience the sense of ease and comfort which
comes at once by taking a few drinks—drinks which they see
others taking with impunity. After they have succumbed to the
desire again, as so many do, and the phenomenon of craving
develops, they pass through the well-known stages of a spree,
emerging remorseful, with a firm resolution not to drink again.
This is repeated over and over, and unless this person can
experience an entire psychic change there is very little hope of
his recovery (italics added).[2]

Silkworth thus concluded that the alcoholic is restless, irritable,
and discontented unless and until he seeks and obtains the *illusory*,
and *often fatal* solution of *peace through alcohol*.

Bill Wilson's principal religious teacher in the days before
A.A.'s Big Book was published was the Reverend Sam
Shoemaker, Jr., the rector of Calvary Episcopal Church in New
York. And Shoemaker often wrote of a much deeper, spiritual
problem causing irritability and discontent in most people of that
day. Shoemaker's first title said:

The modern mind is restless and easily bored. It is also intensely
individualistic. . . . There has always been a large amount of
unhappiness in the world, but it seems as if our modern America
had got more than its share. Look at the sheer irritability you
can find in any city you know! Can you count off half a dozen
really happy, really peaceful people whom you know? So many
"problems," so many "complex situations." Now the thing
which is striking about much of the misery one sees is that it is
spiritual misery. . . . It is the sadness of maladjustment to the
eternal things, and this throws out the whole focus of life. Rest
cures and exercise and motor drives will not help. The only

---

[2] Big Book, pp. xxvi-xxvii.

thing that will help is religion. For the root of the malady is estrangement from God—estrangement from Him in people that were made to be His companions. . . . What you want is simply a vital religious experience. You need to find God. You need Jesus Christ.[3]

Bill Wilson seemed to cover this same religious territory when he wrote the following in A.A.'s Big Book:

[W]e have been not only mentally and physically ill, we have been *spiritually sick*. When the *spiritual malady* is overcome, we straighten out mentally and physically.[4]

Remember that we deal with alcohol—cunning, baffling, powerful! Without help it is too much for us. But there is One who has all power—that One is God. May you find Him now![5]

There was, felt A.A.'s founders, a spiritual problem underlying the alcohol problem. Bill wrote in 1960:

Of course, we have since found that these awful conditions of mind and body invariably bring on the third phase of our malady. This is the sickness of the spirit; a sickness for which there must necessarily be a spiritual remedy. We AAs recognize this in the first five words of Step Twelve of the recovery program. Those words are: "Having had a spiritual awakening. . . ." Here we name the remedy for our threefold sickness of body, mind and soul. Here we declare the necessity for that all-important spiritual awakening.[6]

The spiritual problem, as Shoemaker characterized it, was estrangement from, and lack of contact with, God through Christ.

---

[3] Samuel M. Shoemaker, *Realizing Religion* (New York: Association Press, 1923), pp. 2-9.

[4] Big Book, p. 64 (italics added).

[5] Big Book, pp. 58-59.

[6] *The Language of the Heart*, p. 297.

And though others today have put a different interpretation on the *nature* of the "spiritual problem," there appears to be agreement with Bill Wilson's description of alcoholism as a three-part disease—physical, mental, and *spiritual.*[7]

Our question concerns the Biblical roots, if any, from which A.A.'s sources identified the spiritual problem—a problem epitomized by the Big Book's cry that there was a need for the seemingly hopeless alcoholic to find God. And to find Him *now.*[8]

Some of the early AAs (including Dr. Bob), and a good many religious writers of that day, read and quoted *The Confessions of St. Augustine.*[9] Augustine wrote, "Thou madest us for Thyself, and our heart is restless, until it repose in Thee."[10] This idea struck several of A.A.'s root source writers as the real spiritual problem, for they frequently quoted the foregoing statement by Augustine.[11] Sam Shoemaker added, in connection with this Augustine quote, "The emptiness, loneliness, homesickness, wistfulness, wonderment which all men feel at some time is a hollow place in the human soul that God is meant to fill."[12]

Dr. Leslie D. Weatherhead—whose titles were read by many early AAs, including Henrietta Seiberling and Bill Wilson—quoted the Book of Job to describe man's despairing need to find God:

---

[7] Ernest Kurtz, *Not-God: A History of Alcoholics Anonymous.* Exp. ed. (Minnesota: Hazelden, 1991), pp. 45, 199, 204, 381-82.

[8] See the comment by Harry Emerson Fosdick in the *Meaning of Faith* (New York: The Abingdon Press, 1917), p. 36: "*Men never really find God until they need him*; and some men never feel the need of him until life plunges them into a shattering experience (italics in original)."

[9] See Dick B., *Dr. Bob's Library: Books for Twelve Step Growth* (San Rafael, CA: Paradise Research Publications, 1994), p. 25; and *The Confessions of St. Augustine,* trans. by E. B. Pusey (New York: A Cardinal Edition, Pocket Books, 1952).

[10] *Confessions,* p. 1.

[11] See Harold Begbie, *Twice-Born Men* (New York: Fleming H. Revell, 1909), p. 263; Samuel M. Shoemaker, Jr., *National Awakening* (New York: Harper & Brothers, 1936), p. 46; T. R. Glover, *The Jesus of History* (New York: Association Press, 1919), pp. 97, 121; compare Emmet Fox, *The Sermon on the Mount: The Key to Success in Life* (New York: Harper & Row, 1938), pp. 111, 175.

[12] Shoemaker, *National Awakening,* p. 46.

Even to day *is* my complaint bitter: my stroke is heavier than my groaning. Oh that I knew where I might find him! *that* I might come *even* to his seat![13]

In a book frequently read by early AAs, Dr. Harry Emerson Fosdick quoted Psalm 55:1-5 in describing man's plight without God's listening ear:

Give ear to my prayer, O God; and hide not thyself from my supplication. Attend unto me, and hear me: I mourn in my complaint, and make a noise. Because of the voice of the enemy, because of the oppression of the wicked: for they cast iniquity upon me, and in wrath they hate me. My heart is sore pained within me: and the terrors of death are fallen upon me. Fearfulness and trembling are come upon me, and horror hath overwhelmed me.[14]

The Reverend Sam Shoemaker quoted the Apostle Paul's description of man's spiritual problem and its solution:

O wretched man that I am! who shall deliver me from the body of this death? I thank God through Jesus Christ our Lord . . . (Romans 7:24-25).[15]

And one of the early A.A. pioneer stories in the Big Book's first edition quoted this segment of Romans and indicated the verses marked the turning point toward recovery. *Smile With Me, At Me* wrote:

One morning, after a sleepless night worrying over what I could do to straighten myself out, I went to my room alone—took my

---

[13] Job 23:2-3; Leslie D. Weatherhead, *How Can I Find God?* (London: Hodder & Stoughton, 1933), p. 1. See also *The Upper Room* for 7/2/35.

[14] Fosdick, *The Meaning of Faith*, p. 184.

[15] Shoemaker, *National Awakening*, p. 48; *Religion That Works* (New York: Fleming H. Revell, 1928), p. 45. See also Glover, *The Jesus of History*, p. 149. This latter book was read and recommended by Dr. Bob and Anne Smith.

Bible in hand and asked Him, the One Power, that I might open
to a good place to read—and I read. "For I delight in the law of
God after the inward man. But I see a different law in my
members, warring against the law of my mind and bringing me
into captivity under the law of sin which is in my members.
Wretched man that I am! Who shall deliver me out of the body
of this death?" That was enough for me—I started to
understand. Here were the words of Paul a great teacher. When,
then if I had slipped? Now, I could understand. From that day
I gave and still give and always will, time everyday to read the
word of God and let Him do all the caring. Who am I to try to
run myself or anyone else.[16]

Dr. Carl G. Jung eventually gave AAs an even more specific
Biblical picture of their spiritual problem and the necessary
spiritual solution. Years after Bill Wilson had written the Big Book
and the Twelve Steps, Jung responded to a letter from Bill and
explained to Bill that he (Jung) had told one of Bill's Oxford
Group mentors, Rowland Hazard, the solution to the alcoholic's
spiritual problem. To his spiritual restlessness and discontent. And
to his estrangement from God. Jung wrote:

> His [the alcoholic's] craving for alcohol was the equivalent on
> a low level of the spiritual thirst of our being for wholeness,
> expressed in medieval language: the union with God.[17]

Jung then referred Bill to Psalm 42:1:

> As the hart panteth after the water brooks, so panteth my soul
> after thee, O God.[18]

The bottom line in A.A.'s First Step, then, *was*, very possibly,
biblical. AAs certainly needed to recognize the deadly physical and

---

[16] Big Book, 1st edition, p. 347.

[17] *Pass It On* (New York: Alcoholics Anonymous World Services, 1984), p. 384.

[18] *Pass It On*, p. 384-85.

mental disease that medicine had revealed to them.[19] The alcoholic needed to know he or she was powerless over alcohol because of a mental obsession, coupled with a physical allergy.[20] And that life had become unmanageable.[21] But the alcoholic would never recover, found Bill and Dr. Bob, without spiritual wholeness, without finding God—without union *with* God, as Carl Jung put it. And the spiritual *problem*, which Jung described, had long before been defined in the Bible by Job, by David, and by Paul: Man was wretched of and by himself.[22] And man needed to learn and concede that spiritual fact, those Biblical writers said, in order to see his need for God as the solution to his seeming spiritual hopelessness.

There is a little-discussed talk that Bill Wilson and Dr. Bob Smith made to 4,500 alcoholics, their friends, and relatives on Sunday night at a public meeting of Alcoholics Anonymous in the Shrine Auditorium in Los Angeles, California. The address was reported at length on page 17 of the March 26, 1943, issue of the Roman Catholic paper, *The TIDINGS*. The newspaper reported the following:

> An alcoholic, Bill said, is a fellow who is "trying to get his religion out of a bottle," when what he really wants is unity within himself, unity with God. But he is suffering from a "cancer of the emotions, maybe of the soul."

---

[19] Bill wrote: "[Dr. Silkworth] was soon to contribute a very great idea without which AA could never have succeeded. For years he had been proclaiming alcoholism an illness, an obsession of the mind coupled with an allergy of the body. By now I knew this meant me. I also understood what a fatal combination these twin ogres could be." *The Language of the Heart: Bill W.'s Grapevine Writings* (New York: The A.A. Grapevine, Inc., 1988), p. 197.

[20] Big Book, pp. xxiv, 23, 37, 59.

[21] Big Book, p. 60: "That we were alcoholic and could not manage our own lives."

[22] See also Paul's statement in Ephesians 2:12: "That at that time [when they were Gentiles] ye were without Christ, being aliens from the commonwealth of Israel, and strangers from the covenants of promise, having no hope, and without God in the world."

Alcoholics Anonymous recommends a return to religion, resumption of Church attendance.

"There is a definite religious element here," Bill said. "I pray and I feel released."

He emphasized that Divine Aid was A.A.'s greatest asset, more effective than confinement, environment changes and dietary experiments. . . .

The fame of Dr. Bob is great in A.A.

In soft, confident and unhurried words he too reiterated the principles of Alcoholics Anonymous: "Read religious literature, resume church attendance, cultivate the habit of prayer, and transmit the desires and principles of Alcoholics Anonymous to others." He particularly recommended reading the Bible.

Professor William James—whom Bill Wilson regarded as the father of modern psychology, "a founder" of A.A., and the author of the First Step's "deflation at depth" idea—had described the solution to every person's need for union with God via a conversion experience in the following terms:

To be converted, to be regenerated, to receive grace, to experience religion, to gain an assurance, are so many phrases which denote the process, gradual or sudden, by which a self hitherto divided, and consciously wrong inferior and unhappy, becomes unified and consciously right superior and happy, in consequence of its firmer hold upon religious realities.[23]

And many of A.A.'s spiritual sources, including Anne Smith, quoted this William James definition as an example of man's divided self—which was consciously wrong, inferior, and

---

[23] William James, *The Varieties of Religious Experience* (New York: Vintage Books/The Library of America Edition, 1990), p. 177. For Wilson's views of James as psychology's father, as an A.A. "founder," and as the source of A.A.'s "deflation at depth" idea, see *Pass It On*, pp. 124-25, 197; *Alcoholics Anonymous Comes of Age*, p. 64.

unhappy—and which needed regeneration, change and conversion by the grace of God.[24]

The solution to the divided self problem, said many of A.A.'s sources, was crucifixion of the big "I."[25] Surrender of self.[26] A turning point involving self-surrender of the ego.[27] And at least two of A.A.'s root sources referred to the turning point (which began with a divided, deflated self, requiring such a surrender) as "powerlessness" and loss of power.[28]

Many also declared the unmanageability of a spiritually sick life focused on self—a life of self-centeredness and ego-centricity, in which self constituted God.[29] A common prayer in use at that stage of the path was "O, God, manage me, because I cannot manage myself."[30] Dr. Bob's wife often recommended such a prayer at the point of powerlessness.[31]

---

[24] Dick B., *The Oxford Group & A.A.*, p. 60; *Anne Smith's Journal*, p. 101.

[25] Edgar J. Goodspeed, *The Wonderful Career of Moody and Sankey in Great Britain and America* (New York: Henry S. Goodspeed & Co., 1876), p. 46; Peter Howard, *Frank Buchman's Secret* (Garden City, NY: Doubleday & Company, 1961), p. 43; *The World Rebuilt: The True Story of Frank Buchman and the Achievements of Moral Re-Armament* (New York: Duell, Sloan and Pearce, 1951), p. 242; Paul Campbell and Peter Howard, *Remaking Men* (New York: Arrowhead Books, 1954), p. 75; The Layman with a Notebook, *What Is the Oxford Group?* (London: Oxford University Press, 1933), pp. 23-24; A. J. Russell, *For Sinners Only* (London: Hodder & Stoughton, 1932), p. 60; Bremer Hofmeyr, *How to Change* (New York: Moral Re-Armament, n.d.), p. 3.

[26] Leslie D. Weatherhead, *Discipleship* (London: Student Christian Movement Press, 1934), p. 16. For the many discussions of the self-surrender idea in A.A. roots, see Dick B., *The Oxford Group & A.A.*, pp. 170-75.

[27] *What Is the Oxford Group?*, pp. 23-24; Samuel M. Shoemaker, Jr., *If I Be Lifted Up* (New York: Fleming H. Revell, 1931), p. 28; Weatherhead, *How Can I Find God?*, p. 84; Dick B., *The Oxford Group & A.A.*, pp. 45, 76, 334.

[28] Shoemaker, *If I Be Lifted Up*, pp. 131, 133; *How to Become a Christian* (New York: Harper & Brothers, 1953), p. 77; Dick B., *Anne Smith's Journal*, p. 22.

[29] Dick B., *The Oxford Group & A.A.*, pp. 77, 79, 183, 299, 300, 347; *New Light on Alcoholism*, 2d ed., pp. 158-161, 197, 204, 250; *Anne Smith's Journal*, pp. 19-21. See also Big Book, pp. 52, 53, 60-64, 71, 87-88.

[30] Dick B., *The Oxford Group & A.A.*, pp. 77, 79, 182-83; *New Light on Alcoholism*, 2d ed., pp. 78, 79, 161, 249, 342, 493.

[31] Dick B., *Anne Smith's Journal*, pp. 20-22.

Shoemaker summed up the spiritual problem as follows:

God is God, and self is not God—that is the heart of it. It is an actual fact that we become God to ourselves unless we have God to believe in: the final reference becomes ourselves.[32]

My principles "listened" well but they worked like the devil's own. . . . I realized the horror I was passing through, and suddenly gave up that path because I saw it ending in a blank wall or worse. One is reminded of a very old verse: "There is a way which seemeth right unto a man, but the end thereof are the ways of death."[33]

The Big Book said:

So our troubles . . . are basically of our own making. . . . Neither could we reduce our self-centeredness much by wishing or trying on our own power. We had to have God's help. This is the how and why of it. First of all, we had to quit playing God. It didn't work (p. 62).

In its chapter titled "Get Wisdom, Get Understanding," *The Runner's Bible* pointed to the reproof Jesus gave to the Sadducees:

Ye do err, not knowing the scriptures, nor the power of God.[34]

And we believe the early AAs, with their regular study of Scripture and their search for the power that God could provide, were following exactly the path Jesus suggested.[35] The early AAs

---

[32] Shoemaker, *National Awakening*, p. 48.

[33] Shoemaker, *Realizing Religion*, p. 7, quoting Proverbs 16:25.

[34] Matthew 22:29; Nora Smith Holm, *The Runner's Bible* (New York: Houghton Mifflin, 1915), p. 51.

[35] Note that the Big Book declared that probably no human power could relieve AAs of their alcoholism, but that "God could and would if He were sought" (p. 60).

studied the Good Book; and they sought the power of God for the solution to their spiritual misery and despair.

Step Two, Willingness, Belief, and Seeking

[Step Two: Came to believe that a Power greater than ourselves could restore us to sanity.]

Reduced to its essence, and as described in A.A.'s Big Book, the Second Step required *"willingness* to believe," *belief* in a "Power, which is God," and *"seeking"* the power of God for relief from alcoholism. Some might disagree with our description of the Second Step requirements, but Bill Wilson put those ideas very explicitly in the following Big Book phrases:

> *It was only a matter of being willing to believe in a Power greater than myself. Nothing more was required of me to make my beginning.* I saw that growth could start from that point. Upon a foundation of complete willingness I might build what I saw in my friend [Bill's "sponsor," Ebby Thacher] (p. 12; italics in original).

> Its [the Big Book's] main object is to enable you to find a Power greater than yourself which will solve your problem . . . it means, of course, that *we are going to talk about God* . . . even though it was impossible for any of us to fully define or comprehend that *Power, which is God* (pp. 45-46; italics added).

> We needed to ask ourselves but one short question. "Do I now *believe, or am I even willing to believe,* that there is a Power greater than myself?" As soon as a man can say that he does believe, or is willing to believe, we emphatically assure him that he is on his way (p. 47; italics added).

> Circumstances made him willing to believe. He humbly offered himself to his Maker—then he knew. Even so has God restored us all to our right minds. . . . He has come to all who have honestly *sought* Him (p. 57; italics added).

[P]robably no human power could have relieved our alcoholism.
. . . God could and would *if He were sought* (p. 60; italics added).

All three A.A. concepts—willingness, belief, and seeking—were borrowed by AAs from Bible verses A.A.'s sources had frequently quoted.

Concerning *willingness*, the Reverend Sam Shoemaker was A.A.'s most articulate Bible teacher.[36] Shoemaker said that if one wished to "come to believe," he or she should follow the injunction of Jesus Christ in John 7:17. The essence of Jesus's teaching as Shoemaker and others including early AAs interpreted it, was that if one obeyed the known commandments and doctrines of God by acting upon them, he or she would learn, believe, and know more about God and His will because God would then reveal more.[37] A.A.'s religious sources taught that *obedience* to God's will is the organ of spiritual *knowledge*.[38] They quoted John 7:17:

If any man will do his will, he shall know of the doctrine, whether it be of God, or *whether* I speak of myself.

Concerning *belief*, many of A.A.'s root sources quoted Hebrews 11:6. Oxford Group people, other A.A. sources, and

---

[36] See also the discussion by Shoemaker's Oxford Group friend, Philip Marshall Brown, *The Venture of Belief* (New York: Fleming H. Revell, 1935), pp. 29, 36.

[37] See, for example, Shoemaker, *Religion That Works*, p. 36; Russell, *For Sinners Only*, p. 211; Brown, *The Venture of Belief*, pp. 29, 36; Dick B., *The Oxford Group & A.A.*, pp. 41, 50, 54-56, 70, 149, 164, 190, 217, 272-74, 313, 315-16, 333; *The Upper Room* for 4/26/35, 6/28/37, 12/1/37; Harry Emerson Fosdick, *The Meaning of Prayer* (New York: Association Press, 1915), p. 59; *The Meaning of Faith*, pp. 216-17; Glenn Clark, *I Will Lift Up Mine Eyes* (New York: Harper & Brothers, 1937), p. 27; Oswald Chambers, *Studies in the Sermon on the Mount* (London: Simpkin Marshall, n.d.), p. 37.

[38] See Henry Drummond, *The Ideal Life* (New York: Hodder & Stoughton, 1897), pp. 227-320; F. B. Meyer, *The Secret of Guidance* (New York: Fleming H. Revell, 1896), p. 11; Henry B. Wright, *The Will of God and a Man's Lifework* (New York: The Young Men's Christian Association, 1909), pp. 102-279; Clarence I. Benson, *The Eight Points of the Oxford Group* (London: Oxford University Press, 1936), pp. 134-42.

early AAs subscribed to the idea that they could not come to God without believing that God is.[39] Hebrews 11:6 states:

> But without faith *it is* impossible to please *him*: for he that cometh to God must believe that He is, and *that* he is a rewarder of them that diligently seek him.

And concerning *seeking*, early AAs took their cue from the Sermon on the Mount and religion's countless references to seeking *first* the Kingdom of God. These references can be found in Shoemaker's titles and the other Christian writings of the day which were being studied by the AAs.[40] As we've mentioned, Dr. Bob was very emphatic that A.A.'s well-known "First Things First" slogan came from Matthew 6:33.[41] The verse declares:

> But seek ye first the kingdom of God, and his righteousness; and all these things [earthly needs for food, drink, clothing] shall be added unto you.

Step Three and the Decision to Surrender

[Step Three: Made a decision to turn our will and our lives over to the care of God *as we understood Him.*]

---

[39] Weatherhead, *How Can I Find God?*, p. 72; Samuel M. Shoemaker, *The Gospel According to You* (New York: Fleming H. Revell, 1934), p. 47; *National Awakening*, pp. 40-41; *Religion That Works*, p. 55; *Confident Faith* (New York: Fleming H. Revell, 1932), p. 187; Oswald Chambers, *My Utmost for His Highest* (New Jersey: Barbour and Company, 1963), p. 304; Fosdick, *The Meaning of Faith*, pp. 8, 92; Dick B., *Design for Living*, pp. 165, 331; *New Light on Alcoholism*, pp. 85-86; *DR. BOB and the Good Oldtimers* (New York: Alcoholics Anonymous World Services, 1980), p. 144. The latter title is hereinafter called *DR. BOB.*

[40] Shoemaker, *National Awakening*, p. 41; *The Upper Room* for 9/4/35; 11/19/35; 6/20/37; 12/2/38; Holm, *The Runner's Bible*, p. 127; Chambers, *My Utmost for His Highest*, p. 142; *Studies in the Sermon on the Mount*, pp. 60-61; Fosdick, *The Meaning of Faith*, pp. 192-93; Dick B., *The Oxford Group & A.A.*, p. 284; *Anne Smith's Journal*, pp. 132, 140; *Dr. Bob and His Library*, p. 100.

[41] *DR. BOB*, p. 144.

We have not, among A.A.'s religious sources, located any direct biblical references to the "decision" of Step Three. But, A.A. sources do discuss two verses which mandate a *decision*:

> That if thou shalt confess with thy mouth the Lord Jesus, and shalt believe in thine heart that God hath raised him from the dead, thou shalt be saved (Romans 10:9).[42]

> And be not conformed to this world: but be ye transformed by the renewing of your mind, that ye may prove what is that good, and acceptable, and perfect, will of God (Romans 12:2).[43]

And there are ample Bible verses, adopted by AAs from their root sources, which served as guides for their *making* their decision to surrender to God and to *entrust* their lives to His care.

The *decision* in early A.A.—and today in some cases—involved a surrender made on the knees.[44] The A.A. surrender language came from the Lord's Prayer—a part of the Sermon on the Mount. Several A.A. sources suggested *decision language* that declared simply and humbly, "Thy will be done."[45] A variant involved Jesus's other similar expression, "Not my will, but thine, be done."[46] The root language for these two "decision"

---

[42] Shoemaker, *If I Be Lifted Up*, p. 83; Glenn Clark, *Touchdowns for the Lord: The Story of "Dad" A. J. Elliott* (Minnesota: Macalester Park Publishing Company, 1947), pp. 55-56.

[43] Dick B., *Anne Smith's Journal*, pp. 46, 77, 102, 132, 143; *The Oxford Group & A.A.*, p. 171.

[44] For the history of the A.A. surrender "on the knees," see *Pass It On*, pp. 198-99.

[45] Big Book, pp. 67, 88; compare p. 443; Matthew 6:10; *What Is The Oxford Group*, p. 48; Samuel M. Shoemaker, Jr., *Children of the Second Birth* (New York: Fleming H. Revell, 1927), p. 175-87; *The Upper Room* for 12/3/37; Dick B., *The Oxford Group & A.A.*, p. 181; *The Akron Genesis*, p. 96.

[46] Big Book, p. 85; compare pp. 229, 381; Mary Wilder Tileston, *Daily Strength for Daily Needs*, 1977 Printing (New York: Grosset & Dunlap, 1884), pp. 296, 146; *The Upper Room* for 6/21/38; *What is the Oxford Group?*, p. 48; Shoemaker, *Children of the*
(continued...)

expressions, as rendered in the King James Version of the Bible, came from:

Thy will be done in earth, as *it is* in heaven (Matthew 6:10).

[N]evertheless not my will, but thine, be done (Luke 22:42).

Sam Shoemaker cited Psalm 46:10 as to the *need* for surrendering and finding God. Shoemaker quoted Dr. Moffatt's translation of Psalm 46:10 as follows:

"Give in," he cries, "admit that I am God, high over nations, high over the world."[47]

Both the Big Book and Sam Shoemaker spoke of "abandoning yourself to God," and such language indicated the total surrender of the will that was expected.[48] The Third Step's actual surrender phraseology can be found in A.A. sources which used such language as "turned over to Him her life for His direction" and a "decision to cast my will and my life on God."[49]

Additional Bible verses which A.A.'s sources associated with a decision to surrender were:

I can of mine own self do nothing: as I hear, I judge: and my judgment is just; because I seek not mine own will, but the will of the Father which hath sent me (John 5:30).[50]

---

[46] (...continued)
Second Birth, pp. 58, 182; Glenn Clark, *The Soul's Sincere Desire* (Boston: Little, Brown & Co., 1925), p. 40; *I Will Lift Up Mine Eyes*, p. 27.

[47] Shoemaker, *National Awakening*, pp. 45-54. The better known King James Version of Psalm 46:10 reads: "Be still, and know that I am God: I will be exalted among the heathen, I will be exalted in the earth."

[48] Big Book, pp. 164, 59, 63; Shoemaker, *Religion That Works*, p. 19.

[49] Samuel M. Shoemaker, Jr., *Children of the Second Birth*, p. 82; *Twice-Born Ministers* (New York: Fleming H. Revell, 1929), p. 134.

[50] Meyer, *The Secret of Guidance*, p. 11.

Know ye not, that to whom ye yield yourselves servants to obey, his servants ye are to whom ye obey; whether of sin unto death, or of obedience unto righteousness (Romans 6:16).[51]

Know ye not that ye are the temple of God, and *that* the Spirit of God dwelleth in you? (1 Corinthians 3:16).[52]

God *is* a Spirit: and they that worship him must worship *him* in spirit and in truth (John 4:24).[53]

For in him we live, and move, and have our being; as certain also of your own poets have said, For we are also his offspring (Acts 17:28).[54]

Repent ye therefore, and be converted, that your sins may be blotted out, when the times of refreshing shall come from the presence of the Lord (Acts 3:19).[55]

In connection with this Step, Clarence S. referred to 1 Thessalonians 1:9—"how ye turned to God from idols to serve the living and true God." Clarence also quoted Ephesians 4:22-24—putting off the old man by renewing your mind, and putting on the new man created in righteousness and true holiness.[56]

---

[51] Wright, *The Will of God and a Man's Lifework*, p. 31; Chambers, *My Utmost for His Highest*, p. 283.

[52] Holm, *The Runner's Bible*, p. 17; *What Is The Oxford Group?*, p. 39; Clark, *I Will Lift Up Mine Eyes*, p. 30.

[53] Fosdick, *The Meaning of Faith*, p. 85; *What Is the Oxford Group?*, p. 41; *The Upper Room* for 5/1/35; Holm, *The Runner's Bible*, p. 4.

[54] Fosdick, *The Meaning of Faith*, pp. 86-87; *What Is the Oxford Group?*, p. 42; R. C. Mowat, *Modern Prophetic Voices from Kierkegaard to Buchman* (Great Britain, New Cherwell Press, 1994), pp. 72-73; B. H. Streeter, *The God Who Speaks* (London: Macmillan & Co., Ltd., 1936), p. 12.

[55] Holm, *The Runner's Bible*, p. 88; *What Is The Oxford Group?*, p. 43. On repentance, see discussion in Benson, *The Eight Points*, pp. 7-9; *The Upper Room* for 6/1/37.

[56] See Dick B., *That Amazing Grace*, pp. 68-69.

Step Four and Self-examination

[Step Four: Made a searching and fearless moral inventory of ourselves.]

A.A.'s root sources spoke of taking a *moral* inventory. One was to examine one's life in terms of how it measured up to the "Four Absolutes"—honesty, purity, unselfishness and love. More importantly, Oxford Group members wished to learn of any "sins" or "shortcomings" blocking them from God and from others.[57]

The basic idea that self-examination is required to establish a satisfactory relationship with God came from several verses in the Sermon on the Mount. These verses state that one should look for his own faults, his own part in difficulties, before looking at the faults of another. A.A. sources quoted Matthew 7:3-5:

> And why beholdest thou the mote [speck] that is in thy brother's eye, but considerest not the beam [log] that is in thine own eye? Or wilt thou say to thy brother, "Let me pull out the mote out of thine eye;" and, behold, a beam is in thine own eye? Thou hypocrite, first cast out the beam out of thine own eye; and then shalt thou see clearly to cast out the mote out of thy brother's eye.[58]

The Oxford Group's self-examination "yardsticks" were *positive*. The self-examination was to be in the context of how well a person was living up to the "absolute" moral standards taught by Jesus. The Oxford Group's standards were taken from Dr. Robert

---

[57] See Dick B., *The Oxford Group & A.A.*, pp. 166-70, for the varying Oxford Group definitions of sin, all of which characterized "sin" as that which blocks us from God and from others.

[58] Geoffrey Allen, *He That Cometh* (New York: The Macmillan Company, 1933), pp. 81, 140; Victor C. Kitchen, *I Was a Pagan* (New York: Harper & Brothers, 1934), p. 111; Samuel M. Shoemaker, Jr., *The Church Can Save the World*, 2d ed (New York: Harper & Brothers, 1938), pp. 88-121; *God's Control* (New York: Fleming H. Revell, 1939), pp. 62-72; Dick B., *Anne Smith's Journal*, pp. 30-31.

E. Speer's reconstruction of Jesus's uncompromising teachings on perfection.[59] Speer believed he had identified Jesus's four "absolute" moral standards in the following verses:

> *Honesty* (which Speer spoke of as "an absolute standard of truth"). Speer urged, if Satan is the father of lies, how can any lie be justifiable? Speer's unmistakable reference is to John 8:44: "Ye are of *your* father the devil, and the lusts of your father ye will do. He was a murderer from the beginning, and abode not in the truth, because there is no truth in him. When he speaketh a lie, he speaketh of his own: for he is a liar, and the father of it."[60]

> *Unselfishness*. Speer cited: (1) Mark 10:45: "For even the Son of man came not to be ministered unto, but to minister, and to give his life a ransom for many." (2) Luke 22:27: "For whether *is* greater, he that sitteth at meat, or he that serveth? *is* not he that sitteth at meat? but I am among you as he that serveth." (3) Luke 14:33: "So likewise, whosoever he be of you that forsaketh not all that he hath, he cannot be my disciple."[61]

> *Purity*. Speer cited: (1) Mark 7:15: "There is nothing from without a man, that entering into him can defile him: but the things which come out of him, those are they that defile the man." (2) Matthew 5:29-30: "And if thy right eye offend thee, pluck it out, and cast *it* from thee: for it is profitable for thee that one of thy members should perish, and not *that* thy whole body should be cast into hell. And if thy right hand offend thee, cut it off, and cast *it* from thee: for it is profitable for thee that

---

[59] Robert E. Speer, *The Principles of Jesus* (New York: Association Press, 1902). Speer discussed Jesus's standard of perfection at page 34 and quoted Matthew 5:48 from the Sermon on the Mount: "Be ye therefore perfect, even as your Father which is in heaven is perfect."

[60] Speer, *The Principles of Jesus*, p. 35.

[61] Speer, *The Principles of Jesus*, p. 35. See also Streeter, *The God Who Speaks*, p. 84.

one of thy members should perish, and not *that* thy whole body should be cast into hell."[62]

Love. Speer basically cited (1) John 13:34: "A new commandment I give unto you, That ye love one another; as I have loved you, that ye also love one another." (2) John 13:1: "Now before the feast of the passover, when Jesus knew that his hour was come that he should depart out of this world unto the Father, having loved his own which were in the world, he loved them unto the end."[63]

Later writers, including Sam Shoemaker, thought Speer's four standards actually *came* from Jesus's teachings in the Sermon on the Mount.[64] And the standards did, in the sense that they were founded on the standard of perfection Jesus enunciated in the Sermon. But the verses which Speer himself cited as authority were not all from Matthew 5–7, though they *were* taught by Jesus and were consistent *with* his Sermon on the Mount teachings.

Professor Henry B. Wright, who was a major influence on the thinking of Oxford Group Founder Frank Buchman, examined Speer's four absolute standards in light of the following Gospel verses.[65] (Wright termed the principles in the verses the "Four Absolutes."[66]):

Honesty. Luke 16:10-11: "He that is faithful in that which is least is faithful also in much: and he that is unjust in the least is unjust also in much. If therefore ye have not been faithful in the unrighteous mammon, who will commit to your trust the true *riches*?"[67]

---

[62] Speer, *The Principles of Jesus*, p. 35.

[63] Speer, *The Principles of Jesus*, p. 35.

[64] See Dick B., *The Oxford Group & A.A.*, pp. 237-38.

[65] For a discussion of Wright's immense influence on Frank Buchman, see Dick B., *The Oxford Group & A.A.*, pp. 67-72.

[66] Wright, *The Will of God*, pp. 167-218:

[67] Wright, *The Will of God*, p. 187.

Unselfishness. Luke 9:23-24: "And he said to *them* all, If any man will come after me, let him deny himself, and take up his cross daily, and follow me. For whosoever will save his life shall lose it: but whosoever will lose his life for my sake, the same shall save it."[68]

Purity. Matthew 5:8: "Blessed *are* the pure in heart: for they shall see God."[69]

Love. Matthew 25:41-43, 45: ". . . Depart from me, ye cursed, into everlasting fire, prepared for the devil and his angels; For I was an hungered, and ye gave me no meat: I was thirsty, and ye gave me no drink: I was a stranger, and ye took me not in: naked, and ye clothed me not: sick, and in prison, and ye visited me not. . . . Then shall he answer them, saying, Verily I say unto you, Inasmuch as ye did *it* not to one of the least of these, ye did *it* not to me."[70]

Unsurprisingly, A.A.'s other progenitors in the Oxford Group, including Wright himself, found the same four absolute moral principles in a good many other New Testament verses including the following: Mark 10:19-21; 1 Corinthians 13; Ephesians 4:15-16; Colossians 3:5-14; 1 Thessalonians 4:3-12; and James 3:17.[71]

In his last major address to AAs, Dr. Bob still spoke highly of the Oxford Group's "Four Absolutes" and said they were the "yardsticks" by which AAs could measure their conduct and, in effect, "take their inventory."[72] Dr. Bob's wife, Anne, frequently urged the Four Absolutes as moral standards for conduct.[73] In

---

[68] Wright, *The Will of God*, p. 197.

[69] Wright, *The Will of God*, p. 179. See also Russell, *For Sinners Only*, p. 63.

[70] Wright, *The Will of God*, p. 207.

[71] Wright, *The Will of God*, p. 167; *What is the Oxford Group?*, p. 109; Harry J. Almond, *Foundations for Faith*. 2d ed (London: Grosvenor Books, 1980), p. 12; Benson, *The Eight Points*, pp. 44-57.

[72] *The Co-Founders of Alcoholics Anonymous: Biographical sketches Their last major talks* (New York: Alcoholics Anonymous World Services, 1972, 1975), pp. 12-14.

[73] Dick B., *Anne Smith's Journal*, pp. 31-34, 59-60, 104-06, 108, 115-20.

later years, A.A.'s other co-founder Bill Wilson became quite critical of the Four Absolutes, claiming they were too "absolute" for alcoholics to follow.[74] And perhaps in consequence, Wilson framed the Big Book's moral inventory in terms of *negatives*. AAs were enjoined to examine their lives for: (1) Resentments and grudges; (2) Fears; (3) Selfishness and self-seeking, particularly in the sex area; (4) Dishonesty; and (5) "Harms" they had caused others by their conduct.[75]

The Biblical roots which defined A.A.'s "negative" yardsticks were not as concisely and precisely defined in A.A.'s religious sources as were the four "positive" absolutes. But we believe those negative moral yardsticks do pop out rather clearly from the Bible verses early AAs studied or to which they were exposed.

In their search for objectionable conduct that blocked them from God, AAs were, in their Fourth Step, to *put on paper* their resentments, fears, selfish sex conduct, and harms to others.[76] And the underlying requirement was that they apply rigorous honesty in their inventory.[77]

And we believe the following Biblical teachings by A.A.'s sources had a major influence in defining the negatives AAs were to search for, list in writing, and root out. We believe this because of the pervasive A.A. source teachings *about* these spiritual problems, and the similarity between A.A. language and the Biblical root teachings:

> *Resentments and grudges*: "Grudge not one against another, brethren, lest ye be condemned: behold, the judge standeth before the door" (James 5:9). "But I say unto you, That whosoever is angry with his brother without a cause shall be in danger of the judgment: and whosoever shall say to his brother,

---

[74] *Alcoholics Anonymous Comes of Age*, pp. 74-75; *Pass It On*, pp. 171-74.

[75] See Big Book, pp. 64-70, 84, 86.

[76] Big Book p. 64 (resentments); p. 68 (fears); p. 69 (selfish sex conduct); p. 70 (people hurt by the conduct).

[77] Big Book, pp. 58, 65, 67, 69. See also pp. 84, 86.

Raca, shall be in danger of the council: but whosever shall say,
Thou fool, shall be in danger of hell fire" (Matthew 5:22—in
the Sermon on the Mount).[78]

Fears: "The Lord *is* my light and my salvation; whom shall I
fear? the Lord *is* the strength of my life; of whom shall I be
afraid?" (Psalm 27:1); "Yea, though I walk through the valley
of the shadow of death, I will fear no evil: for thou *art* with
me; thy rod and thy staff they comfort me" (Psalm 23:4); "Fear
not: for I *am* with thee" (Isaiah 43:5); "Be not afraid, only
believe" (Mark 5:36); "For God hath not given us the spirit of
fear; but of power, and of love, and of a sound mind" (2
Timothy 1:7); "There is no fear in love; but perfect love casteth
out fear: because fear hath torment" (1 John 4:18).[79]

Selfishness. "Charity . . . seeketh not her own" (1 Cor. 13:4-
5).[80]

Dishonesty. "Charity . . . rejoiceth not in iniquity, but rejoiceth
in the truth" (1 Corinthians 13:4, 6); "Finally, brethren,
whatsoever things are true, whatsoever things *are* honest,

---

[78] See *The Upper Room* for 10/18/35; Holm, *The Runner's Bible*, p. 82; Shoemaker,
Twice-Born Ministers, p. 182; *How to Become a Christian*, pp. 55-64; Harold Begbie,
Life Changers (London: Mills & Boon, Ltd., 1923), p. 38; Ebenezer Macmillan, *Seeking
and Finding* (New York: Harper & Brothers, 1933), pp. 96-98; E. Stanley Jones, *The
Christ of the Mount* (New York: The Abingdon Press, 1931), p. 136; Dick B., *Anne
Smith's Journal*, pp. 34-36.

[79] Holm, *The Runner's Bible*, pp. 41-44, 132; *The Upper Room* for 7/11/35, 8/22/35,
5/2/37, 8/2/37, 8/6/37, 7/1/38; Tileston, *Daily Strength for Daily Needs*, p. 228;
Fosdick, *The Meaning of Faith*, pp. 191-92, 240; Clark, *The Soul's Sincere Desire*, pp.
8-9, 14; *What is the Oxford Group?*, p. 2; Streeter, *The God Who Speaks*, p. 68; Stephen
Foot, *Life Began Yesterday* (New York: Harper & Brothers, 1935), p. 35; Dick B., *The
Akron Genesis*, p. 94.

[80] Henry Drummond, *The Greatest Thing in the World*, 2d ed (World Bible
Publishers), pp. 26, 32, 33; *DR. BOB*, pp. 96, 310; Dick B., *Anne Smith's Journal*, p.
131.

whatsoever things *are* just . . . if *there be* any virtue, and if *there be* any praise, think on these things" (Philippians 4:8).[81]

Harms caused. Oxford Group writer Olive Jones succinctly defined "restitution" from the Oxford Group viewpoint as follows: "*Restitution*, by which we make amends, restore, so far as human power permits, for the wrong done."[82] The four principal sets of Bible verses from which came the A.A. suggestions as to amends for harm done were: Numbers 5:6-7; Matthew 5:23-24; and Luke, Chapter 15, and 19:1-10. We will quote and discuss these verses at a later point in connection with Step Nine.[83]

Clarence Snyder emphasized Mark 7:18-23 and Galatians 5:16-26, both of which segments emphasize the nature of a person's shortcomings—defiling, defeating, evil things people nurture inside themselves and which need purging.[84]

Step Five and Confession

[Step Five: Admitted to God, to ourselves, and to another human being the exact nature of our wrongs.]

[81] Drummond, *The Greatest Thing in the World*, pp. 27, 39; *DR. BOB*, pp. 96, 310; Clark, *I Will Lift Up Mine Eyes*, pp. 54, 93; *The Upper Room* for 9/12/35, 5/14/36, 7/20/37; Tileston, *Daily Strength for Daily Needs*, p. 364; Holm, *The Runner's Bible*, p. 116; Fosdick, *The Meaning of Prayer*, p. 72.

[82] Olive M. Jones, *Inspired Children* (New York: Harper & Brothers, 1933), p. 136.

[83] See also Weatherhead, *Discipleship*, pp. 114-23; Benson, *The Eight Points*, pp. 30-43.

[84] Dick B., *That Amazing Grace*, pp. 69-71.

Except for scattered mention of a few other verses, AAs and their sources very consistently mentioned James 5:16 as the root of their "confession" step.[85] James 5:16 states:

> Confess *your* faults one to another, and pray for one another, that ye may be healed. The effectual fervent prayer of a righteous man availeth much.

Step Six, Conviction and Readiness to Change

[Step Six: Were entirely ready to have God remove all these defects of character.]

It is difficult to pinpoint the Sixth's Step's Biblical link to A.A. The link, if any, was never discussed by Bill Wilson; and apparently it was not discussed either by Dr. Bob or his wife, Anne. However, A.A.'s link to the Oxford Group's "Five C's" and their "soul-surgery" art is very clear.[86] And the third "C" in the Oxford Group formula for life-change was "Conviction."[87] "Conviction" was mentioned *by name and by concept* by Bill Wilson's wife, Lois, in Lois's "Oxford Group Notes" and

---

[85] J. P. Thornton-Duesbury, *Sharing* (Pamphlet of The Oxford Group, published at Oxford University Press, no date), p. 5; Sherwood Sunderland Day, *The Principles of the Group* (Oxford: University Press, n.d.), p. 6; *What is the Oxford Group?*, pp. 29, 31; Streeter, *The God Who Speaks*, p. 125; Weatherhead, *Discipleship*, p. 32; Almond, *Foundations for Faith*, p. 13; Garth Lean, *Cast Out Your Nets* (London: Grosvenor, 1990), p. 48; Samuel M. Shoemaker, Jr., *The Conversion of the Church* (New York: Fleming H. Revell, 1932), p. 35; Fosdick, *The Meaning of Faith*, p. 190; *The Meaning of Prayer*, pp. 157-58; *The Upper Room* for 12/4/35; *Pass It On*, p. 128; Dick B., *Anne Smith's Journal*, pp. 36, 38, 40, 99, 129, 131-32, 142, 144.

[86] See Dick B., *The Oxford Group & A.A.*, pp. 175-79; *New Light on Alcoholism*, pp. 55, 93; *Anne Smith's Journal*, pp. 96-97; and see also *DR. BOB*, p. 54.

[87] Dick B., *The Oxford Group & A.A.*, pp. 192-97; Howard A. Walter, *Soul Surgery: Some Thoughts on Incisive Personal Work*, 6th ed. (Oxford: University Press, 1940), pp. 64-78.

subsequent 1937 diary entries.[88] Dr. Bob's wife, Anne Smith, addressed the "conviction" subject quite frequently in the spiritual journal she kept between 1933 and 1939.[89]

Shoemaker's Oxford Group colleague Olive M. Jones defined "conviction" as follows: *"Conviction,* by which we come to a conscious realization of our sins which shut God away from us."[90]

Understood from the vantage point of its Oxford Group roots in the Five C's, the Step Six "conviction" idea could have come from several Biblical roots. Repentance or dying to self, is the way Glenn Clark summarized the conviction concept.[91] And note that the Biblical source verses progress from the idea that one must convict himself or herself of sin to the idea that *God* brings people to conviction:

> "Against thee, thee only, have I sinned, and done *this* evil in thy sight . . ." (Psalm 51:4); "Iniquities prevail against me: as *for* our transgressions, thou shalt purge them away" (Psalm 65:3); "And the son said unto him, Father, I have sinned against heaven, and in thy sight, and am no more worthy to be called thy son" (Luke 15:21); "For we know that the law is spiritual: but I am carnal, sold under sin" (Romans 7:14); "Who is weak, and I am not weak? who is offended, and I burn not?" (2 Corinthians 11:29); "And when he [the Comforter] is come, he will reprove [convict] the world of sin, and of righteousness, and of judgment" (John 16:8). "But God commendeth his love

---

[88] Dick B., *New Light on Alcoholism*, pp. 545-49; *The Akron Genesis*, p. 155. For example, during one of his two visits to Stepping Stones Archives at Bedford Hills, New York, the author was allowed by the archivist to inspect and copy entries from Lois Wilson's diary for 1937. That diary contained an entry for February 8, 1937, which stated, "Convicted of trying to be a fixer . . ." For February 13, 1937, Lois wrote, "Convicted of being put out when my personal things have been mishandled . . ."

[89] Dick B., *Anne Smith's Journal*, pp. 41-45, 100-01.

[90] Olive Jones, *Inspired Children*, pp. 135-36.

[91] Clark, *I Will Lift Up Mine Eyes*, p. 77.

toward us, in that, while we were yet sinners, Christ died for us" (Romans 5:8).[92]

Step Seven, Humble Submission and Rebirth

[Step Seven: Humbly asked Him to remove our shortcomings.]

Early AAs believed God was willing and able to change them. They expected the change to occur if they asked Him for it. In his correspondence with Dr. Carl Jung, Bill Wilson wrote the great psychiatrist about "conversion" and "conversion experiences." As to Rowland Hazard and the "conversion experience that released him for the time being from his compulsion to drink," Bill wrote:

> This concept [a spiritual experience] proved to be the foundation of such success as Alcoholics Anonymous has since achieved. This has made conversion experience . . . available on an almost wholesale basis.[93]

A *conversion experience* certainly meant, among other things, to Bill and to Bill's spiritual teachers, that one had been "born again of the spirit."[94]

In an early Big Book manuscript which the author found at Bill's home at Stepping Stones in Bedford Hills, New York, Bill spoke of his *own* conversion experience. He proclaimed of that experience, "For sure, I'd been born again;" and he repeated that

---

[92] Walter, *Soul Surgery*, pp. 64-78; Fosdick, *The Meaning of Faith*, pp. 54, 146; *The Upper Room* for 6/2/37; Chambers, *My Utmost for His Highest*, p. 324; Glover, *The Jesus of History*, p. 149.

[93] *Pass It On*, p. 383.

[94] Shoemaker, *Realizing Religion*, pp. 21, 35; *Children of the Second Birth,* p. 32; *Religion That Works*, p. 14; *Twice-Born Ministers*, pp. 10, 56; *Confident Faith*, pp. 137, 140; *National Awakening*, pp. 55-66; Allen, *He That Cometh*, pp. 19, 32, 48-49; Jones, *Inspired Children*, p. 136; Drummond, *The Ideal Life*, pp. 212-26; Frank Buchman, *Remaking The World* (London: Blandford, 1961), p. 23; Begbie, *Life Changers*, p. 117.

"born again" conclusion in another early manuscript.[95] Neither of Bill's explicit observations about his rebirth was included in A.A.'s Conference Approved literature. However, Bill reached his conclusion after he had made a decision for Christ at Shoemaker's Calvary Rescue Mission in New York, just prior to Bill's entering Towns Hospital for the last time.[96]

This early A.A. idea that one needed to be "converted" and "born again" by the power of God seemed to vanish in later A.A. language. Yet the early A.A. concept that one achieves freedom from sin by the grace of God was firmly rooted in John 3 and the new birth principle. Hence even the third edition of the Big Book—seemingly almost by oversight—proclaimed, "as we became conscious of His presence, we began to lose our fear of today, tomorrow or the hereafter. We were reborn" (p. 63).

The following were the verses most frequently cited by A.A. sources in connection with the conversion experiences to which AAs had been led in their early days:

Jesus answered and said unto him, Verily, verily, I say unto thee, Except a man be born again, he cannot see the kingdom of God. . . . Jesus answered, Verily, verily, I say unto thee, Except a man be born of water and of the Spirit, he cannot enter the kingdom *of* God. . . . Marvel not that I said unto thee, Ye must be born again (John 3:3, 3:5, 3:7).[97]

Submit yourselves therefore to God. Resist the devil, and he will flee from you (James 4:7).[98]

---

[95] Dick B., *Turning Point*, pp. 94-98.

[96] Dick B., *The Akron Genesis,* pp. 157-58.

[97] See Olive Jones, *Inspired Children*, which states at page 136: "*Conversion*, which means simply a changed life. 'Ye must be born again,' said Christ." See also Shoemaker, *Twice-Born Ministers*, pp. 56, 10; *National Awakening*, pp. 55, 57, 58; Buchman, *Remaking the World*, p. 23; Begbie, *Life Changers*, p. 117; Allen, *He That Cometh*, pp. 19-43; Chambers, *My Utmost for His Highest*, pp. 228, 333; *Studies in the Sermon on the Mount*, pp. 16, 31; *The Upper Room* for 6/8/37, 5/22/38.

[98] Holm, *The Runner's Bible*, pp. 59, 94, 112, 115.

Humble yourselves in the sight of the Lord, and he shall lift you up (James 4:10).[99]

Clarence S. illustrated the Seventh Step process by characterizing it as the Step where the New Manager (God) got out the tape eraser and erased the defects identified in Step Four, confessed in Step Five, and renounced in Step Six. He said the assurance of God's help was given in the Sermon on the Mount (Matthew 7:7-11). The fullness of God's forgiveness was set forth in Psalm 103:10-12. And the procedure for praying with other believers to secure removal was set forth in James 5:13-16.[100]

Step Eight, Willingness to Make Amends

[Step Eight: Made a list of all persons we had harmed, and became willing to make amends to them all.]

The Big Book states:

> We have made a list of all persons we have harmed and to whom we are willing to make amends. . . . Now we go out to our fellows and repair the damage done in the past. We attempt to sweep away the debris which has accumulated out of our effort to live on self-will and run the show ourselves (p. 76).

In discussing the approach to others and the reason for making amends even to those we dislike, A.A.'s sources emphasized the following verses:

> Agree with thine adversary quickly, whiles thou art in the way with him; lest at any time the adversary deliver thee to the

---

[99] Samuel M. Shoemaker, *Those Twelve Steps as I Understand Them*; Volume II, *Best of the Grapevine* (New York: The A.A. Grapevine, Inc., 1986), p. 130.

[100] Dick B., *That Amazing Grace*, pp. 72-74.

judge, and the judge deliver thee to the officer, and thou be cast into prison (Matthew 5:25).[101]

If a man say, I love God, and hateth his brother, he is a liar: for he that loveth not his brother whom he hath seen, how can he love God whom he hath not seen? (1 John 4:20).[102]

Step Nine, Restitution

[Step Nine: Made direct amends to such people wherever possible, except when to do so would injure them or others.]

Four sets of verses captured the attention of A.A.'s root sources in connection with straightening out the wreckage of the past and making restitution for harms done to others:

Therefore if thou bring thy gift to the altar, and there rememberest that thy brother hath ought against thee; leave there thy gift before the altar, and go thy way; first be reconciled to thy brother, and then come and offer thy gift (Matthew 5:23-24).[103]

Speak unto the Children of Israel, when a man or a woman shall commit any sin that men commit, to do a trespass against the Lord, and that soul shall be guilty; Then they shall confess their sin which they have done: and he shall make restitution for his

---

[101] Holm, *The Runner's Bible*, p. 67; Chambers, *My Utmost for His Highest*, p. 182; Benson, *The Eight Points*, p. 32; Weatherhead, *Discipleship*, p. 112. See also *The Upper Room* for 1/12/36 or 1/12/39.

[102] Clark, *I Will Lift Up Mine Eyes*, p. 32; Benson, *The Eight Points*, pp. 36-37; Macmillan, *Seeking and Finding*, p. 99; Tileston, *Daily Strength for Daily Needs*, p. 103; Dick B., *The Akron Genesis*, p. 92, n. 10; *New Light on Alcoholism*, p. 272.

[103] Benson, *The Eight Points*, p. 30; MacMillan, *Seeking and Finding*, p. 176; Russell, *For Sinner's Only*, p. 120; Weatherhead, *Discipleship*, p. 113; Shoemaker, *The Conversion of the Church*, pp. 47-48; *The Gospel According to You*, p. 149; Holm, *The Runner's Bible*, p. 82; Chambers, *My Utmost for His Highest*, p. 268; *DR. BOB*, p. 308; *RHS* (the dedication page); E. Stanley Jones, *The Christ of the Mount*, p. 140.

guilt in full, and add unto it the fifth part thereof, and give it unto him in respect of whom he hath been guilty (Numbers 5:6-7, as the translation is rendered in Russell, *For Sinners Only*, p. 119).

For Sinners Only also referred to the Prodigal Son story in Luke, chapter 15. Russell said, "Sending prodigal sons back to their earthly as well as their Heavenly Father is a specialty of the Oxford Group."[104]

For Sinners Only also cited the conversation between Jesus and Zacchaeus recorded in Luke 19:1-10. Zacchaeus had told Jesus that if he had taken anything from any man by false accusation, he had restored the man fourfold. Jesus responded approvingly, "This day is salvation come to thy house."[105]

Step Ten and Daily Corrective Action

[Step Ten: Continued to take personal inventory and when we were wrong promptly admitted it.]

The elements of the Tenth Step can be found on page 84 of the Big Book. The Tenth Step instructions call primarily for a daily application of the spiritual principles learned in the previous nine steps; and the instructions add that AAs should strive to be helpful, loving, and tolerant toward others.

Thus the Big Book's Tenth Step directions state the alcoholic is to *continue* to watch for resentment, selfishness, dishonesty, and fear (tests derived from Step Four). If the "defects of character" are encountered, he or she is to confess the problem to another (derived from Step Five). Then God is to be asked for help in

---

[104] Russell, *For Sinners Only*, p. 129. See also *What is the Oxford Group?*, pp. 63-64.

[105] Russell, *For Sinners Only*, p. 135; Lean, *Cast out Your Nets*, pp. 87-88; Macmillan, *Seeking and Finding*, p. 111; Weatherhead, *Discipleship*, pp. 115-16; Almond, *Foundations for Faith*, p. 13.

eliminating the shortcoming (derived from Steps Six and Seven). If harm has been caused, amends are to be made promptly (derived from Steps Eight and Nine). The alcoholic is then to think of, and help others (derived from Steps Nine and Twelve). And a code of love and tolerance is proclaimed. In short, continuing surrender, continuing recourse to God for help, and continuing corrective behavior are specified as the elements for taking this step.

These ideas involving daily inventory and housecleaning can be found in the Oxford Group concept of "Conservation."[106] Later, Oxford Group writers began speaking of "Continuance" as their Fifth "C," rather than "Conservation."[107] They called for *continuing* repentance, "dying of self," as A.A.'s religious sources might have put it.[108] And the significant Bible verses from which continuance ideas seem to have come are these:

I am crucified with Christ: nevertheless I live; yet not I, but Christ liveth in me: and the life which I now live in the flesh I live by the faith of the Son of God, who loved me, and gave himself for me (Galatians 2:20).[109]

Watch and pray, that ye enter not into temptation: the spirit indeed *is* willing, but the flesh *is* weak (Matthew 26:41).[110]

---

[106] Dick B., *The Oxford Group & A.A.*, pp. 221-24; *New Light on Alcoholism*, p. 433; *Anne Smith's Journal*, pp. 49-53, 107, 143; Walter, *Soul Surgery*, 89-100.

[107] The Five C's have alternately been said to include either Conservation or Continuance. But Oxford Group historian and writer K. D. Belden of Great Britain recently wrote the author and explained that the later and preferred usage had become "Continuance." "Continuance" had supplanted "conservation" in usage; and this change may explain A.A.'s emphasis on the word "continued" in connection with the Tenth Step.

[108] Clark, *I Will Lift Up Mine Eyes*, p. 77.

[109] Howard J. Rose, *The Quiet Time* (Sussex, England, n.d.), p. 3; Streeter, *The God Who Speaks*, p. 92; Fosdick, *The Meaning of Faith*, p. 269; *The Upper Room* for 3/27/36 or 3/27/39 and 5/30/36 or 5/30/39.

[110] Rose, *The Quiet Time*, p. 3; Tileston, *Daily Strength for Daily Needs*, p. 100. See also Luke 21:36 and Holm, *The Runner's Bible*, p. 61; *The Upper Room* for 6/13/35.

Howbeit when he, the Spirit of truth, is come, he will guide you into all truth: for he shall not speak of himself; but whatsoever he shall hear, *that* shall he speak: and he will shew you things to come. He shall glorify me: for he shall receive of mine, and shall shew *it* unto you. All things that the Father hath are mine: therefore said I, that he shall take of mine, and shall shew *it* unto you (John 16:13-15).[111]

If ye continue in the faith grounded and settled, and *be* not moved away from the hope of the gospel, which ye have heard, *and* which was preached to every creature which is under heaven; whereof I Paul am made a minister (Colossians 1:23).[112]

Being confident of this very thing, that he which hath begun a good work in you will perform *it* until the day of Jesus Christ (Philippians 1:6).[113]

Step Eleven, Prayer, Guidance, Growth, Power

[Step Eleven: Sought through prayer and meditation to improve our conscious contact with God *as we understood Him*, praying only for knowledge of His will for us and the power to carry that out.]

The Effectiveness of Prayer

The Big Book states: "*Step Eleven* suggests prayer and meditation. We shouldn't be shy on this matter of prayer. Better men than we are using it constantly. It works, if we have the proper attitude and

---

[111] Rose, *The Quiet Time*, p. 3; Holm, *The Runner's Bible*, pp. 16, 129; Clark, *I Will Lift Up Mine Eyes*, p. 134; Streeter, *The God Who Speaks*, p. 113; Dick B., *The Akron Genesis*, p. 93; *New Light on Alcoholism*, p. 433.

[112] Dick B., *Anne Smith's Journal*, p. 52.

[113] Benson, *The Eight Points*, pp. 162-63.

work at it."[114] And many A.A. sources quoted the verse in the Book of James which confirmed the effectiveness of prayer:

> The effectual fervent prayer of a righteous man availeth much (James 5:16).[115]

A.A. sources also quoted from 1 John:

> And this is the confidence that we have in him, that, if we ask any thing according to his will, he heareth us: And if we know that he hear us, whatsoever we ask, we know that we have the petitions that we desired of him (1 John 5:14-15).[116]

Eleventh Step Guidance Elements

In one sense, the Eleventh Step (as the Big Book presents the instructions for taking it) contains four elements: (1) *In the evening, before retiring* the alcoholic is to review his or her day, essentially to see how well the Tenth Step was practiced. Then ask forgiveness where there were mistakes or failures. And see what can be done to improve the situation for the future. (2) *In the morning, on awakening*, he or she is to ask for the guidance of God at that time *and* for the rest of the day. (3) *For spiritual growth*, there is to be prayer, meditation, study of "helpful books," and religious observances if the latter are part of one's belief system. (d) *In times of stress throughout the day*, he or she is to deal with agitation and doubt by turning to God for direction and strength.

---

[114] Big Book, pp. 85-86.

[115] Holm, *The Runner's Bible*, p. 62; *The Upper Room* for 8/19/35; Fosdick, *The Meaning of Faith*, p. 190; *The Meaning of Prayer*, pp. 157-58; Walter, *Soul Surgery*, p. 29; Macmillan, *Seeking and Finding*, p. 128; Roger Hicks, *How to Read the Bible* (London: Moral Re-Armament, n.d.), p. 35; Dick B., *Anne Smith's Journal*, pp 36-37.

[116] Holm, *The Runner's Bible*, p. 64; Clark, *I Will Lift Up Mine Eyes*, p. 24; Dick B., *The Oxford Group & A.A.*, p. 162.

1. The End of Day Review. We have already dealt with what we believe were A.A.'s Tenth Step Biblical origins and here need only to point to 1 John 1:9 as a source for the idea that God will forgive *future* shortcomings as they occur. In its Eleventh Step instructions, the Big Book states: "After making our review we ask God's forgiveness and inquire what corrective measures should be taken."[117] On this subject of forgiveness, the Good Book states:

> And the prayer of faith shall save the sick, and the Lord shall raise him up; and if he have committed sins, they shall be forgiven him (James 5:15).[118]

> But if we walk in the light, as he is in the light, we have fellowship one with another, and the blood of Jesus Christ his Son cleanseth us from all sin (1 John 1:7).[119]

> If we confess our sins, he is faithful and just to forgive us *our* sins, and to cleanse us from all unrighteousness (1 John 1:9).[120]

2. Morning Quiet Time and Guidance. The "Morning Watch," or "Quiet Time," as it was called in the Oxford Group, had ancient origins in the Book of Psalms. The verse most commonly said to be the origin of the "morning watch" idea was Psalm 5:3:

---

[117] Big Book, p. 86. See also the Big Book discussion on page 70 concerning sex conduct which falls "short of the chosen ideal." The text adds: "If we are sorry for what we have done, and have the honest desire to let God take us to better things, we believe we will be forgiven and will have learned our lesson."

[118] Holm, *The Runner's Bible*, p. 114; Fosdick, *The Meaning of Faith*, p. 190.

[119] Chambers, *My Utmost for His Highest*, p. 361; Howard, *Frank Buchman's Secret*, p. 109; Miles Phillimore, *Just for Today*, (Privately published pamphlet, 1940) p. 7; Almond, *Foundations for Faith*, p. 15.

[120] Almond, *Foundations for Faith*, p. 13.

My voice shalt thou hear in the morning, O Lord; in the morning will I direct *my prayer* unto thee, and will look up.[121]

There was another verse from the Book of James that was frequently quoted concerning the importance of going to God for wisdom and guidance:

If any of you lack wisdom, let him ask of God, that giveth to all *men* liberally, and upbraideth not; and it shall be given him (James 1:5).[122]

And there were an immense number of Bible verses, segments, and ideas that supported the belief that God does guide and provide when His will is sought in the Bible or listened to.[123]

The following are precise biblical references to revelation from God:

For I [the Apostle Paul] neither received it [my gospel] of man, neither was I taught *it*, but by revelation of Jesus Christ (Galatians 1:12).[124]

All scripture *is* given by inspiration of God . . . (2 Timothy 3:16).[125]

---

[121] Holm, *The Runner's Bible*, p. 158; *The Upper Room* for 5/9/35, 7/1/35, 7/22/37; Fosdick, *The Meaning of Prayer*, p. 75.

[122] Holm, *The Runner's Bible*, p. 51; Fosdick, *The Meaning of Prayer*, p. 118; *The Meaning of Faith*, p. 239; Clark, *I Will Lift Up Mine Eyes*, p. 137.

[123] Oxford Group Founder Frank Buchman's biographer said, for example: "To Sam Shoemaker in 1920, Buchman wrote a seven-page foolscap letter, citing a formidable array of Biblical and theological authority for the practice" [listening to God]. Garth Lean, *On the Tail of a Comet: The Life of Frank Buchman* (Colorado Springs, CO: Helmers & Howard, 1988), p. 75

[124] Streeter, *The God Who Speaks*, p. 91; Macmillan, *Seeking and Finding*, p. 140.

[125] See discussion as to Dwight L. Moody, the evangelist, in Dick B., *The Oxford Group & A.A.*, p. 44.

For to one is given by the Spirit the word of wisdom; to another
the word of knowledge by the same Spirit . . . (1 Corinthians
12:8).[126]

For the prophecy came not in old time by the will of man: but
holy men of God spake *as they were* moved by the Holy Ghost
(2 Peter 1:21).[127]

The following were the better known verses quoted to show that
God guides and provides:

Trust in the Lord with all thine heart; and lean not unto thine
own understanding. In all thy ways acknowledge him, and he
shall direct thy paths (Proverbs 3:5-6).[128]

I will instruct thee and teach thee in the way which thou shalt
go: I will guide thee with mine eye (Psalm 32:8).[129]

Commit thy way unto the Lord; Trust also in him; and he shall
bring *it* to pass (Psalm 37:5).[130]

---

[126] Streeter, *The God Who Speaks*, p. 123; compare Holm, *The Runner's Bible*, p. 138

[127] Holm, *The Runner's Bible*, p. 18.

[128] *The Upper Room* for 5/15/35, 10/17/35; Holm, *The Runner's Bible*, pp. 39, 41, 61, 126; Tileston, *Daily Strength for Daily Needs*, p. 31; Clark, *The Soul's Sincere Desire*, p. 10; *I Will Lift Up Mine Eyes*, pp. 9, 28, 89, 151; Brown, *The Venture of Belief*, p. 40; Streeter, *The God Who Speaks*, p. 135; Benson, *The Eight Points*, p. 81.

[129] Drummond, *The Ideal Life*, p. 282; Wright, *The Will of God*, p. 9; Streeter, *The God Who Speaks*, p. 115; Benson, *The Eight Points*, p. 80; Holm, *The Runner's Bible*, p. 128; Tileston, *Daily Strength for Daily Needs*, p. 184; *The Upper Room* for 4/22/35.

[130] Holm, *The Runner's Bible*, pp. 127, 136; Clark, *I Will Lift Up Mine Eyes*, p. 28; Benson, *The Eight Points*, p. 81; Samuel M. Shoemaker, Jr., *The Experiment of Faith* (New York: Harper & Brothers, 1957), pp. 28-29; *How You Can Find Happiness* (New York: E. P. Dutton, 1947), p. 149; *The Upper Room* for 11/9/35, 9/25/38, 11/3/38.

For as many as are led by the Spirit of God, they are the sons of God (Romans 8:14).[131]

But as it is written, Eye hath not seen, nor ear heard, neither have entered into the heart of man, the things which God hath prepared for them that love him (1 Corinthians 2:9).[132]

For we walk by faith, not by sight (2 Corinthians 5:7).[133]

But the wisdom that is from above is first pure, then peaceable, gentle, *and* easy to be intreated, full of mercy and good fruits, without partiality, and without hypocrisy (James 3:17).[134]

As to receiving God's wisdom, A.A.'s sources suggested getting quiet, listening, and expecting to *receive*: i.e., "Speak, Lord, thy servant heareth." Not "Hear Lord, thy servant speaketh."[135]

The Big Book said: "We relax and take it easy. We don't struggle. We are often surprised how the right answers come . . ." (p. 86). A.A.'s sources for these ideas were:

Be still, and know that I *am* God (Psalm 46:10).[136]

---

[131] *What is the Oxford Group?*, p. 65; Jack C. Winslow, *Why I Believe in the Oxford Group* (London: Hodder & Stoughton, 1934), p. 39.

[132] *What is the Oxford Group?*, p. 65; Lean, *Cast Out Your Nets*, p. 30; Dick B., *The Akron Genesis*, p. 100; Holm, *The Runner's Bible*, p. 142.

[133] *What is the Oxford Group?*, p. 67.

[134] Holm, *The Runner's Bible*, p. 46; Wright, *The Will of God*, p. 167; Clark, *I Will Lift Up Mine Eyes*, p. 63; *The Upper Room* for 9/25/35.

[135] See Shoemaker, *National Awakening*, p. 86; Benson, *The Eight Points*, p. 66.

[136] Chambers, *My Utmost for His Highest*, p. 53; Holm, *The Runner's Bible*, p. 112; Howard Rose, *The Quiet Time*; Brown, *The Venture of Belief*, p. 37; Benson, *The Eight Points*, pp. 63, 68, 72, 87; *The Upper Room* for 6/23/35, 9/7/35, 1/16/36 or 1/16/39, 3/20/36 or 3/20/39, 4/10/37, 7/3/37, 12/13/38.

Speak, Lord; for thy servant heareth (1 Samuel 3:9).[137]

Lord, what wilt thou have me to do? (Acts 9:6).[138]

What shall I do, Lord? (Acts 22:10).[139]

3. Further Work for Spiritual Growth. Big Book "spirituality" did not end with surrender, prayer, or meditation. It suggested spiritual *growth*—through work with one's priest, minister, or rabbi; and study of "helpful books" (p. 87). Anne Smith mentioned these.[140] For her, the Bible was "the main Source Book of all."[141] Support for these aids to growth was certainly suggested by the following source verses:

> Study to shew thyself approved unto God, a workman that needeth not to be ashamed, rightly dividing the word of truth (2 Timothy 2:15).[142]

---

[137] Tileston, *Daily Strength for Daily Needs*, p. 157; Fosdick, *The Meaning of Prayer*, p. 66; Shoemaker, *Children of the Second Birth*, p. 16; *The Church Can Save the World*, p. 30; *National Awakening*, pp. 78, 83, 86, 88; *God's Control*, pp. 115-16; 121; Cecil Rose, *When Man Listens* (New York: Oxford University Press, 1937), p. 30; Foot, *Life Began Yesterday*, p. 4; Jack C. Winslow, *When I Awake* (London: Hodder & Stoughton, 1938), p. 48; Bremer Hofmeyr, *How to Listen* (New York: Moral Re-Armament, n.d.), p. 1; K. D. Belden, *Reflections on Moral Re-Armament* (London: Grosvenor, 1983), p. 35; Benson, *The Eight Points*, p. 66; *The Upper Room* for 4/2/37; Dick B., *The Akron Genesis*, pp. 95-96.

[138] Drummond, *The Ideal Life*, p. 306; Shoemaker, *A Young Man's View of the Ministry*, p. 80; *Religion That Works*, p. 65; Dick B., *Anne Smith's Journal*, p 124; *The Upper Room* for 6/5/36 or 6/5/39.

[139] Shoemaker, *Confident Faith*, pp. 107, 110, 115; *How to Find God*, p. 10; *Extraordinary Living for Ordinary Men* (Michigan: Zondervan, 1965), pp. 40-44, 46, 48.

[140] Dick B., *Anne Smith's Journal*, p. 83.

[141] Dick B., *Anne Smith's Journal*, p. 60.

[142] Tileston, *Daily Strength*, p. 68; *The Upper Room* for 4/27/38, 9/20/38. *Going through the Steps* said: "Read the Bible . . . know the Word of God so that you will understand it when you meditate." Clarence S., (NV: Roger Bunn, n.d.), p. 7.

Search the scriptures . . . (John 5:39).[143]

And ye shall know the truth, and the truth shall make you free (John 8:32).[144]

4. When Agitated and Doubtful. The Big Book did not end its Eleventh Step instructions with the end-of-the-day review, morning prayer and meditation, and suggestions for spiritual growth. For the major spiritual battles occur *all through the day.*[145] As to these situations, the Big Book suggested continued reliance on the guidance of God, stating:

> As we go through the day we pause, when agitated or doubtful, and ask for the right thought or action. We constantly remind ourselves we are no longer running the show, humbly saying to ourselves many times each day "Thy will be done." We are then in much less danger of excitement, fear, anger, worry, self-pity, or foolish decisions. We become much more efficient. We do not tire so easily, for we are not burning up energy foolishly as we did when we were trying to arrange life to suit ourselves (pp. 87-88).

And there were some well-accepted and much relied upon Biblical precedents for this thinking:

> Be careful [anxious] for nothing; but in everything by prayer and supplication with thanksgiving let your requests be made known unto God. And the peace of God, which passeth all

---

[143] Holm, *The Runner's Bible*, p. 51; *The Upper Room* for 8/12/38; Dick B., *New Light on Alcoholism*, p. 432.

[144] Holm, *The Runner's Bible*, pp. 46, 107; Clark, *I Will Lift Up Mine Eyes*, p. 58; *The Upper Room* for 5/20/36, 6/28/36.

[145] See Ephesians 6:10-18; and discussion of the spiritual battle by Shoemaker, *God's Control*, pp. 27-32; and Clark, *I Will Lift Up Mine Eyes*, p. 38.

understanding, shall keep your hearts and minds through Christ Jesus (Philippians 4:6-7).[146]

Take no thought for [be not anxious about] your life, what ye shall eat, or what ye shall drink; nor yet for your body, what ye shall put on. . . . for your heavenly Father knoweth that ye have need of all these things. But seek ye first the kingdom of God, and his righteousness; and all these things shall be added unto you (Matthew 6:25, 32-33).[147]

Thou wilt keep *him* in perfect peace, *whose* mind *is* stayed on *thee*: because he trusteth in thee (Isaiah 26:3).[148]

Step Twelve, Awakening, Witness, Practice of Principles

[Step Twelve: Having had a spiritual awakening as the result of these steps, we tried to carry this message to alcoholics, and to practice these principles in all our affairs.]

In one sense, the Twelfth Step has three elements: (1) The spiritual awakening which occurs when the alcoholic has taken the previous eleven Steps; (2) The message of hope as to such a spiritual awakening that he or she is to carry to another alcoholic; (3) The

---

[146] Holm, *The Runner's Bible*, pp. 61, 115, 147, 155; Tileston, *Daily Strength for Daily Needs*, pp. 53, 361; *The Upper Room* for 10/7/35, 10/20/35, 11/24/35; Fosdick, *The Meaning of Prayer*, p. 72; Clark, *I Will Lift Up Mine Eyes*, p. 93.

[147] Tileston, *Daily Strength for Daily Needs*, p. 61; Chambers, *My Utmost for His Highest*, p. 144; *Studies in the Sermon on the Mount*, pp. 54-57; Fosdick, *The Meaning of Faith*, pp. 192-93; Holm, *The Runner's Bible*, p. 144; *The Upper Room* for 5/10/37; Glover, *The Jesus of History*, p. 91; Streeter, *The God Who Speaks*, p. 81; E. Stanley Jones, *The Christ of the Mount*, p. 200; Dick B., *The Akron Genesis*, pp. 91-92.

[148] Holm, *The Runner's Bible*, pp. 112, 145; Tileston, *Daily Strength for Daily Needs*, p. 321; *The Upper Room* for 6/30/35, 7/13/35; 9/15/35; 10/22/35; 10/20/37; Clark, *The Soul's Sincere Desire*, pp. 10, 83; *I Will Lift Up Mine Eyes*, p. 93; Dick B., *The Akron Genesis*, pp. 91-92.

practice of the principles he or she has learned from the Steps and is to apply in all of life's affairs.

The Spiritual Awakening

There are many possible definitions of A.A.'s "spiritual awakening." It was described as a spiritual "experience" in the First Edition of the Big Book.[149] And the terms "spiritual experience" and "spiritual awakening" are both Oxford Group expressions.[150] For the author, at least, based on his own experience and much language in the Big Book, a spiritual experience has meant to him consciousness and *knowledge* of the power and presence of God in his life.[151] Another less easily understood expression for this consciousness was "God Consciousness."[152]

Early AAs and their spiritual sources referred to several Biblical segments dealing with the change in attitude and receipt of power that had entered their lives as the result of their conversion experiences:

> But ye shall receive power, after that the Holy Ghost is come upon you: and ye shall be witnesses unto me both in Jerusalem,

---

[149] See discussion in Appendix II of the Third Edition, pp. 569-70.

[150] Dick B., *The Oxford Group & A.A.*, pp. 276-77.

[151] See Big Book, pp. 25, 47, 51, 56, 63, 130, 162, 164; Kitchen, *I Was a Pagan*, pp. 157, 68; Brown, *The Venture of Belief*, pp. 24-26; Samuel M. Shoemaker, Jr., *With the Holy Spirit and with Fire* (New York: Harper & Brothers, 1960), p. 27. For other Oxford Group ideas expressions for the experience, see Dick B., *The Oxford Group & A.A.*, pp. 276-77.

[152] Big Book, p. 570; Begbie, *Life Changers*, pp. 41, 20; Philip Leon, *The Philosophy of Courage or the Oxford Group Way* (New York: Oxford University Press, 1939), pp. 110-11; Kitchen, *I Was a Pagan*, pp. 41, 75; Robert H. Murray, *Group Movements Throughout the Ages* (New York: Harper & Brothers, 1935), p. 349; Shoemaker, *Twice-Born Ministers*, p. 123; *How to Become a Christian*, p. 52; Clark, *The Soul's Sincere Desire*, p. 47.

and in all Judaea, and in Samaria, and unto the uttermost part of the earth (Acts 1:8).[153]

And when they had prayed, the place was shaken where they were assembled together; and they were all filled with the Holy Ghost, and they spake the word of God with boldness. . . . And with great power gave the apostles witness of the resurrection of the Lord Jesus: and great grace was upon them all (Acts 4:31, 33).[154]

I beseech you therefore, brethren, by the mercies of God, that ye present your bodies a living sacrifice, holy, acceptable unto God, *which is* your reasonable service. And be not conformed to this world: but be ye transformed by the renewing of your mind, that ye may prove what *is* that good, and acceptable, and perfect, will of God (Romans 12:1-2).[155]

Therefore if any man *be* in Christ, *he is* a new creature: old things are passed away; behold, all things are become new (2 Corinthians 5:17).[156]

[153] Holm, *The Runner's Bible*, p. 16; *The Upper Room* for 6/9/35, 11/12/35, 4/23/37, 10/29/37, 6/6/38, 12/31/38; Benson, *The Eight Points*, p. 101; Streeter, *The God Who Speaks*, p. 111; compare Dick B., *Anne Smith's Journal*, p. 22.

[154] Shoemaker, *Religion That Works*, pp. 66-76; Macmillan, *Seeking and Finding*, pp. 162-63.

[155] *The Upper Room* for 12/17/35, 4/18/63, 4/4/38; Tileston, *Daily Strength for Daily Needs*, pp. 98, 196; Holm, *The Runner's Bible*, p. 106; Fosdick, *The Meaning of Faith*, p. 219; Phillimore, *Just for Today* (portion containing a study of Romans chapter 12); Hicks, *How to Read the Bible*, p. 32; Dick B., *Anne Smith's Journal*, pp. 46, 77-78, 108, 132; Chambers, *Studies in the Sermon on the Mount*, pp. 23, 60.

[156] *The Upper Room* for 7/16/35, 5/1/38, 7/29/38; Holm, *The Runner's Bible*, p. 93; Chambers, *My Utmost for His Highest*, pp. 297, 317; Hicks, *How to Read the Bible*, p. 32; Streeter, *The God Who Speaks*, p. 111; E. Stanley Jones, *The Christ of the Mount*, p. 107. See also Dick B., *The Akron Genesis*, p. 205, containing a discussion of the verse by early AA, William V. H. in *Going through the Steps*, Clarence S. quoted this verse—saying, "You are Reborn." (NV: Roger Bunn, n.d.), pp. 6-7.

Now unto him that is able to do exceeding abundantly above all that we ask or think, according to the power that worketh in us (Ephesians 3:20).[157]

Carrying the Message

As part of the AA's Twelfth Step, there was the critical importance of witnessing, of carrying to another the message of deliverance. "You have to give it away to keep it," said the early AAs and their sources.[158] Action was called for; and the following Bible verses spelled out the duty to get into action and witness:

And he [Jesus] saith unto them, Follow me, and I will make you fishers of men (Matthew 4:19).[159]

But wilt thou know, O vain man, that faith without works is dead? (James 2:20).[160]

Having therefore obtained the help of God, I continue unto this day, witnessing both to small and great, saying none other things than those things which the prophets and Moses did say should come: That Christ should suffer, *and* that he should be the first that should rise from the dead, and shew light unto the people, and to the Gentiles (Acts 26:22-32).[161]

---

[157] For the frequency of Oxford Group founder Frank Buchman's reference to this verse, see Dick B., *The Oxford Group & A.A.*, pp. 369-70; Phillimore, *Just for Today*, pp. 12-13.

[158] See Dick B., *The Oxford Group & A.A.*, p. 294; *Anne Smith's Journal*, pp. 69, 65, 72-73, 85, 121, 138; *New Light on Alcoholism*, p. 168.

[159] Shoemaker, *Realizing Religion*, p. 82; *Twice-Born Ministers*, p. 16; Almond, *Foundations for Faith*, 2d ed., p. 25; Glenn Clark, *Fishers of Men* (Boston: Little, Brown, 1928); Dick B., *New Light on Alcoholism*, pp. 139, 202.

[160] Big Book, pp. 14-15, 76, 88, 93; *What Is The Oxford Group?*, p. 36; *DR. BOB*, p. 71; *Pass It On*, p. 147; Nell Wing, *Grateful to Have Been There*, pp. 70-71.

[161] *What Is The Oxford Group?*, p. 25; Dick B., *Anne Smith's Journal*, p. 131.

Now then we are ambassadors for Christ, as though God did beseech *you* by us: we pray *you* in Christ's stead, be ye reconciled to God (2 Corinthians 5:20).[162]

Practicing the Principles

Finally, there were spiritual principles to be practiced in daily living. Principles from the Sermon on the Mount, from 1 Corinthians 13, from the Book of James, from the Oxford Group's Four Absolutes, and from a number of other biblical sources as well.

The Big Book really does not specifically list the "principles" or describe the "works" that are to the follow the attaining of "faith." But we believe the following are *among* the principles the Big Book suggests should be practiced: (1) Relying upon God (Big Book, pp. 46, 50, 51-53, 68, 80, 98, 100, 120); (2) Being rigorously honest (pp. 58, 64, 67, 69, 73, 84, 86); (3) Eliminating selfishness and self-centeredness (pp. 67-68, 84, 86, 145); (4) Eliminating resentment, jealousy, and envy (pp. 64-67, 84, 86, 145); (5) Eliminating fear (pp. 67-68, 84, 86, 145); (6) Practicing patience, tolerance, kindliness, understanding, love, forgiveness, and helpfulness to others (pp. 20, 77, 83, 84, 97, 118, 153). And there are additional Twelfth Step principles embodying ideas of humility, forgiveness, and service (Big Book, pp. 73, 77). Also, stressing overcoming the bondage of self, sharing by confession, making restitution, reconciling, seeking guidance, and so on (Big Book, pp. 63, 73, 76, 77, 85-88).

The Rev. Harry Almond said, of the biblical principles of the Oxford Group (which contained many of A.A.'s roots): "A good place to start is with the Ten Commandments." In modern words, Almond summarized them as follows: (1) You shall have no other gods before me. (2) You shall not make for yourself a graven image . . . or . . . likeness. You shall not bow down to them or

---

[162] *What Is The Oxford Group?*, p. 35; *The Upper Room* for 8/28/38; Dick B., *Anne Smith's Journal*, p. 131.

serve them. (3) You shall not take the name of the Lord your God in vain. (4) Remember the sabbath day, to keep it holy. (5) Honor your father and mother. (6) You shall not kill. (7) You shall not commit adultery. (8) You shall not steal. (9) You shall not bear false witness against your neighbor. (10) You shall not covet.[163]

And there were the Oxford Group's own spiritual principles of absolute honesty, purity, unselfishness, and love from the Oxford Group's Four Absolutes, which we have already discussed.

As we have also discussed at length, Professor Drummond in his *The Greatest Thing in the World*—which was widely read and recommended in early A.A.—summarized the "love elements" of 1 Corinthians 13 as follows: (1) *Patience.* (2) *Kindness.* (3) *Generosity.* (4) *Humility.* (5) *Courtesy.* (6) *Unselfishness.* (7) *Good Temper.* (8) *Guilelessness.* (9) *Sincerity.*[164] These, said Drummond *and* Dr. Bob, were vital elements in living the principles which Dr. Bob said could be simmered down to "love and service."[165]

Many A.A. principles, detailed elsewhere, came from the Book of James and include: (1) Patience. (2) Seeking the wisdom of God. (3) Avoiding temptation. (4) Telling the truth. (5) Avoiding anger. (6) Studying the word of God and "doing" it. (7) Helping the unfortunate. (8) Loving your neighbor. (9) Avoiding adultery and killing. (10) Backing up faith with works. (11) Bridling the tongue. (12) Avoiding envy and strife. (13) Avoiding lying. (14) Avoiding selfish lusts. (15) Avoiding pride. (16) Submitting to God. (17) Purifying hearts. (18) Being humble. (19) Avoiding speaking evil of another. (20) Doing good. (21) Avoiding

---

[163] Almond, *Foundations for Faith*, 2d ed., p. 10. For the Ten Commandments themselves, see Exodus 20:3-17; Deuteronomy 5:6-21.

[164] Drummond, *The Greatest Thing in the World*, pp. 26-27; 1 Corinthians 13:4-6. See comment in Benson, *The Eight Points*, p. 47: "The perfect life is simply a life of perfect love. Love is all in all. Jesus said that the whole law is summed up in the one word *love*. It embraces everything, as St. Paul teaches in his glorious hymn to love" (1 Corinthians 13). See similar discussions in Clark, *I Will Lift Up Mine Eyes*, pp. 65-66; Dick B., *Anne Smith's Journal*, p. 131.

[165] *DR. BOB*, p. 338.

riches for the sake of riches. (22) Avoiding grudges. (23) Avoiding swearing and false oaths. (24) Relying on prayer. (25) Confessing faults. (26) Converting sinners from the error of their ways.

The following A.A. principles, detailed elsewhere, seem to have come from the Sermon on the Mount: (1) Humility. (2) Compassion. (3) Meekness. (4) Spotless conduct. (5) Making peace with enemies. (6) Harmonizing actions with God's will. (7) Overcoming resentments. (8) Making restitution. (9) Avoiding retaliation. (10) Conducting prayers and good works anonymously. (11) Forgiving. (12) Seeking God first. (13) Utilizing self-examination. (14) Doing the will of God. (15) Being rigorously honest. (16) Avoiding evil. (17) Being unselfish. (18) Loving.[166]

---

[166] See also Almond, *Foundations for Faith*, pp. 10-11, setting forth additional Oxford Group views of "Sin—the Disease" and urging avoidance of conduct such as murder, adultery, deceit, envy, slander, pride, theft, and greed.

Part Four

A Vision for You

The Process

[Speaking of Dr. Bob, AA Number Two] "Some time later, and just as he thought he was getting control of his liquor situation, he went on a roaring bender. For him, this was the spree to end all sprees. He saw that he would have to face his problems squarely that God might give him mastery." . . . [Speaking of Bill Dotson, AA Number Three] "Next day found the prospect more receptive. He had been thinking it over. 'Maybe you're right,' he said. 'God ought to be able to do anything. . . .' On the third day the lawyer gave his life to the care and direction of his Creator, and said he was perfectly willing to do anything necessary. . . . [H]e found God—and in finding God had found himself. That was in June, 1935. He never drank again. He too has become a respected and useful member of his community. He has helped other men recover, and is a power in the church from which he was long absent." ". . . These men [the first, four successful members] had found something brand new in life. [Speaking of the growing fellowship members] Though they knew they must help other alcoholics if they would remain sober, that motive became secondary. It was transcended by the happiness they found in giving themselves for others. . . . They knew they had a host of new friends; it seemed they had known these strangers always. They had seen miracles, and one was to come to them. They had visioned the Great Reality—their loving and All Powerful Creator. . . . See that your relationship with Him is right, and great events will come to pass for you and countless others." (*Alcoholics Anonymous*, 3rd ed., pp. 155-164).

The Cure. . . . Yes, Cure!

"The medicine the AAs use is unique. Though it should be all-powerful, it has never been tried with any consistent success against any other major sickness. The medicine is no triumph of chemical science; has needed no billion dollar scientific foundation to discover it; does not come in capsules or syringes. It is free as air—with this provision: that the patients it cures have to nearly die before they can bring themselves to take it. The AAs' medicine is God and God alone. This is their discovery" (Medical writer Paul de Kruif, July, 1991, *Volume II, Best of the Grapevine*, pp. 202-03).

"There is a definite religious element here," Bill said. "I pray and I feel released. He emphasized that Divine Aid was A.A.'s greatest asset. . ." (The Tidings, March 26, 1943—a Roman Catholic newspaper reporting Bill and Bob's talks to 4500 alcoholics, their friends, and relatives at the Shrine Auditorium in Los Angeles).

11

Can There Be Pioneer Groups in Today's A.A.?

"There is no reason why a group of A.A.'s shouldn't get together for Bible study; no reason at all why a group of A.A.'s in a church should not associate themselves into a sort of spiritual kindergarten fellowship, into which anyone might be invited. As a matter of fact, I am anxious to see this sort of thing tried." [Writing, as above, to Sam Shoemaker, Bill Wilson added] "Have you ever thought of inaugurating something like this in your own congregation? Could you open up your church basement to a group operating on strictly A.A. principles? This would be a spiritual kindergarten of the ABC kind. No theology involved" (Letter to Sam Shoemaker, dated May 2, 1958, located in the Episcopal Church Archives, Austin, Texas).

In the foregoing letter, Wilson was writing Shoemaker after the death of both Dr. Bob and Anne Smith. Wilson often spoke about his own work as being in a "spiritual kindergarten," while Dr. Bob's was far more advanced. Wilson's remark should be understood in the light of his own lack of experience with, and reading of the Bible, whereas early A.A. *stressed* Bible study in its meetings, its Quiet Times, and in the homes of its families.

We repeat below portions of the remarks Bill and Bob made to 4,500 alcoholics, their friends, and relatives at the Shrine Auditorium in Los Angeles on March 20, 1943 (as reported on page 17 of the March 26, 1943, issue of *The TIDINGS*):

195

An alcoholic, Bill said, is a fellow who is "trying to get religion out of a bottle," when what he really wants is unity within himself and unity with God. . . .

Alcoholics Anonymous recommends a return to religion, resumption of church attendance.

"There is a definite religious element here," Bill said. "I pray and I feel released."

He emphasized that Divine Aid was A.A.'s greatest asset.

[Dr. Bob said:] "Read religious literature. Resume church attendance, cultivate the habit of prayer, and transmit the desires and principles of Alcoholics Anonymous to others." He particularly emphasized reading the Bible.

Facts about the Earliest Group—Akron No. 1

Dr. Bob said this:

At that point, our stories didn't amount to anything to speak of. When we started in on Bill D., we had no Twelve Steps, either; we had no Traditions. But we were convinced that the answer to our problems was in the Good Book. To some of us older ones, the parts that we found absolutely essential were the Sermon on the Mount, the thirteenth chapter of First Corinthians, and the Book of James (*The Co-Founders of Alcoholics Anonymous*, p. 13).

It wasn't until 1938 that the teachings and efforts and studies that had been going on were crystallized in the form of the Twelve Steps. I didn't write the Twelve Steps. I had nothing to do with the writing of them. But I think I probably had something to do with them indirectly. After my June 10th episode, Bill came to live at our house and stayed for about three months. There was hardly a night that we didn't stay up until two or three o'clock talking. It would be hard for me to conceive that, during these nightly discussions around our kitchen table, nothing was said that influenced the writing of the Twelve Steps. We already had the basic ideas, though not in terse and tangible form. We got them, as I said, as a result of our study of the Good Book. We *must* have had them. Since then, we have learned from experience that they are very important in maintaining sobriety. We *were* maintaining sobriety—therefore, we must have had them (*The Co-Founders of Alcoholics Anonymous*, p. 14).

Members of Alcoholics Anonymous begin the day with a prayer for strength and a short period of Bible reading. They find the basic messages they need in the Sermon on the Mount, in Corinthians and the Book of James (Dick B., *The Good Book and The Big Book*, p. 21).

Both Dr. Bob and Bill frequently said that Jesus' Sermon on the Mount (Matthew 5-7) contained the underlying philosophy of A.A. At every meeting, there was reading from the Bible (*DR. BOB and the Good Oldtimers*, p. 142). The Bible was stressed as reading material (*Dr. Bob*, pp. 139-41). The following are specific recollections by oldtimers of three different people, who led the first part of pioneer meetings, reading from the Bible before them:

Alex M. said [of the meetings at a later point], "Doc talked much at regular meetings. He would come just at a regular meeting and speak. About 40 minutes, and he was a simple talker. He had the Bible in front of him and wasn't afraid to read from it. It [the Bible] was at King School. It was always on the podium" (Dick B., *The Akron Genesis of Alcoholics Anonymous*, p. 189).

Wally G. said, "I remember the first meeting I attended was led by Dick S. He opened the meeting with a short prayer, read a passage from the Bible which I do not recall, and talked about that in its relationship to the everyday life of those present" (*The Akron Genesis*, p. 189).

Earl T. [who founded A.A. in Chicago] said, "I remember most distinctly the first meeting that I attended—Bill D. [A.A. Number Three] sat with the Holy Bible in his lap. The meeting had been opened with a prayer. Bill read excerpts from the

Bible and translated them into everyday life. After half an hour
of this, the meeting was thrown open to everyone in the room
and they in turn picked up some of these passages from the
Bible that he had discussed and gave their interpretation" (*The
Akron Genesis*, p. 190).

There was regular quiet time and also discussion of biblical
topics The A.A. members of that time did not consider meetings
necessary to maintain sobriety. They were simply "desirable."
Morning devotion and "quiet time," however, were musts (*DR.
BOB*, p. 136).

Usually, the person who led the Wednesday meeting took
something from *The Upper Room* [the Methodist periodical
mentioned earlier] or some other literature as a subject.
Sometimes, they selected a theme such as "My Utmost Effort"
or "My Highest Goal." There would be a quiet time. Then
different people would tell something out of their own
experience (*DR. BOB*, p. 139).

The meeting picture was described in various ways. But invariably, the meetings opened with a prayer and with reading from the
Bible, whether from the Bible itself or from Scripture in the Bible
devotionals. Someone led the meetings and the ensuing discussions. There was quiet time, prayer, and listening for guidance.
Literature of the Oxford Group and other Christian literature was
discussed and passed out to those present or was exchanged. The
meeting closed with the Lord's Prayer. Bob E., an Akron oldtimer
whom Dr. Bob sponsored, rendered this description:

The general set up [of] a meeting was done by Dr. Smith & a
few others in an upstairs bed room just before the regular 8:30
meeting & it usually followed a page of the Upper Room which
was supplied to us by Ernie G.'s mother (@ 5 cents a piece) &
we all carried them. They fit in our side pocket, they were the
size of a *Reader's Digest* only not so thick. Each page was
called a "thought for the day." 1st there was a short quote of
scripture, next a short prayer, next the short story for the day

was read. Next if the group was still small enough we would
hold hands in a circle and have a short quiet time during which
we silently asked God for guidance. Then we shared or
witnessed whatever we felt guided to talk about, a problem or
an experience with a point worth sharing. If it didn't help
anybody it helped you. Then came instructions from Dr. Smith
& announcements and asking for help or suggestions in handling
a new man. (Letter from Bob E. to Nell Wing, dated March 14,
1975; see *The Akron Genesis*, pp. 197-98).

Many oldtimers told of their own quiet times and prayers, usually
accompanied by the guidance of the daily devotionals such as *The
Upper Room* or *The Runner's Bible* (See, for example, the
recollections of Bill Wilson, Henrietta D. [wife of A.A. No. 3],
William V. H., Wally G., Duke P., and Dick S., *The Akron
Genesis*, pp. 204-08). To which, Bill Wilson added:

I think there may have been times when we attributed it [the
many successes of Wally and Annabele G.] to their morning
meditation. I sort of always felt that something was lost from
A.A. when we stopped emphasizing the morning meditation
(*DR. BOB*, p. 178).

Rockefeller's Frank Amos (later an A.A. Trustee) described the
pioneer "Program" as follows:

1. An alcoholic must realize that he is an alcoholic, incurable
from a medical viewpoint, and that he must never again drink
anything with alcohol in it. 2. He must surrender himself
absolutely to God, realizing that in himself there is no hope. 3.
Not only must he want to stop drinking permanently, he must
remove from his life other sins such as hatred, adultery, and
others which frequently accompany alcoholism. Unless he will
do this absolutely, Smith and his associates refuse to work with
him. 4. He must have devotions every morning—a "quiet time"
of prayer and some reading from the Bible and other religious
literature. Unless this is faithfully followed, there is grave
danger of backsliding. 5. He must be willing to help other

alcoholics get straightened out. This throws up a protective barrier and strengthens his own willpower and convictions. 6. It is important, but not vital, that he meet frequently with other reformed alcoholics and form both a social and a religious comradeship. 7. Important, but not vital, that he attend some religious service at least once weekly (*DR. BOB*, p. 131).

The Arrival of Splinter Groups and Special Groups

Not long after A.A. published its textbook in the Spring of 1939 and grew in size, splinter groups and special groups grew as well. In Akron, AAs retained the Bible and the "Four Absolutes" of the Oxford Group. Then Dr. Bob's sponsee Clarence Snyder left Akron No. 1 and held the first meeting (called Alcoholics Anonymous) in Cleveland. The masthead of the *Cleveland Central Bulletin* highlighted the Oxford Group's "Four Absolutes." And that messenger for the Cleveland A.A. groups frequently quoted Scripture. Furthermore, writing to Clarence Snyder (founder of Cleveland A.A. in May, 1939), Bill Wilson said:

> You folks who started the Cleveland group had been under the Oxford Group influence at T. Henry's. When you shifted to Cleveland, you merely changed your address and then had a meeting composed of alcoholics only. In fact, you carried the Oxford Group Absolutes with you and have used them ever since (Letter, Wilson to Snyder, March 20, 1957).

Thus while Cleveland A.A. grew by leaps and bounds, there was still the Bible-oriented Akron No. 1 led by Dr. Bob (and soon called the King School Group). Among the many new Cleveland A.A. groups, there was the Oxford Group influence of the Four Absolutes which obviously certainly through at least 1957; and literature is still distributed by Cleveland and Akron A.A. offices today that refers to the Four Absolutes and quotes Scripture. On January 15, 1945, writing on the stationary of The Alcoholic Foundation, National Headquarters—Alcoholics Anonymous, Bill

Wilson wrote the Rev. Sam Shoemaker, Jr. (whom Bill called a "co-founder" of A.A.):

> Saving some of our Catholic members and a few others, we are, as a group, pretty deficient on the prayer meditation side. Quite a number of older AAs run into a period of seeming spiritual bankruptcy, indeed, one might guess, by excessive activity not balanced by sufficient intake. Apparently it is possible to get very bad indigestion on a straight died of "good works." (Letter, Wilson to Sam Shoemaker, January 15, 1945, Episcopal Church Archives, Texas).

Speaking for himself only at that point, Wilson seemed to admit that there was a third influence in A.A. that had insufficient spiritual input and was deficient in prayer and meditation.

However, as early as April, 1946, Bill began pushing for adoption by A.A. of his "Twelve Traditions." About his proposed Traditions 5 and 10, Wilson wrote:

> 5. Each Alcoholics Anonymous group ought to be a spiritual entity *having but one primary purpose*—that of carrying its message to the alcoholic who still suffers.

> 10. No AA group or member should ever, *in such a way as to implicate AA*, express any opinion on outside controversial issues—particularly those of politics, alcohol reform or sectarian religion. The Alcoholics Anonymous groups oppose no one. Concerning such matters they can express no views whatever (from an article, dated April, 1946, reported in *The Language of the Heart*, pp. 22-23).

In September 1948, Bill wrote as to Tradition Ten:

> To this end, none could be more vital than our Tenth Tradition, for it deals with the subject of controversy—serious controversy. . . . Political controversy and reform by compulsion have reached an all-time high. And eternal, seemingly, are the flames of religious dissension (*The Language of the Heart*, p. 90).

On May 14, 1957, Wilson wrote the Roman Catholic priest Father John C. Ford, S.J., who was editing Bill's proposed *Alcoholics Anonymous Comes of Age* (soon to become official A.A. literature). Bill said:

> Another doubtful item had to do with the question of Catholic A.A. groups, Protestant A.A. groups, Republican A.A. groups, Democratic A.A. groups, etc. For good measure, I have added Communist A.A. groups. In an abstract way such groups would be no different from actors groups, priests groups, or carpenters groups. But in a mighty practical way, they *are* quite different. It is in the realms of religion and politics that men have usually gone mad—the twentieth century being a notable example. Political and religious groups have ideologies and dogma. The minute you hitch the A.A. name to Catholicism or Protestantism or Communism or what-have-you, you actually start to push around A.A.'s Tradition of no alliances or endorsements. Theoretically we shouldn't be specially endorsing priests, actors, or plumbers. But in practice such A.A. groups do no harm at all. To these kind of group names, nobody ever made much objection. It is generally recognized, too, that the vocational necessities of priests, actors, surgeons and the like, may really require private groups. After a careful consideration of whether to bring up the question of Catholic and Protestant groups, I feel that the risk of inviting controversy is less than would be the risk if I omitted an outright warning against religious and political endorsements.

> You will remember there was another spot in the manuscript where the Buddhists wanted to substitute the word "Good" for "God" in the Twelve Steps. Here I felt I could make only a partial accommodation. To begin with, the Steps are not enforceable upon anyone—they are only suggestions. A belief in the Steps or in God is not in any way a requisite for A.A. membership. Therefore we have no means of compelling anyone to stay away from A.A. because he does not believe in God or the Twelve Steps. . . . By practicing the program with "Good" in mind, they almost invariably come back to some kind of a concept of God—usually a personal God. Whether this will

happen to our Buddhist members, I don't know. But it certainly can't make the least difference to any of us what the Buddhists do with the Steps. The Steps are for everybody to take or leave alone as they wish, in whole or in part.

On May 2, 1958, Wilson wrote to his friend and mentor Sam Shoemaker as follows:

> Concerning your last inquiry, I might say that A.A. does have a species of splinter groups. . . . In A.A. these are of several kinds. For example, we have clubs, Half-Way Houses for derelict folk, and that sort of thing. Groups have also been formed for the special benefit of people with serious dual problems—narcotics, plus alcohol addiction, for example. Another sort of operation is the A.A. Retreat. You must know about the Cooks Forest business and there is a similar undertaking at San Francisco. The Catholic Church also provides several retreat facilities for members of A.A. . . . Although under Catholic auspices, they are pretty much A.A. affairs. Very often the retreat leader is a priest member of A.A.. . . . Older members also join in formal groups who wish to make spiritual progress by greater attention to deep analysis, prayer, and meditation. As you can see, these are not exactly splinter groups. But they do allow us to function in many fields of endeavor related to A.A. interests.
>
> So it is now pretty well established that groups of A.A.'s can do anything under the sun they wish, with these simple provisos: That they do not attach the name Alcoholics Anonymous to any of these groups, and that they do not use the A.A. name to secure publicity or raise money. If these conditions are carefully observed, there is no splintering effect whatever. There is no reason why a group of A.A.'s shouldn't get together for Bible study; no reason at all why a group of A.A.'s in a church should not associate themselves into a sort of spiritual kindergarten fellowship, into which anyone might be invited. As a matter of fact, I am anxious to see this sort of thing tried.

Have you ever thought of inaugurating something like this in your own congregation? Could you open up your church basement to a group operating on strictly A.A. principles? This would be a spiritual kindergarten of the ABC kind. No theology involved. It could be that many who are having theological difficulties would find that they disappear if they only had a good A.A. bath. You might find a lot of people coming upstairs for the complete treatment. Any number of individuals in A.A., especially the indifferent or agnostic sort, are doing the same thing, one by one.

A.A.'s Own Remarks to the Clergy (via Bill Wilson)

In the Episcopal Church Archives at Austin, Texas, in the Shoemaker collection, is a Draft # 1, January 31, 1961, that Wilson sent to Sam Shoemaker. Here are some of the comments in that proposed official A.A. publication (*A Clergyman Asks about Alcoholics Anonymous*):

> Many clergymen are already familiar with the informal Fellowship of Alcoholics Anonymous and with the Twelve Step program of recovery from Alcoholism. They know A.A. as a non-sectarian, non-denominational ally in their own efforts to help problem drinkers. . . .

> Alcoholics Anonymous is a fellowship of men and women who share their experience, strength and hope with each other that they may solve their common problem and help others to recover from alcoholism. The only requirement for membership is a desire to strop drinking. There are no dues or fees for A.A. membership; we are self-supporting through our own contributions. A.A. is not allied with any sect, denomination, politics, organization or institution; does not wish to engage in any controversy, neither endorses nor opposes any causes. Our primary purpose is to stay sober and help other alcoholics to achieve sobriety.

A.A. is not a religious society or movement in the *denominational* sense although the recovery program includes suggestions that reflect the spiritual insights of many spiritual leaders. . . . Members frequently describe A.A. as a "spiritual" program. They do *not* mean that it is in any way *sectarian or denominational*. . . . The Fellowship does not actively recruit adherents to a formal body of beliefs (emphasis added).

A.A. members are not asked to accept any formal creed or statement of beliefs beyond the admission that they have a drinking problem and want help. Members are free to interpret the A.A. recovery program, as expressed in the Twelve Suggested Steps, in any manner they choose.

As a Fellowship, A.A. welcomes alcoholics of all faiths and those who profess no faith. Locally, of course, each A.A. group is autonomous in all matters not affecting the welfare of the Society as a whole. Although no information on the religious composition of local groups has ever been sought by the General Service Office, it is possible that *in certain areas all members of a group may be members of the same faith*. Such a group would not be considered typical of "traditional" A.A., however (emphasis added).

It is also understandable that in a group where various faiths are represented, those alcoholics *who share the same communion may be drawn together for spiritual exercises distinctive to their faith*. So long as they do not jeopardize the integrity of the Twelve Step recovery program, these groupings would not be considered to violate A.A. Tradition (emphasis added).

Traditionally, any two or more alcoholics meeting together for purposes of sobriety may consider themselves an A.A. group, provided that, as a group, they are self-supporting and have no outside affiliation.

**Some Documented Practices and Statements
in A.A. after Dr. Bob's Death**

— A.A. is not a "religious" society.

— A.A. *groups* are not headed or sponsored by clergy.

— A.A. is non-sectarian.

— A.A. is non-denominational.

— A.A. is not affiliated with any outside church,
   denomination, or clergy.

— Any two alcoholics meeting together for sobriety may
   consider themselves an A.A. group.

— Such groups have been characterized as groups of priests,
   beginners, young people, men, women, gays and lesbians,
   atheists, lawyers, airline pilots, and doctors.

— The Bible has been read and is still studied in some A.A.
   groups.

— The Lord's Prayer (from Matthew 6:10) has typically
   marked the close of a group meeting.

— The "Serenity Prayer" which derives from Protestant
   Reinhold Niebuhr is commonly recited at the beginning of
   A.A. meetings.

— The "St. Francis Prayer" of Roman Catholic St. Francis
   is found in A.A. literature and recited at the close of some
   A.A. meetings.

— The song "Amazing Grace" was sung at the close of the International Convention of A.A. in Seattle in 1990.

— Two Roman Catholic Jesuits (Father John C. Ford, S.J., and Father Ed Dowling, S.J.), edited Bill Wilson's *Twelve Steps and Twelve Traditions* and his *Alcoholics Anonymous Comes of Age* (both Conference Approved publications of A.A. today).

— The Episcopal priest, Dr. Samuel M. Shoemaker, and the Roman Catholic priest, Father Edward Dowling, S.J., addressed A.A.'s International Convention in St. Louis in 1955. And Dr. Shoemaker, as well as the Roman Catholic priest, the Right Reverend Monsignor John J. Dougherty, addressed A.A.'s International Convention in Long Beach (1960).

— "Eleventh Step" prayer meetings, some with candlelight, are commonly held by some A.A. groups today.

The foregoing statements and practices–documented in other writings by this author–, among others, have been influential in causing several courts to rule that A.A. is a religious organization and that the courts, cannot under First Amendment Separation of Church and State principles, order attendance at A.A. and similar meetings. The items are mentioned here to demonstrate that study of the Bible, by itself, and in relation to A.A.'s Big Book and Steps, and with reference to A.A. history, can hardly be condemned today. The reader can judge this for himself of herself.

That there will be howls of protest and objection from some A.A. quarters seems quite probable. As just one example, in May, 1993, the "Chairperson of the Traditions Committee" of an Arizona Intergroup removed a meeting that studied Emmet Fox from the meeting list, with the approval of "the Steering Committee and endorsed by the Intergroup." But one need only ask what Dr. Bob would have said to that. In fact, when confronted with questions about the program, Dr. Bob's usual response was: "What does the Good Book say?" He also quoted Scripture freely in meetings and with reference to the program and pointed out that most A.A. slogans themselves come directly from the Bible. Such zealots as those in the Arizona group quite simply do not know their A.A. history or what our co-founders said.

What About Early A.A. Groups Today?
Good Book/Big Book Groups?

Suppose a group of today's AAs formed a group which utilizes the format of early A.A.? Suppose they wanted to study the Biblical roots of A.A.? Suppose they wanted to see and understand the Big Book language and the Twelve Steps in light of their biblical and Oxford Group origins? Suppose they just wanted to hear the Bible read?

The meeting might open with a Christian prayer. There would be reading from Scripture. There might be the reading of Christian devotionals such as *The Upper Room*, *My Utmost for His Highest*, *The Meaning of Prayer*, *The Runner's Bible*, and *Victorious Living*. There would be a discussion of topics from the devotionals. There would be a Quiet Time in which prayers to God and listening for guidance were involved. There might be surrenders to Jesus Christ. There might be group prayers for healing and elimination of "sins."

Tools might include the First Edition of the Big Book. Also, the presently available materials from Cleveland and Akron AA on the Four Absolutes and the guidelines. Also, a Big Book Step Guide such as *The Steps We Took* or *Twelve Steps and the Older Member*. Also a Big Book study guide such as *A Program for You*. Also, spiritual history books such as *The Good Book and The Big Book: A.A.'s Roots in the Bible* and *Turning Point: A History of Early A.A.'s Spiritual Roots and Successes*. Also, the King James Version of the Bible, *The Upper Room*, and the other devotionals mentioned above. And finally, A.A.'s *own DR. BOB and the Good Oldtimers*.

Would such a group bring down the wrath of A.A. General Services or a Trustee or a Delegate? Would such a group stir up controversy? Would such a group be subjected to criticism by other groups or by individual AAs or by A.A. "bleeding deacons?"

This is a certainly a real possibility.

Yet there is general acceptance—without such condemnation—in A.A. today of Gay and Lesbian Groups, Atheist Groups, Young People's Groups, Lawyers, Pilots, and priests groups, and so on? Such groups hardly represent "traditional" A.A. (whatever that is) whether that A.A. be of the formative years or today.

Is there any reason to suppose that a non-sectarian, non-denominational, non-affiliated, old-time A.A. group with God, Bible, prayer, quiet time, devotionals, surrenders, the Big Book, and the Twelve Steps would not survive in present-day A.A. when the period of yesteryear's maximum success rates in Akron and in Cleveland involved most if not all these items?

What's the Alternative?

Kick them out and/or let them go?

Well go they have! There are, outside of A.A., Al-Anon, N.A., and so on, "Christ-centered" 12 Step groups. There are Overcomers groups. There are Overcomers Outreach groups. There are Alcoholics for Christ groups. There are Alcoholics Victorious Groups. There are the dozens of other "anonymous" groups for people who do not meet the "singleness of purpose" litmus test in A.A. today. There are Roman Catholic retreats "for AAs." There are Christian retreats "for AAs and their families"—the latter sponsored by Clarence Snyder to the date of his death in the 1980's (Clarence being one of the 40 pioneers, the founder of Cleveland A.A., and a life-time supporter of Dr. Bob). Specific books on or about such groups are included in our Resources List.

More important than these facts is the substantial hunger among many AAs today for something other than "any god," "psychobabble," "group therapy," "child within," "self-help," foul language, and just plain "group depression" and "dumping" meetings. For these have become common in present-day Twelve Step groups, and they often give rise to criticism *in* A.A. and other publications.

Is an "old fashioned meeting" a real possibility today in A.A. for those who don't want to hear one language in their church and another in A.A.? Are meetings describing the early A.A. Christian Fellowship principles and practices a real possibility for those who feel lost when they mention God, the Bible, Jesus Christ, or church in many A.A. meetings today?

This booklet attempts to describe the factors involved in answering such questions. Neither the booklet nor its comments can in any way change the A.A. fellowship or the views of those in the fellowship or the well-known power of the New York office to pressure, publicize, and (in the case of Germany and Mexico) promulgate very punitive legal action, both civil and criminal. A.A.'s lawyers of today have teeth. And they use them—much to the consternation of many in the fellowship. And certainly not in keeping with the A.A. Tradition of avoiding "public controversy." Putting people in jail or on the witness stand over A.A. issues is hardly consistent with A.A.'s principles of anonymity, *spirituality* and avoidance of public disputes.

For those who are interested in the facts, the challenge, and the format, the material here may be of substantial value.

12

Guides for Groups
Direct from A.A.'s Pioneers

"'The leader would open with a prayer, then read Scripture,' Clarence recalled. 'Then he would spend 20 to 30 minutes giving witness—that is, telling about his past life. Then it would open for witness from the floor." "Their witnessing would have nothing to do with alcohol. . . . We were more interested in our everyday life than we were in reminiscings about drinking. . . . After the meeting closed with the Lord's Prayer, all the men beat it to the kitchen for coffee, and most of the women sat around talking to each other," said Wally [G.]" (*DR. BOB and the Good Oldtimers.*, A.A. World Services, Inc., pp. 139-41).

When you first arrive in A.A. today, you hear many things repeated, over and over. If you are foggy, bewildered, afraid, and anxious, you may have no idea where the things came from or how the people learned about them. Eventually you learn that almost every meeting has a set format to guide the Secretary or Chair of the meeting. The reading of the Twelve Steps or of the Twelve Traditions comes from the Big Book. The Preamble comes most frequently from the *AA Grapevine*. The Serenity Prayer apparently came from an obscure Protestant origin. The moment of silence at the beginning of meetings is probably the last vestige of "Quiet Time"—which was a "must" in the earliest meetings. The Lord's Prayer comes from Jesus's Sermon on the Mount and can be found in Matthew 6:9-13. The telling of stories or "leads"

211

or "sharing of experience" comes from the Oxford Group story-telling technique of "Sharing for Witness."

In other words, there appears to be great accuracy in Bill Wilson's frequent statement that everything in A.A. was borrowed and that no one invented A.A. That fact becomes quite clear if you know your history—something that very few AAs do.

The point is that it is quite appropriate to suggest a format for proposed meetings and groups. The early AAs did it at a setup meeting on Monday nights, and they sought God's guidance for topics and speakers. Today, A.A. General Services and also local Central Offices make available suggested guides for secretaries, manuals for "leaders," and pamphlets for newcomers explaining sponsorship, the group, and many other things.

Consistent with these approaches, here then are some possibilities for early A.A. groups—Good Book/Big Book Groups—in today's A.A.

Possible Meeting Resources

Basic Works

A Concordance to Alcoholics Anonymous. Compiled by Stephen E. Poe and Frances E. Poe. Reno, NV: Purple Salamander Press, 1990.

Alcoholics Anonymous. New York City: Works Publishing Co., 1939.

Alcoholics Anonymous. 3rd ed. New York City: Alcoholics Anonymous World Services, Inc., 1976.

Authorized (King James) Version of the Bible

B., Dick. *The Good Book and The Big Book: A.A.'s Roots in the Bible*. Kihei, HI: Paradise Research Publications, 1997.
 [The following histories by the author would also be helpful]:
 Good Morning!: Meditation, Quiet Time, Morning Watch and Early A.A.
 The Oxford Group & Alcoholics Anonymous: A Design for Living That Works

New Light on Alcoholism: God, Sam Shoemaker, and A.A.
Anne Smith's Journal, 1933-1939: A.A.'s Principles of Success
The Books Early AAs Read for Spiritual Growth, 7th ed.
Turning Point: A History of Early A.A.'s Spiritual Roots and
    Successes
Utilizing Early A.A.'s Spiritual Roots for Recovery Today
Young's Analytical Concordance to the Bible. Newly Revised and
Corrected. Nashville: Thomas Nelson, 1982.

Key Resources Used by Early A.A. Pioneers **

Chambers, Oswald. *My Utmost for His Highest*. London: Simpkin
    Marshall, 1927. [This book contains Bible topics.]
Drummond, Henry. *The Greatest Thing in the World and Other*
    Addresses. London: Collins, 1953.]
Holm, Nora Smith. *The Runner's Bible*. New York: Abingdon-
    Cokesbury Press, 1942. [This book is a Bible topic guide.]
Tileston, Mary W. *Daily Strength for Daily Needs*. Boston:
    Roberts Brothers, 1893. [This book is a daily devotional.]
The Upper Room: Daily Devotions for Family and Individual Use.
    [The first issue of this Methodist periodical was April-June,
    1935.]

Other Resources **

Authorized (King James) Version of the Bible on audio cassette
    tapes–narrated by Alexander Scourby.
Video and audio cassettes tapes and series on A.A.:
    Bill's Story. (Obtainable from A.A. World Services, Inc.,
        New York.)
    Dawn of Hope: The Founding of Alcoholics Anonymous–an
        Historical Perspective. Cinemark, Inc., Akron, Ohio.
        (Obtainable from Dr. Bob's Home, 855 Ardmore Ave.,
        Akron, Ohio.)

Dick B.

>   *The Historical Picture of Early A.A.'s Spiritual Ideas &
>   Successes* Seminar (East Dorset, VT: The Wilson
>   House, February 9-11, 1996--Obtainable from Glenn
>   K. Audio Tapes, 1-800-257-TAPE.)
>   *Turning Point: A History of Early A.A.'s Spiritual Roots
>   and Successes* Seminar (East Dorset, VT: The Wilson
>   House, May 17-18, 1997--Obtainable from Glenn K.
>   Audio Tapes, 1-800-257-TAPE.)
>   *Utilizing Early A.A.'s Spiritual Roots* Seminar (East
>   Dorset, VT: The Wilson House, May 15-17, 1998--
>   Obtainable from Glenn K. Audio Tapes, 1-800-257-
>   TAPE.)
>   *The Golden Text of A.A.: Yesterday's Message for
>   Tomorrow's Recovery* Seminar (East Dorset, VT: The
>   Wilson House, May 15-16, 1999--Obtainable from
>   Glenn K. Audio Tapes, 1-800-257-TAPE.)

** The periodical, books, and video and audio cassette tapes listed
in the previous two sections are all still in print.

Possible Types of Meetings for Such Groups

1. Beginners Meeting (see below).
2. Pioneer A.A. Meeting (Prayer, Scripture, Quiet Time,
    devotionals, discussion, surrenders, focus on newcomers).
3. Early A.A. History Meeting (see below).
4. Bible Study meeting (see below).
5. Good Book/Big Book/Step Study meeting (see below).
6. Prayer, Scripture reading, and Sharing meeting.

The reader should be aware that, without any particular guidelines,
most of such meetings are presently in existence within A.A.
today. Some are listed in meeting schedules.

Possible Approaches in Meetings

1. Listening to the reading of Scripture. Perhaps to segments suggested by the Oxford Group book, *How to Read the Bible* [Roger Hicks, *How to Read the Bible* (London: Moral Re-Armament, 1940)]; or perhaps as suggested by Sam Shoemaker, or by Anne Smith and described in the present author's titles on early A.A.

2. Listening to books and tapes on Scripture passages regularly studied in early A.A., such as Matthew chapters 5-7 (i.e., "the Sermon on the Mount"), 1 Corinthians 13, and the Book of James.

3. Examining some of the books which analyze these Bible segments, such as books on the Sermon on the Mount [by Oswald Chambers (*Studies in the Sermon on the Mount*), Glenn Clark (*I Will Lift Up Mine Eyes*), Emmet Fox (*The Sermon on the Mount*), E. Stanley Jones (*The Christ of the Mount*)—which titles are cited in full in the present title's "Selected Bibliography"]; books on 1 Corinthians 13 such as Henry Drummond's *The Greatest Thing in the World*; and study segments from the Book of James in Nora Smith Holm's *The Runner's Bible*. All these resources were commonly used in early A.A.

The possibilities are as endless as the roving minds of those who want to be in "spiritual kindergarten" and also of those who want to make a move toward graduating from that "spiritual kindergarten" and getting on with the Bible and religion themselves, whether in church, fellowships, classes, or individual study such as that done by Dr. Bob and other early AAs and their families.

Topics

Dr. Bob placed great stock in topics such as the following, which are taken from the early A.A. devotional, *The Runner's Bible*:

In the Morning Will I Order My Prayer to Thee
God, the Creator
Jesus Christ, His Son
The Spirit of God
God's image and Likeness
The Divine Commands (Walk in Love, Rejoice Always, In Everything Give Thanks, Fear Not, Only Believe, Get Wisdom and Understanding, Ask and You Shall Receive, He That is the Greatest Among You Shall Serve, Forgiveness)
Be of Good Cheer, Thy Sins Be Forgiven Thee
I will Help Thee
Behold, I will Heal Thee
For Thine is the Power
The Lord Shall Guide Thee Continually
Thou shalt Walk in thy Way Safely
All Things are Yours
Peace Be Unto You
Happy Shalt Thou Be
The Lord will Lighten My Darkness

Possible Meeting Formats

Beginners Meetings

Prayer, Scripture reading, Devotional Page for Day, Discussion of Rules of the Road:

FILL YOUR HOURS with good nutrition, good exercise, a job or volunteer work, service in A.A., fellowship at clubs, church, family, movies, time with sponsor, coffee with others, reading, school, phones, internet, libraries.

OBTAIN A SPONSOR AND SPEND TIME WITH YOUR SPONSOR (Visits, calls, meetings, prayer, Bible, Big Book, Steps, study and explanations, emergency problems).

HALT: Hungry? (eat). Angry? (pray and share). Lonely? (join winners).Tired? (sleep or rest).

AVOID SLIPPERY PLACES AND PEOPLE: Hang with believers and winners.

READ WHAT YOU ARE ABLE TO READ: Bible, devotionals, Big Book.

SURRENDER (Romans 10:9).

PRAY: For sobriety, health, guidance, forgiveness, healing, deliverance, family, friends.

THANK GOD:

> *"CONTINUE IN PRAYER, AND WATCH IN THE SAME WITH THANKSGIVING"* (Colossians 4:2).

> *"AND WHATSOEVER YE DO, DO IT HEARTILY, AS TO THE LORD, AND NOT UNTO MEN"* (Colossians 3:23).

> *"AND WHATSOEVER YE DO IN WORD OR DEED, DO ALL IN THE NAME OF THE LORD JESUS, GIVING THANKS TO GOD AND THE FATHER EVEN BY HIM"* (Colossians 3:17).

STICK TO FILLING BASIC NEEDS: Food, clothing, shelter, company of believers, meetings, financial resources for these.

GO TO MEETINGS WHEN TIME IS ON YOUR HANDS

SHARE with a sponsor, believers, clergy, physicians, therapists, counselors.

WORK: A job, a school, a volunteer position, service.

HAVE WHOLESOME FUN: Sports events, movies, shows, baseball, football, soccer, basketball, skiing, water sports, bowling, pool, cards, TV or radio in company with others, golf, chess, monopoly, trivia, theme parks and museums, barbecues, celebrations of birthdays and anniversaries.

CHECK ON YOUR HEALTH, AND GET MEDICAL ADVICE WHERE NECESSARY.

DON'T DRINK OR USE NO MATTER WHAT

HELP OTHERS WHEREVER POSSIBLE: Give rides, take to others to meetings and wholesome events, make phone calls, do errands, pray together, study together, make visits, read the Bible and Big Book together.

(If you wonder where such ideas came from, just read your own A.A.'s early history and some fine suggestions in its current literature).

Not all meetings need be on Rules of the Road. How about the following for the beginner:

What A.A. can offer you and you can offer A.A.
A sketch of early A.A.
A.A. Tools: Big Book, Twelve Steps, Sponsor, Meetings, Fellowship.
Christian tools (Bible, prayer, quiet time, fellowship, church, clergy, and literature).

Questions about A.A., sobriety, sponsor, Bible, Steps, filling time.

Emphasis on honesty (not lying, cheating, stealing, denying, hiding, embezzling, evading, falsifying documents).

Close with Lord's Prayer.

Bible Study Meeting

Open with prayer, quiet time, Scripture.

Tapes on the Bible, or subjects in *The Runner's Bible*, Read Genesis, Psalms, Gospels, Acts, Church Epistles.

Subjects: What the Bible is; how it was written; the Creator; His Son Jesus Christ; Books in the Bible; God's will (1 Timothy 2:4; Romans 10:9; John 17:17); The Ten Commandments; the Two Great Commandments from Jesus (Mark 12:28-31); the Sermon on the Mount (Matthew 5 to 7); 1 Corinthians 13; Book of James; The accomplishments of Jesus Christ for us; Forgiveness, healing, deliverance (Psalm 103).

Close with Lord's prayer

Early A.A. History Meeting

Beginnings of A.A.

Six Major Biblical Roots of A.A.

Early A.A. Program and Meetings

Basic Elements: Licked; Surrender to God; Change life; do God's will; love and serve others.

From the Bible and A.A.'s roots to the Steps

Movies: *Bill's Story* and *Dawn of Hope*

Good Book/Big Book/Step Study Meeting

Utilize a Big Book study book or tape, and a Step guide or tape. Study the actual sources of the Twelve Steps in the Bible. Study the First Edition of *Alcoholics Anonymous* (1939). Take a look at one of the following Bibles/New Testaments which endeavor to relate a host of particular verses to each particular step: (1) *Recovery Devotional Bible* (Zondervan); (2) *The Life Recovery Bible* (Tyndale House); and (3) *Serenity: A Companion for Twelve Step Recovery: Complete with New Testament, Psalms & Proverbs* (Thomas Nelson). Study the author's resources on each of A.A.'s six biblical roots: (1) the Bible, (2) Quiet Time, (3) Sam Shoemaker's teachings, (4) the Oxford Group's life-changing program, (5) Anne Smith's journal, and (6) Christian literature the pioneers read.

Pioneer A.A. Meeting

Prayer, Scripture, Quiet Time, Devotional, Topic, Surrender, Newcomer visits, needs, locations, outreach.

13

What Such Meetings Can Accomplish

"Wherefore lay apart all filthiness and superfluity of naughtiness, and receive with meekness the engrafted word [of God], which is able to save your souls. But be ye doers of the word, and not hearers only, deceiving your own selves" (James 1:21-22). "For this cause also thank we God without ceasing, because, when ye received the word of God which ye heard of us, ye received it not as the word of men, but as it is in truth, the word of God, which effectually worketh also in you that believe" (1 Thessalonians 2:13).

The Profit

Is there a profit to A.A. and AAs in starting, maintaining, or returning to the kind of group that flourished in Akron in the earliest days? A type of group and program which produced astonishing success rates when the "program" had been tested and found to work? The following could be considered the objectives of such groups today. For we believe such groups could and would:

- Teach anyone and everyone what early AAs did when they succeeded so astonishingly well.

- Give people a better handle on the real nature of, and *cure* for alcoholism.

- Document the real origins of A.A. and the "rock" on which it was founded.

- Demonstrate how today's drifting A.A. differs from the pioneer A.A. which achieved the phenomenal successes.

- Show people what early AAs read in the Bible; how they prayed; how they used devotionals; why they were encouraged to graduate from kindergarten to spiritual reading and church.

- Show people how to come to God as early AAs presented the path.

- Show people God's nature as early AAs spoke of Him: Creator, Maker, Spirit, Father.

- Show people what the Bible is, what it contains, and what can be learned.

- Enable people to know precisely what principles and practices early AAs actually took from the Bible.

- Make it possible for people to understand the language of the Steps, the Big Book, and the Fellowship much better and to clothe all these tools with their Biblical roots.

- Return to the spiritual expertise available to early AAs and all but ignored today.

- Enable people to overcome and be delivered from fear, anxiety, sickness, and despair rather attending meetings which continue their experiencing, recounting, and dwelling upon these negatives.

- Offer to AAs today the same moral standards that the early AAs insisted on observing.

- Help people understand honesty, purity, unselfishness, and love with the same tools from the Bible originally used to explain these yardsticks.

- Accurately depict the Bible's ideas about surrender, belief, decision, self-examination, confession, conviction, conversion, restitution, communion with God, receiving power, attaining healing and forgiveness and deliverance, experiencing the presence of God, understanding how to learn His will and promises from the Bible, from revelation, and from other believers, and being able to fellowship and witness and live love and serve in the Biblical sense.

- Overcome fear, enjoy peace and the love of God, communicate with God, receive and operate God's power and have the same sound mind that God wishes all mankind to have.

- End the ceaseless babble in Twelve Step Groups about what God's will is, how to find it, where to find it, and what to do with it after it is found.

Would Such Groups Further A.A.'s Primary Purpose?

A.A. exists today for the sole purpose of helping people who want to stop drinking. It is supposed to carry the message, through the mouths of those who have recovered, as to just how to do that. And over and over the Founders said that the entire program was *spiritual*. Belief in God was essential. Surrender to God was essential. Study of God's Word was essential. A quiet time of prayer to, and hearing from, God was a must. Dr. Bob called every meeting of early A.A. a Christian Fellowship. And many wanted to call that fellowship "The James Club," after the Book of James.

When people would come to Dr. Bob and say: "I don't get the spiritual angle," Dr. Bob said again and again, "There is no spiritual angle. It's a spiritual program" (*DR. BOB*, p. 194). Ebby Thacher's message (the message from the man Bill called his sponsor) to Bill was that God had done for him what he could not do for himself. Bill's message to Bill D. (A.A. No. 3) was that the Lord had cured him of his terrible disease. Dr. Bob's message to all AAs for all time was: "Your Heavenly Father will never let you down."

How could anyone possibly claim today that studying early A.A. history, studying the Bible, praying and listening to God, reading books about these subjects, surrendering to God, practicing the principles of the Bible, and telling newcomers how the oldtimers got well by relying on Almighty God be construed as defeating A.A.'s primary purpose? Whatever an AA may believe today, and whatever he or she may want to say or hear, there surely ought to be no objection to groups that practice the principles and program originally practiced—all to the end of helping others get sober and learn the meaning of the spiritual program developed by the Founders!

Just consider how often Bill Wilson himself adverted to the power of God. You will find the *golden text of A.A.*, as stated by Bill Wilson and A.A. Number Three (Bill Dotson) on page 191 of the Third Edition of A.A.'s Big Book—the *Lord cured them*. You will find Bill Wilson's explanation to a Cleveland pioneer who asked what it was the worked so many wonder on pages 216-17 of the Third Edition of A.A.'s Big Book—Bill pointed to a picture of Jesus Christ at Gethsemane and said: *There it is*. In our appendix, you will see what Bill and Bob and Bill Dotson wrote in the copy of Dr. Bob's Bible which was symbolically given to A.A.'s First Group-the King School Group, Akron No. 1. All these graphic symbols have deep and significant meaning: Recovery God's Way!

14

What You Can Do Today

Let's Suppose

Let's just suppose you are or want to become a Christian. Suppose too that you are an "alcoholic Christian." A *real*, medically incurable alcoholic, as early AAs used to call them. One who can recover only by Divine help, as A.A.'s own Big Book continues to mention. And you want to study the Bible. You want to rely on God. You want to say freely that you came to God by His son Jesus Christ. Most importantly, you want to rely on the power of God, the truth in His Word, and the promises in the Good Book that God heals all diseases, forgives all iniquities, and redeems lives from destruction. You want more than anything to get well, to feel well, to be "cured," to be released from the bondage of fear that has encased your life. You want to be delivered from the power of darkness.

Let's also suppose you decide, on your own, to try A.A. Or, that a judge, probation officer, or correctional agency—mindful of the First Amendment—has strongly "suggested" that you go to A.A. and quietly "hinted" that your alternative is incarceration. Or, that an in-patient or out-patient treatment or rehab has "brought you" or conveyed you to an A.A. meeting. Or, that your counselor or therapist suggests that you *also* need A.A. Or, that your physician has suggested A.A. with the comment that he or she knows of nothing else that really works.

There are many other stimuli to entry: an intervention, an employer, a partner, a wife or relative, a military unit, and so on.

Finally, let's suppose that you enter A.A., get yourself a sponsor, buy a Big Book, obtain a meeting schedule, resolve to go to "90 meetings in 90 days," decide to stay away from "slippery places and slippery people," and are willing to "go to any lengths." You go to meetings. You study the Big Book. You "take" the Twelve Steps with your sponsor. And so on. Finally, your mind clears somewhat and you face *reality*.

Without a drink, you are lonely, afraid, filled with guilt and shame and beset with all the problems you had when you quit drinking: bankruptcy, divorce, court judgments against you, income taxes unreported and unpaid, debts over-due, court dates still pending but long ignored, baskets full of traffic tickets, creditors hounding you, drivers license suspended, reputation ruined, can't get insurance, lost your job, lost your friends, lost your self esteem, lost your self respect, and lost your self confidence. "Worthless." "Helpless." "Hopeless." "Confused." "Resentful." "Revengeful." "Rejected." "Forgetful." "Bewildered." "Overwhelmed." And Terrified." Especially if you still have the paranoia that accompanied heavy drug use. Ask any of us if these problems are commonplace. There's only one answer. Yes!

People in the Fellowship make these comments or suggestions: "This too shall pass." "Keep coming back, it works." "You need more meetings." "What Step are you on?" "Are you keeping any secrets?" "Participate in your own recovery." "Get into *service*." "Find a newcomer." "Help someone." "Stop saying 'poor me.'" "It's really: Poor me, poor me, pour me another drink." "Stop living in the problem, and get into the solution." "Do what's in front of you." "Don't get too hungry, angry, lonely, or tired." "One day at a time." "ODAAT." "HALT." "Easy does it." "First things first." "Kiss: Keep it simple, stupid." "Take the cotton out of your ears and put it in your mouth." "Learn to listen and listen to learn." "Sit down, shut up, and listen." "Suit up, show up, and tell the truth." "If you'd like to try it, just go out and drink, and we'll gladly refund your misery." (I have personally heard all of these at literally hundreds of meetings. So has anyone else that has been an active AA for several years.) And there are dozens more! All somewhat helpful at times if you understand what the expressions mean or someone explains. Meanwhile, the problems are still there, and so are you—the newcomer!

Let's change the circumstances a bit.

Let's suppose you've been around the rooms for several years. You've been a sponsor. You've been a leader or "trusted servant," if you like that expression. You've been to Big Book Seminars, Conferences, Unity Days, Gratitude Nights, and Conventions. And you have begun to ask yourself, "What about God?" "What about Jesus Christ?" "What about the Bible?" "What do they mean when they say that A.A. is spiritual, and not religious?" If you've dabbled in some early A.A. history, you notice God is mentioned, one way or another, over 400 times in the Big Book. Jesus Christ used to be the subject of *the* surrenders. The Bible was read at every meeting in the old days. And you ask, "And what's wrong with *religion*?" Bill Wilson said A.A.'s spiritual ideas were borrowed from religion. And he said almost every principle of A.A. could be found in the Oxford Group and that the very material for the Steps came from Sam Shoemaker.

Maybe you think, "Am I stupid enough to go for this higher power is a lightbulb or doorknob stuff?" "No one *really* says or means or believes that, do they?" "Came to believe that a lightbulb can restore me to sanity?" "Turn my will and my life over to the care of a doorknob?" "Admit to Gertrude or Santa Claus the exact nature of my wrongs?" "Become entirely ready to have a chair remove my shortcomings?" "Ask a bulldozer to remove my character defects?" "Seek through prayer and meditation to improve my conscious contact with a radiator?" "Having had a spiritual awakening as the result of establishing a relationship with Ralph?"

Then you bravely start to talk in meetings about God—your God—the Bible, Jesus Christ, the Holy Spirit. But the cyclone hits. You read A.A.'s new *Daily Reflections* book and find all the stuff that you heard in meetings has been put in print for daily consumption. You read the myriad official pamphlets, and they say you can believe in something or anything or nothing at all.

In conclusion, let's suppose, you've finally become an elder statesman—double-digit sobriety. "Been there. Done that." You've seen the newcomers go out, drink and use in droves, and never return. You've seen others go out, "do research," and return after months and years saying it was worse out there than ever. Moreover, you've noticed that practically none of the people who got sober with you are still in the meetings. If they are still there, they may still be pumping in the same expressions, the same "higher power" stuff, and the same gruff warnings to the newcomer. Furthermore, there's swearing. There's psychobabble. There's incessant talk of *relationships*. And what has all this to do with the Twelve Steps, with recovery, even with A.A., you might ask?

Now exactly what can you do? What *can* you do?

You can go out and drink. But you are too sane for that. You can simply stop going to A.A., and most do. You can join a church or Bible fellowship and still go to A.A., but you can't talk about church sermons on Bible verses in meetings. Your comments about prayer life, sermons, the Bible, God, Christ, healing, Divine forgiveness, and salvation would simply fall on deaf or unfriendly ears. You know that because you've seen it happen over the years.

Or you can search for helpful books and outside alternatives. If you read long enough, you will see that Rational Recovery says A.A. is religious. It offers an "irreligious" solution. You will see that Martin and Deidre Bobgan's title, *Twelve Steps to Destruction*, says A.A. is neither religious nor Christian. It suggests you avoid A.A. like the plague. You observe that many *in* A.A. want the Lord's Prayer and Christianity *out* of A.A. In fact, they're voting it out quite frequently these days. And you see that churches and clergy are forming Twelve Step Groups that are "Christ-centered," or that they expand on the Twelve Steps, or that they use special Bibles which contain whole segments supposedly teaching on, consistent with, or explanatory of the Twelve Steps. You see some trying to establish a spiritual kindergarten *outside* of A.A., instead of inside it, as Bill Wilson suggested be done.

Where does it end? And exactly what can *you* do if you know what A.A. has done for you. If you are aware of A.A.'s biblical roots and Christian beginnings. If you would rather help yourself and the newcomers by staying *in* A.A. and proclaiming that AAs still *can* be Christians, still *can* read the Bible, still can try to grow spiritually in church or by religious reading or by retreats—just as the early AAs did. And still can talk about it, openly, frankly, and freely—in their *own* A.A. group. Also, if you wish to pass along A.A. history instead of A.A. garbage. Also if you want to learn and study the basic ideas and practices and principles that produced a 75% success rate among medically incurable, real alcoholics before there were *any* Steps—when the pioneers simply belonged to the Oxford Group and developed ideas from the Bible.

What Can You Do, Then, If You Don't Want to Leave A.A.?

An answer is shaping up in many parts of the United States today. From my listening post, on the phone, by fax, by email, on the internet, and by mail, it is becoming a hunger. The answer may or may not survive in Twelve Step Anonymous Fellowships themselves.

You can decide that secret agent Christianity or Catholicism or Protestantism or Judaism are not for you. You can start sharing *your* experience, strength, and hope. You can point out that criticism inside the fellowship leads to public controversy outside the fellowship. And has! Reams of articles and books by AAs criticizing A.A. You can point out that A.A. is just as capable of dying through universalism, fragmentation, atheism, compromise, religious prejudice, and mollifying placebos as any other institution or society. Some of the very groups A.A. thinks it does not

resemble perished in exactly that way—the Washingtonians, the
Oxford Group of the 1930's, and many many other respected
institutions in America we dare not mention, which still have well-
known names, attractive buildings, prestigious boards of directors,
and bountiful endowments. *And*, empty rooms. Even churches!
What can you do? Here are some possibilities:

- Resolve to stay with the ship and help it regain strength
  and course.

- Resolve to keep learning, studying, and disseminating
  early A.A. history.

- Resolve to stay as close to the principles that worked as
  those who said, "It works."

- Accept the idea that the Twelve Steps contain biblical
  principles and can profitably be studied in that light.

- Accept the same idea for the Big Book and the Fellowship.

- Organize seminars and conferences of AAs where history
  is taught accurately.

- Organize groups which focus on early A.A. practices.

- Organize groups which want to study the Good Book as
  well as the Big Book.

- Promote the idea that the same language should be spoken
  in a well-informed A.A. that is spoken in religious,
  psychological, and medical circles, whatever their
  differences. For that is what occurred when Bill Wilson
  spoke and wrote to clergy, scholars, and medical groups.
  People are leaving A.A. because God is mentioned in their
  church and in society at large and even in the dictionary,

while "Gertrude" and her likes has become an acceptable god in many A.A. conversations and books.

- Gather together a number of A.A. friends who don't want to leave A.A. Who understand and want to further its strengths in carrying the message about alcoholism and its solution. Who want to pass *that very message* on to new people, instead of leaving it to churches, treatment centers, rehabs, and therapists who don't understand or agree with it or even know about it.

- Seek God's guidance at every step.

- Fear not to reject such misunderstood, misused, and improperly defined terms as "higher power," "spirituality," "meditation," and other veiled sources of confusion.

- Use the materials that Dr. Bob and other early AAs used to produce such wonderful fellowship, moral growth, and spiritual strength. Use the Bible, prayer, the devotionals, Quiet Time, the Christian literature of early A.A., and the principles that lead to a relationship with, and knowledge of God Almighty.

- Identify yourselves as AAs, not as heretics or naysayers. Follow A.A. Traditions. Use the A.A. format, beginning meetings with solid prayer, an expanded Quiet Time, the Bible, and then some of the approaches and topics covered above. Close with the Lord's Prayer if you like. Bring people to Jesus Christ if you like. Every AA in pioneer A.A. did those things. Why not you and your group?

- Don't be afraid to reach out and offer healing to those in your group whom you know how to help through the power of God. Don't be afraid to offer prayer for them.

Don't be afraid to give them Scripture when it can be
helpful and is appropriate.

- List your group with the A.A. Central Office, in meeting
  schedules, and in flyers. Be a General Service
  Representative for your group. Donate to A.A. in accord
  with the Seventh Tradition. Be a participant and not a
  critic. Stand tall. Dr. Bob did. Bill Dotson did. Clarence
  Snyder did. And many are today, believe it or not.

- Don't concern yourself about A.A.'s atheist groups, young
  people's groups, policemen's groups, airline pilot groups,
  loners, gay and lesbian groups, Roman Catholic retreats,
  Christian retreats, lawyers groups, or men and women's
  groups. They are not concerned with you as long as you
  are not beating down A.A., are contributing to it, and are
  focused on the primary purpose of helping the alcoholic
  who still suffers.

- Stand for what Bill Wilson, Dr. Bob, and A.A. Number
  Three stood for before the editing and compromising
  began. Alcoholism can be cured! Alcoholism can be cured!
  Bill Wilson said the Lord had cured him of his terrible
  disease. Dr. Bob said "Your Heavenly Father will never
  let you down." Bill Dotson said that God can do anything;
  Bill believed that; and he never drank again! Why be "in
  recovery" for the rest of your life. Why not be
  "recovered"—which is what the early AAs said they were.
  Why have a disease for the rest of your life. Why not be
  healed of it, as the Bible says you can be. Read Psalm
  103. Read Mark 16. Read Acts 4. Read Colossians 1:13.
  Read James 5:15. Read 1 Peter 2:24. Early AAs did. If
  the early AAs read that God heals all our diseases; if Jesus
  instructed his followers to heal; if Peter said the man lame
  from birth was made whole by the name of Jesus Christ;
  if the Book of Colossians said the Father has delivered us

from the power of darkness; if the Book of James said the prayer of faith shall save the sick; if Peter said by Christ's stripes we were healed, why not read what the early AAs read in those and many other parts of the Bible. And believe, just as they did?

• Alcoholism can be cured. Today's people have just changed the language to satisfy the unbelievers. Today's people have just rejected the foundations of A.A. to placate those who want an easier softer way. They have often just spurned the Divine help that early AAs were told they *had* to have. "God could and would if he were sought," those A.A. pioneers wrote.

• Don't substitute human inadequacy and earthly unbelief for God's power. Whether you call uncontrolled or binge drinking a sin or a disease or a relapse or a predictable thing. Early AAs proved that, by the power of God, they could stop drinking. They said they were *recovered*. They didn't continue in sin or with a disease or have a relapse or look forward to the next drink. They needed not to be cocky nor afraid. They didn't need liquor any more. They didn't want liquor any more. They didn't drink liquor any more. God healed them. God cured them. God restored them to sanity, and they used the sanity that God gave them to live happy, joyous, free, and useful lives.

• As Sam Shoemaker wrote more than once, the Devil comes back along familiar paths. But James 4:7, which the pioneers loved to read, said: "Submit yourselves therefore to God. Resist the devil, and he will flee from you." The verse was popular in early A.A. The pioneers did submit and resist, and the devil did flee. Many pioneers lived long, sober, happy lives. So have I. And dozens of young men who accepted the early AA premise and whom I have sponsored are on that path also.

- Combine Big Book Study with Historical Roots study. Put the Good Book first on the study list. Learn the early A.A. technique for Quiet Time. Examine Anne Smith's journal. Look on the Oxford Group for understanding, not theology. Get an understanding of God as God understands Himself and tells us about Himself in the Bible. Go and show. Give news, not views.

- And you can follow the early A.A. path too. Healed of a dreadful malady!

Let the Bible be your guide:

O Lord my God, I cried unto thee, and thou hast healed me (Psalm 30:2).

He sent his word, and healed them, and delivered *them* from their destructions (Psalm 107:20).

You decide whether the God of the Bible, our Creator, can help you. And you *can* tell others *in* A.A.

The End

Appendix

Dr. Bob's Bible and A.A. Group No. 1 in Akron

When I first went to Founders Day in Akron, Ohio, in the early 1990's, Dr. Bob's daughter Sue took me to the Wednesday meeting of Dr. Bob's own A.A. Group. The group was and is called the King School Group. There, for many many years, Dr. Bob's Bible was brought to the podium before the meeting started. And it was returned to its place of safekeeping when the meeting was over. Recently, I asked Sue to send me pictures of the dedications that were signed in the Bible by Dr. Bob, by Bill Wilson, and by A.A. Number Three, Bill Dotson. And here is what they say:

> It is the hope of the King School Group whose property this is that this book may never cease to be a source of wisdom, gratitude, humility & guidance as when fulfilled in the life of the Master. Dr. Bob Smith

> Dear Friends at Akron Group # 1 This is the anniversary of the founding of AA-the 24th. As I stand here in King School memory is at flood tide. On behalf of all AAs I give thanks for the gifts of grace beyond [?] that had their beginning here. Gratefully Bill Wilson. Akron, June/59

> It is a great pleasure and privilege to be permitted to extend to the King School Group my deep appreciation of their very dear friendship and fellowship and to hope that we may all grow in grace and brotherly love. Bill Dotson

The Bible itself and the believing fellowship in the King School Group demonstrated results that could be achieved by all suffering alcoholics and their families if they chose to hear and *do* the Word (James 1:22).

Selected Bibliography

A Guide to the Twelve Steps of Alcoholics Anonymous. Akron: AA of Akron, n.d.

A Manual for Alcoholics Anonymous. Akron: AA of Akron, n.d.

A Program for You: A Guide to the BIG BOOK'S Design for Living. Hazelden, 1991.

Alcoholics Anonymous. New York City: Works Publishing Company, 1939. Reproduction published by The Anonymous Press, PO Box 1212, Malo, WA, 99150, 1-800-800-4398, www.anonpress.org.

Alcoholics Anonymous, 3rd ed. New York: Alcoholics Anonymous World Services, Inc., 1976.

Alcoholics Anonymous: An Interpretation of Our Twelve Steps. Washington, D.C.: Paragon Creative Printers, 1944.

Alcoholics Anonymous Comes of Age. New York: Alcoholics Anonymous World Services, Inc., 1957.

As Bill Sees It: The A.A. Way of Life. New York: Alcoholics Anonymous World Services, Inc., 1967.

Authorized King James Version of the Bible. New York: Thomas Nelson, 1984.

B., Dick. *Anne Smith's Journal, 1933-1939*. 3rd ed. Kihei, HI: Paradise Research Publications, 1998.

———. *Dr. Bob and His Library*. 3rd ed. Kihei, HI: Paradise Research Publications, 1998.

———. *Good Morning!: Quiet Time, Morning Watch, Meditation, and Early A.A.*. 2d ed. Kihei, HI: Paradise Research Publications, 1998.

———. *New Light on Alcoholism: God, Sam Shoemaker, and A.A.* 2d ed. Kihei, HI: Paradise Research Publications, 1999.

———. *That Amazing Grace: The Role of Clarence and Grace S. in Alcoholics Anonymous*. San Rafael, CA: Paradise Research Publications, 1996.

———. *The Akron Genesis of Alcoholics Anonymous*. 3rd ed. Kihei, HI: Paradise Research Publications, 1998.

———. *The Books Early AAs Read for Spiritual Growth*. 7th ed. Kihei, HI: Paradise Research Publications, 1998.

———. *The Golden Text of A.A.* Kihei, HI: Paradise Research Publications, 1999.

———. *The Good Book and The Big Book: A.A.'s Roots in the Bible*. 2d ed. Kihei, HI: Paradise Research Publications, 1998.

———. *The Oxford Group & Alcoholics Anonymous*. 2d ed. Kihei, HI: Paradise Research Publications, 1998.

———. *Turning Point: A History of Early A.A.'s Spiritual Roots and Successes*. Kihei, HI: Paradise Research Publications, 1997.

——. *Utilizing Early A.A.'s Spiritual Roots for Recovery Today*. Kihei, HI: Paradise Research Publications, 1998.

Baker, John. *Celebrate Recovery* (4 pamphlets). Lake Forest, CA: Celebrate Recovery Books, 1994.

Bartosch, Bob & Pauline. *Overcomers Outreach: A Bridge to Recovery*. La Habra, CA: Overcomers Outreach, Inc., 1994.

Best of the Grapevine, Volume II. New York: The A.A. Grapevine, Inc., 1986.

Bobgan, Martin and Deidre. *12 Steps to Destruction*. Santa Barbara, CA: EastGate Publishers, 1991.

Bufe, Charles. *Alcoholics Anonymous: Cult or Cure*. 2d ed. Tucson, AZ: Sharp Press, 1998.

Burns, Cathy. *Alcoholics Anonymous Unmasked: Deception and Deliverance*. Mt. Carmel, PA: Sharing, 1991.

Central Bulletin, Volumes I-III. Cleveland Central Committee, October, 1942-December, 1945.

Chambers, Oswald. *My Utmost for His Highest*. London: Simpkin Marshall, Ltd., 1927.

——. *Studies in the Sermon on the Mount*. London: Simpkin, Marshall, Ltd., n.d.

Clark, Glenn. *I Will Lift Up Mine Eyes*. New York: Harper & Brothers, 1937.

Comparative Study Bible: NIV, Amplified, KJV, Updated NASB. Rev. ed. Grand Rapids: Zondervan, 1999.

Daily Reflections. New York: Alcoholics Anonymous World Services, Inc., 1991.

Davis, Martin M. *The Gospel and the Twelve Steps: Developing a Closer Relationship with Jesus*. San Diego, CA: Recovery Publications, Inc., 1993.

Dinger, Clare M. *Moral Re-Armament: A Study of Its Technical and Religious Nature in light of Catholic Teaching*. Washington, D.C.: The Catholic University of America Press, 1961.

DR. BOB and the Good Oldtimers. New York: Alcoholics Anonymous World Services, Inc., 1980.

Drummond, Henry. *The Greatest Thing in the World and Other Addresses*. London: Collins, 1953.

Fosdick, Harry Emerson. *The Meaning of Prayer*. New York: Association Press, 1915.

Fox, Emmet. *The Sermon on the Mount*. New York: Harper & Row, 1934.

Helmfelt, Robert and Fowler, Richard. *Serenity: A Companion for Twelve Step Recovery*. Nashville, TN: Thomas Nelson, 1990.

Holm, Nora Smith. *The Runner's Bible*. New York: Houghton Mifflin, 1915.

Ishee, John, & Paul Barton Doyle. *Spirituality in Recovery: A Twelve Step Approach*. Brentwood, TN: John Ishee & Associates, 1997.

Jones, E. Stanley. *The Christ of the Mount*. New York: Abingdon Press, 1930.

——. *Victorious Living*. New York: Abingdon Press, 1936.

Kurtz, Ernest. *Not-God: A History of Alcoholics Anonymous*. Exp. ed. Minnesota: Hazelden, 1991

McQ., Joe. *The Steps We Took*. Little Rock, AR: August House Publishers, 1990.

O., Peter. *Serenity's Prayer: Asking for Recovery*. Brooklyn, NY: East River/Saratoga, Inc., 1997.

Pass It On. New York: Alcoholics Anonymous World Services, Inc., 1984.

P., Wally. *Back to Basics: The Alcoholics Anonymous Beginners' Classes. Take All 12 Steps in Four One-Hour Sessions.* Tucson, AZ: Faith With Works Publishing Company, 1997.

Peale, Norman Vincent. *The Positive Power of Jesus Christ.* Pauling, NY: Foundation for Christian Living, 1980.

Pittman, Bill. *AA The Way It Began.* Seattle: Glen Abbey Books, 1988.

Poe, Stephen E. and Frances E. Poe. *A Concordance to Alcoholics Anonymous.* Nevada: Purple Salamander Press, 1990.

Ragge, Ken. *More Revealed: A Critical Analysis of Alcoholics Anonymous and the Twelve Steps.* Henderson, NV: Alert! Publishing, 1991.

Recovery Devotional Bible. Grand Rapids, MI: Zondervan Publishing House, 1993.

S., Clarence. *Going through the Steps.* 2d ed. Altamonte Springs, FL: Stephen Foreman, 1985.

———. *My Higher Power—The Lightbulb.* 2d ed. Altamonte Springs, FL: Stephen Foreman, 1985.

S., Jerry & Pittman, Bill. *Prayers for the Twelve Steps—A Spiritual Journey.* San Diego, CA: Recovery Publications, 1993.

Second Reader for Alcoholics Anonymous. Akron: AA of Akron, n.d.

Speer, Robert E. *The Principles of Jesus.* New York: Fleming H. Revell, 1902.

Spiritual Milestones in Alcoholics Anonymous. Akron: AA of Akron, n.d.

The Co-Founders of Alcoholics Anonymous. New York: Alcoholics Anonymous World Services, Inc., 1972.

The Language of the Heart: Bill W.'s Grapevine Writings. New York: The A.A. Grapevine, Inc., 1988.

The Life Recovery Bible. Wheaton, IL: Tyndale House, 1992.

The Upper Room: Daily Devotions for Family and Individual Use. Quarterly (1935-1939). Edited by Grover Carlton Emmons. Nashville: General Committee on Evangelism through the Department of Home Missions, Evangelism, Hospitals, Board of Missions, Methodist Episcopal Church, South.

The Way Home: A Spiritual Approach to Recovery. Orlando, FL: Bridge Builders, Inc., 1996.

Tileston, Mary W. *Daily Strength for Daily Needs.* Boston: Roberts Brothers, 1893.

Trimpey, Jack. *Rational Recovery: The New Cure for Substance Addiction.* New York: Pocket Books, 1996.

Twelve Steps and Twelve Traditions. New York: Alcoholics Anonymous World Services, Inc., 1953.

What Others Think of A.A. Akron: Friday Forum Luncheon Club, circa 1941.

Young's Analytical Concordance to the Bible. New York: Thomas Nelson, 1982.

The text of this present book refers to many other source materials pertaining to A.A.'s roots, and to the research and writing the author has done. For specific bibliographic references to these works, in addition to what is included herein, the reader should refer to the following titles by Dick B.: (1) *The Books Early AAs Read for Spiritual Growth*; (2) *New Light on Alcoholism: God, Sam Shoemaker, and A.A.*; (3) *The Oxford Group & Alcoholics Anonymous: A Design for Living That Works*; and (4) *Turning Point: A History of Early A.A.'s Spiritual Roots and Successes.*

About the Author

Dick B. writes books on the spiritual roots of Alcoholics Anonymous. They show how the basic, biblical ideas used successfully by early AAs can be valuable tools for success in today's A.A. His research can also help the religious and recovery communities work more effectively with alcoholics, addicts, and others involved in Twelve Step programs.

The author is an active, recovered member of A.A.; a retired attorney; and a Bible student. He has sponsored more than eighty men in their recovery from alcoholism. Consistent with A.A.'s traditions of anonymity, he uses the pseudonym "Dick B."

He has had fourteen titles published: *Dr. Bob and His Library*; *Anne Smith's Journal, 1933-1939*; *The Oxford Group & Alcoholics Anonymous: A Design for Living That Works*; *The Akron Genesis of Alcoholics Anonymous*; *The Books Early AAs Read for Spiritual Growth*; *New Light on Alcoholism: God, Sam Shoemaker, and A.A.*; *Courage to Change* (with Bill Pittman); *The Good Book and The Big Book: A.A.'s Roots in the Bible*; *That Amazing Grace: The Role of Clarence and Grace S. in Alcoholics Anonymous*; *Good Morning!: Quiet Time, Morning Watch, Meditation, and Early A.A.*; *Turning Point: A History of Early A.A.'s Spiritual Roots and Successes*, *Hope!: The Story of Geraldine D., Alina Lodge & Recovery*, *Utilizing Early A.A.'s Spiritual Roots for Recovery Today*, and *The Golden Text of A.A.: God, the Pioneers, and Real Spirituality*. The books have been the subject of newspaper articles, and have been reviewed in *Library Journal*, *Bookstore Journal*, *For a Change*, *The Living Church*, *Faith at Work*, *Sober Times*, *Episcopal Life*, *Recovery News*, *Ohioana Quarterly*, *The PHOENIX*, *MRA Newsletter*, and the *Saint Louis University Theology Digest*.

Dick is the father of two married sons (Ken and Don) and a grandfather. As a young man, he did a stint as a newspaper reporter. He attended the University of California, Berkeley, where he received his A.A. degree, majored in economics, and was elected to Phi Beta Kappa in his Junior year. In the United States Army, he was an Information-Education Specialist. He received his A.B. and J.D. degrees from Stanford University, and was Case Editor of the Stanford Law Review. Dick became interested in Bible study in his childhood Sunday School and was much inspired by his mother's almost daily study of Scripture. He joined, and was president of, a Community Church affiliated with the United Church of Christ. By 1972, he was studying the origins of the Bible and began traveling abroad in pursuit of that subject. In 1979, he became much involved in a Biblical research, teaching, and fellowship ministry. In his community life, he was president of a merchants' council, Chamber of Commerce, church retirement center, and homeowners' association. He served on a public district board and was active in a service club.

In 1986, he was felled by alcoholism, gave up his law practice, and began recovery as a member of the Fellowship of Alcoholics Anonymous. In 1990, his interest in A.A.'s Biblical/Christian roots was sparked by his attendance at A.A.'s International Convention in Seattle. He has traveled widely; researched at archives, and at public and seminary libraries; interviewed scholars, historians, clergy, A.A. "old-timers" and survivors; and participated in programs on A.A.'s roots.

The author is the owner of Good Book Publishing Company and has several works in progress. Much of his research and writing is done in collaboration with his older son, Ken, who holds B.A., B.Th., and M.A. degrees. Ken has been a lecturer in New Testament Greek at a Bible college and a lecturer in Fundamentals of Oral Communication at San Francisco State University. Ken is a computer specialist.

Dick is a member of the American Historical Association, Maui Writers Guild, and The Authors' Guild. He is available for conferences, panels, seminars, and interviews.

Dick B.'s Historical Titles on Early A.A.'s Spiritual Roots and Successes

Dr. Bob and His Library: A Major A.A. Spiritual Source (Third Edition)
Foreword by Ernest Kurtz, Ph.D., Author, *Not-God: A History of Alcoholics Anonymous*.
A study of the immense spiritual reading of the Bible, Christian literature, and Oxford Group books done and recommended by A.A. co-founder, Dr. Robert H. Smith. Paradise Research Publications, Inc.; 156 pp.; 6 x 9; perfect bound; $15.95; 1998; ISBN 1-885803-25-7.

Anne Smith's Journal, 1933-1939: A.A.'s Principles of Success (Third Edition)
Foreword by Robert R. Smith, son of Dr. Bob & Anne Smith; co-author, *Children of the Healer*.
Dr. Bob's wife, Anne, kept a journal in the 1930's from which she shared with early AAs and their families ideas from the Bible and the Oxford Group. Her ideas substantially influenced A.A.'s program. Paradise Research Publications, Inc.; 180 pp.; 6 x 9; perfect bound; 1998; $16.95; ISBN 1-885803-24-9.

The Oxford Group & Alcoholics Anonymous (Second Edition)
Foreword by Rev. T. Willard Hunter; author, columnist, Oxford Group activist.
A comprehensive history of the origins, principles, practices, and contributions to A.A. of "A First Century Christian Fellowship" (also known as the Oxford Group) of which A.A. was an integral part in the developmental period between 1931 and 1939. Paradise Research Publications, Inc.; 432 pp.; 6 x 9; perfect bound; 1998; $17.95; ISBN 1-885803-19-2. (Previous title: *Design for Living*).

The Akron Genesis of Alcoholics Anonymous (Newton Edition)
Foreword by former U.S. Congressman John F. Seiberling of Akron, Ohio.
The story of A.A.'s birth at Dr. Bob's Home in Akron on June 10, 1935. Tells what early AAs did in their meetings, homes, and hospital visits; what they read; how their ideas developed from the Bible, Oxford Group, and Christian literature. Depicts roles of A.A. founders and their wives; Henrietta Seiberling; and T. Henry Williams. Paradise Research Pub.; 400 pp., 6 x 9; perfect bound; 1998; $17.95; ISBN 1-885803-17-6.

The Books Early AAs Read for Spiritual Growth (Fwd. by John Seiberling; 7th Ed.)
The most exhaustive bibliography (with brief summaries) of all the books known to have been read and recommended for spiritual growth by early AAs in Akron and on the East Coast. Paradise Research Publications, Inc.; 126 pp.; 6 x 9; perfect bound; 1998; $15.95; ISBN 1-885803-26-5.

New Light on Alcoholism: God, Sam Shoemaker, and A.A. (2d Ed.)
Forewords by Nickie Shoemaker Haggart, daughter of Rev. Sam Shoemaker; and Mrs. W. Irving Harris.
A comprehensive history and analysis of the all-but-forgotten specific contributions to A.A. spiritual principles and practices by New York's famous Episcopal preacher, the Rev. Dr. Samuel M. Shoemaker, Jr.—dubbed by Bill W. a "co-founder" of A.A. and credited by Bill as the well-spring of A.A.'s spiritual recovery ideas. Paradise Research Publications, Inc.; 672 pp.; 6 x 9; perfect bound; 1999; $24.95; ISBN 1-885803-27-3.

The Good Book and The Big Book: A.A.'s Roots in the Bible (Bridge Builders Ed.)
Foreword by Robert R. Smith, son of Dr. Bob & Anne Smith; co-author, *Children of the Healer*.
The author shows conclusively that A.A.'s program of recovery came primarily from the Bible. This is a history of A.A.'s biblical roots as they can be seen in A.A.'s Big Book, Twelve Steps, and Fellowship. Paradise Research Publications, Inc.; 264 pp.; 6 x 9; perfect bound; 1997; $17.95; ISBN 1-885803-16-8.

That Amazing Grace: The Role of Clarence and Grace S. in Alcoholics Anonymous
Foreword by Harold E. Hughes, former U.S. Senator from, and Governor of, Iowa.
Precise details of early A.A.'s spiritual practices—from the recollections of Grace S., widow of A.A. pioneer, Clarence S. Paradise Research Pub; 160 pp.; 6 x 9; perfect bound; 1996; $16.95; ISBN 1-885803-06-0.

Good Morning!: Quiet Time, Morning Watch, Meditation, and Early A.A. (2d Ed.)
A practical guide to Quiet Time—considered a "must" in early A.A. Discusses biblical roots, history, helpful books, and how to. Paradise Research Pub; 154 pp.; 6 x 9; perfect bound; 1998; $16.95; ISBN: 1-885803-09-5.

Turning Point: A History of Early A.A.'s Spiritual Roots and Successes
Foreword by Paul Wood, Ph.D., President, National Council on Alcoholism and Drug Dependence.
Turning Point is a comprehensive history of early A.A.'s spiritual roots and successes. It is the culmination of six years of research, traveling, and interviews. Dick B.'s latest title shows specifically what the Twelve Step pioneers borrowed from: (1) The Bible; (2) The Rev. Sam Shoemaker's teachings; (3) The Oxford Group; (4) Anne Smith's Journal; and (5) meditation periodicals and books, such as *The Upper Room*. Paradise Research Publications, Inc.; 776 pp.; 6 x 9; perfect bound; 1997; $29.95; ISBN: 1-885803-07-9.

Inquiries, orders, and requests for
catalogs and discount schedules
should be addressed to:

Dick B.
c/o Good Book Publishing Company
P.O. Box 837
Kihei, Maui, Hawaii 96753-0837
1-808-874-4876 (phone & fax)
email: dickb@dickb.com

Internet Web Site: "http://www.dickb.com"

Other Dick B. Historical Titles on Early A.A.

Order Form

Qty.

Send: ___ *By the Power of God: A Guide to Early A.A.*   @ $16.95 ea. $____
         Groups & Forming Similar Groups Today

         Paradise Research Publications, Inc.; approx. 250 pp.;
         6 x 9; perfect bound; 2000; ISBN: 1-885803-30-3.

___   *Utilizing Early A.A.'s Spiritual Roots for Recovery*   @ $14.95 ea. $____
         Today

         Paradise Research Publications, Inc.; 106 pp.; 6 x 9; perfect
         bound; 1999; ISBN: 1-885803-28-1.

___   *The Golden Text of A.A.: Early A.A., God, and*   @ $14.95 ea. $____
         Real Spirituality

         Paradise Research Publications, Inc.; 94 pp.; 6 x 9; perfect
         bound; 1999; ISBN: 1-885803-29-X.

                                            Subtotal $_____

Shipping and Handling (within the U.S.)   Shipping and Handling $_____
     Add 10% of retail price (minimum $3.75)

                                     Total Enclosed $_____

Name: _____ (as it appears on your credit card, if using one)

Address: _____   E-mail: _____

City: _____   State: ____   Zip: _____

CC Acct. #: _____   **Circle**: MC VISA AMEX Exp. ____

Tel.: _____   Signature _____

Please mail this Order Form, along with your check or money order, to: Dick B., c/o Good Book Publishing Company, P.O. Box 837, Kihei, HI 96753-0837. Please make your check or money order payable to **"Dick B."** in U.S. dollars drawn on a U.S. bank. Please contact us for Shipping and Handling charges for orders being shipped outside of the United States. If you have any questions, please phone or fax: 1-808-874-4876. Dick B.'s email address is: dickb@dickb.com. The **"Dick B. [Internet] Web Site on Early A.A."**: "http://www.dickb.com".

How to Order Dick B.'s Historical Titles on Early A.A.

Order Form

Qty.

Send:

___	*Turning Point* (a comprehensive history)	@ $29.95 ea. $_____
___	*New Light on Alcoholism* (Sam Shoemaker)	@ $24.95 ea. $_____
___	*The Oxford Group & Alcoholics Anonymous*	@ $17.95 ea. $_____
___	*The Good Book and The Big Book* (Bible roots)	@ $17.95 ea. $_____
___	*The Akron Genesis of Alcoholics Anonymous*	@ $17.95 ea. $_____
___	*That Amazing Grace* (Clarence and Grace S.)	@ $16.95 ea. $_____
___	*Good Morning!* (Quiet Time, etc.)	@ $16.95 ea. $_____
___	*Anne Smith's Journal, 1933-1939*	@ $16.95 ea. $_____
___	*Books Early AAs Read for Spiritual Growth*	@ $15.95 ea. $_____
___	*Dr. Bob and His Library*	@ $15.95 ea. $_____

***Shipping and Handling (S & H) ***   Subtotal $_____

Add 10% of retail price (minimum US$3.75). ** U.S. only.
For "The Set," add US$18.67 per Set. ** U.S. only   **S & H** $_____
Please call, fax, or email for shipments outside the U.S.

                                          Total Enclosed $_____

Name: _____ (as it appears on your credit card)

Address: _____

City: _____ State: ___ Zip: _____

Credit Card #: _____ (MC VISA AMEX) **Exp.** _____

Tel. #: _____ Signature _____

Email address: _____

Special Value for You!

If purchased separately, the author's ten titles sell for US$191.50, plus Shipping and Handling. Using this Order Form, you may purchase sets of all ten titles for **only US$149.95 per set, plus US$19.15** Shipping and Handling. Please contact us for Shipping and Handling charges for orders being shipped outside of the United States.

Send Order Form (or copy), with check or money order, to: Dick B., P.O. Box 837, Kihei, HI 96753-0837. Please make check or money order payable to **"Dick B."** in U.S. dollars drawn on a U.S. bank. For questions, please phone or fax: 1-808-874-4876. Our email: dickb@dickb.com. **Dick B.'s Web Site**: "http://www.dickb.com".